To Donnie
from Peggy with love

Dec 2008

365 days with **Wilberforce**

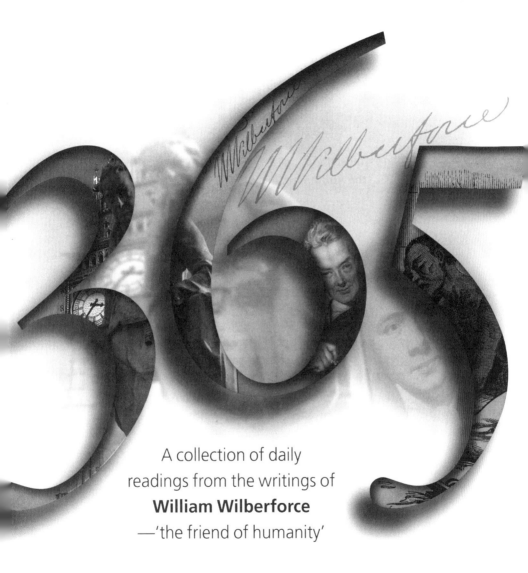

A collection of daily
readings from the writings of
William Wilberforce
—'the friend of humanity'

DayOne

© Day One Publications 2006
First printed 2006

ISBN 978-1-84625-058-3

9 781846 250583 >

Unless otherwise stated, all Scripture quotations are from
the Authorised Version, Crown Copyright

British Library Cataloguing in Publication Data available

Published by Day One Publications
Ryelands Road, Leominster, HR6 8NZ
☎ 01568 613 740 FAX 01568 611 473
email—sales@dayone.co.uk
web site—www.dayone.co.uk
North American—e-mail—sales@dayonebookstore.com
North American web site—www.dayonebookstore.com

Chief Sub-Editor: David Simm
Designed by Steve Devane and printed by Gutenberg Press, Malta

In some ways, *365 Days with Wilberforce* is quite unlike its predecessors in the series of which it is a part. The great anti-slavery reformer William Wilberforce (1759–1833) never intended to write a work of a purely devotional nature. Nor did he preach sermons for decades, as Charles Haddon Spurgeon did, so that such sermons could have been drawn upon to assemble a collection of daily readings.

Wilberforce did write a book, *A Practical View of Christianity* (1797) that has been called 'the manifesto of the Evangelical Movement' by no less an authority than Sir Leslie Stephen in his celebrated essay in *The Dictionary of National Biography*. *A Practical View* was a book with a dual purpose. It was both an apologia for evangelical Christianity and it also set forth a blueprint for the good society—based upon the first principles Wilberforce gleaned from his reading of the Scriptures and other writers who held to a Judeo-Christian worldview. Many passages from this classic work lend themselves to a collection of daily readings, and they are included in the pages that follow.

The other sources that have been drawn upon for this book are letters and diary entries contained in *The Life of William Wilberforce* (5 vols, 1838). *The Correspondence of William Wilberforce* (2 vols, 1840) has also been consulted, as has *The Private Papers of William Wilberforce* (1897). Many passages of an autobiographical nature are contained within John Harford's *Recollections of William Wilberforce* (1864). Lastly, Wilberforce published many little-known articles in the *Christian Observer*, which commenced publication in 1802 and continued beyond Wilberforce's death in 1833. I have drawn upon some of these articles as well.

It also needs to be said that since Wilberforce never intended to write a purely devotional work, with passages of a uniform length, some of the citations selected for this book are rather concise. But then, these passages are often arresting and prompt much thought. To exclude them on account of their brevity would be a loss, and hopefully this has been in some measure compensated for by expanded sections 'For Meditation' that provide a context in which to gain an added benefit from the more succinct entries that occasionally follow below. Like Pascal, Wilberforce was a master of terse and pithy statements. Often these statements cast a particular point in sharp relief, and they are all the more memorable for that. Apart from this, I should say I have edited many of the entries in this book for the sake of clarity. I have also rounded out some entries with kindred thoughts from writers well known in Wilberforce's day, whose writings shaped his understanding of Christianity.

Dedication

For Samuel—our child of promise.
May you come to know the Lord early, love and follow him all the days of
your life.

As a biographer of Wilberforce, I have long understood how central his faith was to his career as a reformer. Indeed it is not too much to say that were it not for his faith he never would have become a reformer, much less the man who has been called 'the greatest reformer in history' by Oxford scholar Dr Os Guinness.

Taken as a whole, the selections contained in this book reveal a great deal about the character of Wilberforce's faith. His habits of the heart, both in the place of prayer and his devotional life, can be clearly seen. His deep and searching knowledge of the Scriptures, as well as many classic devotional works, is readily apparent. His diary entries provide a close view of the diligent ways he sought first the kingdom of God during the years of his pilgrim's progress. He had experienced powerful instances of God's grace in his life, and felt that God's mercy was his constant attendant. Always, the eloquence for which Wilberforce was celebrated shines through.

For all these reasons, the selections given below are most compelling, and they make for a book that is rich in deep views of the Christian life. It has been my privilege to compile these glimpses into Wilberforce's pilgrimage and commend them to a new generation of readers. May this book honour Wilberforce's memory and above all, the Lord whom he so faithfully served.

Kevin Belmonte

Woodholme,
York, Maine, U.S.A.
8 July 2006

Watch and pray

'And be not conformed to this world: but be ye transformed by the renewing of your mind, that ye may prove what is that good, and acceptable, and perfect, will of God.' Romans 12:2
SUGGESTED FURTHER READING: Romans 12:1–12

Watch and pray, read the word of God, imploring that true wisdom which may enable you to comprehend and fix it in your heart, that it may gradually produce its effect under the operation of the Holy Spirit, in renewing the mind and purifying the conduct. This it will do more and more the longer we live under its influence.

It is to the honour of religion, that those who when they first began to run the Christian course were in extremes, or rigidly severe, will often by degrees lose their several imperfections like some of our Westmorland evenings, when though in the course of the day the skies have been obscured by clouds and vapours, yet towards its close the sun beams forth with unsullied lustre, and descends below the horizon in the full display of all his glories.

Shall I pursue the metaphor, just to suggest, that this is the earnest of a joyful rising, which will not be disappointed? The great thing we have to do, is to be perpetually reminding ourselves that we are but strangers and pilgrims, having no abiding city, but looking for a city which hath foundations; and by the power of habit which God has been graciously pleased to bestow upon us, our work will every day become easier, if we accustom ourselves to cast our care on him, and labour in a persuasion of his cooperation. The true Christian will desire to have constant communion with his Saviour. The eastern nations had their talismans, which were to advertise them of every danger, and guard them from every mischief. Be the love of Christ our talisman.

FOR MEDITATION: Each day of our life in Christ is a pilgrim's progress, and the Lord himself is our guide. We have this assurance from the Scriptures. Psalm 48:14 tells us: *'For this God is our God for ever and ever: he will be our guide even unto death.'*

REFERENCE: *The Life of William Wilberforce* (1838)

'I am not as I was'

'Brethren, I count not myself to have apprehended: but this one thing I do, forgetting those things which are behind, and reaching forth unto those things which are before, I press toward the mark for the prize of the high calling of God in Christ Jesus.' Philippians 3:13–14
SUGGESTED FURTHER READING: Philippians 3:7–14

I seem to myself to have awakened about nine or ten years ago from a dream, to have recovered, as it were, the use of my reason after a delirium. In fact till then I wanted first principles; those principles at least which alone deserve the character of wisdom, or bear the impress of truth. Emulation, and a desire of distinction, were my governing motives; and ardent after the applause of my fellow-creatures, I quite forgot that I was an accountable being; that I was hereafter to appear at the bar of God; that if Christianity were not a fable, it was infinitely important to study its precepts, and when known to obey them; that there was at least such a probability of its not being a fable, as to render it in the highest degree incumbent on me to examine into its authenticity diligently, anxiously, and without prejudice. I know but too well that I am not now what I ought to be; yet I trust I can say,

'Non sum qualis eram'
(I am not as I was)

and I hope, through the help of that gracious Being who has promised to assist our weak endeavours, to become more worthy of the name of Christian; more living above the hopes and fears, the vicissitudes and evils of this world; more active in the discharge of the various duties of that state in which the providence of God has placed me, and more desirous of fulfilling his will and possessing his favour.

FOR MEDITATION: Truly, when we come to faith in Christ we are not as we were. The Scriptures tell us: 'Therefore if any man be in Christ, he is a new creature: old things are passed away; behold, all things are become new.' (2 Corinthians 5:17) Added to this, we read in Romans 6:4 'we also should walk in newness of life.'

REFERENCE: *The Life of William Wilberforce* (1838)

'The song of praise and thanksgiving'

'Cause me to hear thy lovingkindness in the morning; for in thee do I trust: cause me to know the way wherein I should walk; for I lift up my soul unto thee.' Psalm 143:8

SUGGESTED FURTHER READING: Psalm 139:1–10

The day has been delightful. I was out before six, and made the fields my oratory, the sun shining as bright and as warm as at Midsummer. I think my own devotions become more fervent when offered in this way amidst the general chorus, with which all nature seems on such a morning to be swelling the song of praise and thanksgiving ...

The Sabbath is a season of rest, in which we may be allowed to unbend the mind, and give a complete loose to those emotions of gratitude and admiration, which a contemplation of the works, and a consideration of the goodness, of God cannot fail to excite in a mind of the smallest sensibility ...

May every Sabbath be to me, and to those I love, a renewal of these feelings, of which the small tastes we have in this life should make us look forward to that eternal rest, which awaits the people of God; when the whole will be a never-ending enjoyment of those feelings of love and joy and admiration and gratitude, which are, even in the limited degree we here experience them, the truest sources of comfort ...

FOR MEDITATION: Of God's many gifts to his people, the Sabbath is particularly intended to be a source of blessing. Rest, renewal and reflection are to be its hallmarks. For it is on the Lord's Day that we consider anew through worship, fellowship and rest what God has done for us. It is on this day that we are accorded the high privilege of communing with him, and asking him to help us, in the week ahead, to live for him and in him.

REFERENCE: *The Life of William Wilberforce* (1838)

Looking unto Jesus

'But mine eyes are unto thee, O GOD the Lord: in thee is my trust.'
Psalm 141:8
SUGGESTED FURTHER READING: Psalm 25:4–10

If then we would indeed be 'filled with wisdom and spiritual understanding'; if we would 'walk worthy of the Lord unto all well pleasing, being fruitful in every good work, and increasing in the knowledge of God'; here let us fix our eyes! 'Laying aside every weight, and the sin which doth so easily beset us, and let us run with patience the race that is set before us, LOOKING UNTO JESUS, the author and finisher of our faith; who, for the joy that was set before him, endured the cross, despising the shame, and is set down at the right hand of the throne of God.'

Here best we may learn the infinite *importance* of Christianity; how little it deserves to be treated in that slight and superficial way, in which it is in these days regarded by the bulk of nominal Christians, who are apt to think it enough, and almost equally pleasing to God, to be religious in *any way*, and upon *any* system. What exquisite folly must it be, to risk the soul on such a presumption, in direct opposition to the dictates of reason, and the express declaration of the word of God! 'How shall we escape, if we neglect so great salvation?'

Here also we shall best learn the duty and reasonableness of an absolute and unconditional surrender of soul and body to the will and service of God—'We are not our own'; for 'we are bought with a price', and must therefore make it our grand concern to 'glorify God with our bodies and our spirits, which are God's.'

FOR MEDITATION: In Luke 10:24 Jesus said to his disciples: 'many prophets and kings have desired to see those things which ye see.' As Christians, we have been blessed beyond measure. Ours is the redemption of the cross— the matchless gift for those who look to Jesus—to all who call upon his name and are saved (Romans 10:13). Jesus is, in himself, the desire of nations. Modern history takes its beginning from his birth. For two millennia, we have spoken of our days as being *anno domini*—'in the year of our Lord.' He is the author of time. He is the maker of the world, and the hope of the world.

REFERENCE: *A Practical View of Christianity* (1797)

'To give an account of our stewardship'

'Jesus said unto him, Thou shalt love the Lord thy God with all thy heart, and with all thy soul, and with all thy mind.' Matthew 22:37
SUGGESTED FURTHER READING: Psalm 119:1–7

It must be confessed by all who believe that we are accountable creatures ... that we shall have to answer hereafter to the Almighty for all the means we have here enjoyed of improving ourselves, or of promoting the happiness of others. And if, when summoned to give an account of our stewardship, we shall be called upon to answer for the use which we have made of our bodily organs, and of the means of relieving the wants and necessities of our fellow-creatures; how much more for the exercise of the nobler faculties of our nature, of invention, and judgment, and memory, and for our employment of every instrument and opportunity of diligent application, and serious reflection, and honest decision.

And to what subject might we in all reason be expected to apply more earnestly, than to that wherein our eternal interests are at issue? When God has granted us such abundant means of instruction, in that which we are most concerned to know, how great must be the guilt, and how awful the punishment of voluntary ignorance!

And why are we in this pursuit alone to expect knowledge without inquiry, and success without endeavour? The whole analogy of nature inculcates a different lesson, and our own judgments in matters of temporal interest and worldly policy confirm the truth of her suggestions. Bountiful as is the hand of Providence, its gifts are not so bestowed as to seduce us into indolence, but to rouse us to exertion; and no one expects to attain to the height of learning, or arts, or power, or wealth, or military glory, without vigorous resolution, and strenuous diligence, and steady perseverance.

FOR MEDITATION: Our lives, Wilberforce knew from his reading of the Scriptures, should be marked by grateful returns to the Author of our salvation. Our gifts and talents, as with our material possessions, have been given us in trust. We ought to carefully cultivate our gifts—to strive to make the best use of them—and in so doing to honour the Giver of them. So too we ought to share of our material possessions, whether tithing to our local church or in acts of service to the less fortunate.

REFERENCE: *A Practical View of Christianity* (1797)

'God's bounty to mankind'

'For unto us a child is born, unto us a son is given: and the government shall be upon his shoulder: and his name shall be called Wonderful, Counsellor, The mighty God, The everlasting Father, The Prince of Peace.' Isaiah 9:6
SUGGESTED READING: Matthew 1:18–25

Christianity is always represented in Scripture as the grand, the unparalleled instance of God's bounty to mankind. This unspeakable gift was graciously held forth in the original promise to our first parents; it was predicted by a long continued series of prophets; the subject of their prayers, inquiries, and expectations. In a world which opposed and persecuted them, it was their source of peace, and hope, and consolation.

The gospel is everywhere represented in Scripture by such figures as are most strongly calculated to impress on our minds a sense of its value; it is spoken of as light from darkness, as life from death.

With what exalted conceptions of the importance of Christianity ought we to be filled by such descriptions as these? Thus predicted, this heavenly treasure, though poured into our lap in rich abundance, we scarce accept. We turn from it coldly, or at best profess it negligently as a thing of no estimation. But a due sense of its value would be assuredly impressed on us by the diligent study of the Word of God, that blessed repository of divine truth and consolation. Thence it is that we are to learn our duty, what we are to believe and what to practise.

FOR MEDITATION: One of the most tragic passages of Scripture is that addressed to the ancient church of Ephesus: 'Thou hast left thy first love', the passage reads, 'remember therefore from whence thou art fallen, and repent, and do the first works' (Revelation 2:4–5). So many things in life compete for our attention, and we can so easily be diverted from that which is the primary business of life—striving to seek the Lord and to honour him in every facet of our lives. May we always love the Lord as we ought, and may he hold the first place in our affections.

REFERENCE: *A Practical View of Christianity* (1797)

'His thoughts, and words, and actions'

'Let the words of my mouth, and the meditation of my heart, be acceptable in thy sight, O LORD, my strength, and my redeemer.' Psalm 19:14
SUGGESTED FURTHER READING: Colossians 3:8–17

On the first promulgation of Christianity, it is true, some of her early converts seem to have been in danger of so far mistaking the genius of the new religion, as to imagine, that in future they were to be discharged from an active attendance on their secular affairs. But the apostle most pointedly guarded them against so gross an error, and expressly and repeatedly enjoined them to perform the particular duties of their several stations with increased alacrity and fidelity, that they might thereby do credit to their Christian profession.

This he did, at the same time that he prescribed to them that predominant love of God and of Christ, that heavenly-mindedness, that comparative indifference to the things of this world, that earnest endeavour after growth in grace, and perfection in holiness, which have already been stated as the essential characteristics of real Christianity.

It cannot therefore be supposed by any who allow to the apostle even the claim of a consistent instructor, much less by any who admit his divine authority, that these latter precepts are incompatible with the former. Let it be remembered, that the grand characteristic mark of the true Christian is *his desiring to please God in all his thoughts, and words, and actions; to take the revealed word to be the rule of his belief and practice; to 'let his light shine before men'; and in all things to adorn the doctrine which he professes.* No calling is proscribed, no pursuit is forbidden, no science or art is prohibited, no pleasure is disallowed, provided it be such as can be reconciled with this principle.

FOR MEDITATION: The apostle Paul wrote memorably of the ways in which athletes compete. 'Know ye not,' he asked, 'that they which run in a race run all, but one receiveth the prize? So run, that ye may obtain' (1 Corinthians 9:24). Not everyone can be an athlete, but each of us can earnestly ask for God's help daily as we seek to honour him in our life's calling. Seeking his wisdom and his strength, we can run our 'race' as we ought to.

REFERENCE: *A Practical View of Christianity* (1797)

'The origin of all that is excellent and lovely'

'Finally, brethren, whatsoever things are true, whatsoever things are honest, whatsoever things are just, whatsoever things are pure, whatsoever things are lovely, whatsoever things are of good report; if there be any virtue, and if there be any praise, think on these things.'
Philippians 4:8
SUGGESTED FURTHER READING: Psalm 8:1–9

Never let it be forgotten, the main distinction between real Christianity and the system of the bulk of nominal Christians chiefly consists in the different place which is assigned in the two schemes to the peculiar doctrines of the gospel. These, in the scheme of nominal Christians, if admitted at all, appear but like the stars of the firmament to the ordinary eye. They twinkle to the common observer with a vain and 'idle' lustre; and except in the dreams of the astrologer, have no influence on human happiness, or any concern with the course and order of the world.

But to the *real* Christian, on the contrary, THESE peculiar doctrines constitute the centre to which he gravitates! the very sun of his system! the origin of all that is excellent and lovely! the source of light, and life, and motion! Dim is the light of reason, and cold and comfortless our state, while left to her unassisted guidance.

But the blessed truths of the gospel are now unveiled to *our* eyes, and *we* are called upon to behold, and to enjoy 'the light of the knowledge of the glory of God, in the face of Jesus Christ.' The words of inspiration best express our highly favoured state; 'We all, with open face, beholding as in a glass the glory of the Lord, are changed into the same image, from glory to glory, even as by the Spirit of the Lord.'

FOR MEDITATION: The words of William Cowper in *The Task* are also appropriate:

THOU art the source and centre of all minds, But O thou bounteous Giver of all good,
Their only point of rest, ETERNAL WORD! Thou art of all thy gifts, thyself the crown!
From thee departing, they are lost, and rove Give what thou canst, without thee we are poor;
At random without honour, hope, or peace. And with thee rich, take what thou wilt away.

REFERENCE: *A Practical View of Christianity* (1797)

'Our peculiar situations'

'But ye are a chosen generation, a royal priesthood, an holy nation, a peculiar people; that ye should shew forth the praises of him who hath called you out of darkness into his marvellous light.' 1 Peter 2:9
SUGGESTED FURTHER READING: Psalm 4:1, 3–8

It is not, believe me, to my own imagination, or to any system formed in my closet, that I look for my principles; it is to the Scriptures ... All that I contend for is, that we should really make this book the criterion of our opinions and actions, and not read it and then think that we do so of course.

But if we do this, we must reckon on not finding ourselves able to comply with all those customs of the world, in which many who call themselves Christians are too apt to indulge without reflection ... we must of course be subject to the charge of excess and singularity. But in what will this singularity consist? Not merely in indifferent things; no, in these our Saviour always conformed, and he took occasion to check an unnecessary strictness into which he saw men were led by overstraining a good principle.

In what then will these peculiarities appear? Take our great Master's own words; 'Thou shalt love the Lord thy God with all thy heart, with all thy mind, and with all thy strength; and thy neighbour as thyself.' It would be easy to dilate on this text; and I am afraid that we should find at the close of the discourse that the picture was very unlike the men of this world. 'But who is my neighbour?' Here, too, our Saviour has instructed us by the parable which follows. It is evident we are to consider our peculiar situations, and in these to do all the good we can.

FOR MEDITATION: To be 'a peculiar people' is but another way of saying there ought to be things that are distinctive about those who profess the name of Christ. Our love for God, to cite one very important example, should inform the way we love others. Or, as the Scriptures tell us: 'By this shall all men know that ye are my disciples, if ye have love one to another' (John 13:35). Are we loving others as we should? In our 'peculiar situations', are we doing all the good we can? These are questions we should ask ourselves consistently.

REFERENCE: *The Life of William Wilberforce* (1838)

'He will lead on his people'

'Being confident of this very thing, that he which hath begun a good work in you will perform it until the day of Jesus Christ.' Philippians 1:6
SUGGESTED FURTHER READING: Psalm 25:1–10

Some men are thrown into public life, some have their lot in private life. These different states have their corresponding duties; and he whose destination is of the former sort, will do as ill to immure himself in solitude, as he who is only a village Hampden would, were he to head an army or address a senate.

If I were thus to fly from the post where Providence has placed me, I know not how I could look for the blessing of God upon my retirement: and without this heavenly assistance, either in the world or in solitude our own endeavours will be equally ineffectual. When I consider the particulars of my duty, I blush at the review; but my shame is not occasioned by my thinking that I am too studiously diligent in the business of life; on the contrary, I then feel that I am serving God best when from proper motives I am most actively engaged in it. What humbles me is, the sense that I forego so many opportunities of doing good; and it is my constant prayer, that God will enable me to serve him more steadily, and my fellow-creatures more assiduously.

I trust that my prayers will be granted through the intercession of that Saviour 'by whom' only 'we have access with confidence into this grace wherein we stand'; and who has promised that he will lead on his people from strength to strength, and gradually form them to a more complete resemblance of their divine original.

FOR MEDITATION: Wherever we find ourselves, in public or private life, ours is to be an active faith. As we read in 1 Corinthians 10:31:'whatsoever ye do, do all to the glory of God.' This is our Father's world, and it is a world in which we can do so much to commend our faith to others. The Dutch Prime Minister and theologian Abraham Kuyper captured this powerfully when he said: 'There is not a square inch on the whole plain of human existence over which Christ, who is Lord over all, does not proclaim: "This is mine!"'

REFERENCE: *The Life of William Wilberforce* (1838)

'Amidst all our sorrows'

'These things I have spoken unto you, that in me ye might have peace. In the world ye shall have tribulation: but be of good cheer; I have overcome the world.' John 16:33
SUGGESTED FURTHER READING: John 16:25–33

Even by those who feel concerning the events of this chequered life as real Christians, such an incident as the death of a parent, or even of a near and dear friend, will be felt severely; and, indeed, it ought to be so felt, for here, as in so many other instances, it is the glorious privilege of Christianity, and the evidence of its superior excellence, that it does not, like the systems of human fabrication, strive to extinguish our natural feelings, from a consciousness that it is only by lessening them that it can deal with them—if I may so express myself—and enable us to bear the misfortune as we ought; but it so softens, and sweetens, and increases the ability of our hearts and tempers as to make us love our friends better, and feel more keenly the loss for the whole of this life of our former delightful intercourse with them; and yet it, at the same time, so spiritualizes and elevates our minds as to cheer us amidst all our sorrows, and enabling us on these as on other occasions to walk by faith and live by the spirit, it raises us to the level of our ascended friends, till we hear almost their first song of exultation, and would not even wish to interrupt it, while we rather indulge the humble hope of one day joining in the chorus.

FOR MEDITATION: So often, some element of our blessed hope as Christians has been beautifully expressed in a hymn. Horatio Spafford understood well many of the sentiments expressed in Wilberforce's words above. That he did is shown in the words of his timeless hymn, *It is Well with my Soul*:

But, Lord, 'tis for thee, for thy coming we wait,
The sky, not the grave, is our goal;
Oh trump of the angel! Oh voice of the Lord!
Blessèd hope, blessèd rest of my soul!

REFERENCE: *Recollections of William Wilberforce* (1864)

'Holiness of heart and life'

'But we are bound to give thanks alway to God for you, brethren beloved of the Lord, because God hath from the beginning chosen you to salvation through sanctification of the Spirit and belief of the truth.'
2 *Thessalonians 2:13*
SUGGESTED FURTHER READING: 2 Thessalonians 2:13–17

The best preparation for being a good politician, as well as a superior man in every other line, is to be a truly religious man. For this includes in it all those qualities which fit men to pass through life with benefit to others and with reputation to ourselves. Whatever is to be the effect produced by the subordinate machinery, the mainspring must be the desire to please God, which, in a Christian, implies faith in Christ and a grateful sense of the mercies of God through a Redeemer, and an aspiration after increasing holiness of heart and life.

FOR MEDITATION: Holiness ... to be set apart unreservedly for the service of God. John Wesley, from whom Wilberforce received the last letter Wesley ever wrote, said: 'I determined, through his grace (the absolute necessity of which I was deeply sensible of;), to be all-devoted to God, to give him all my soul, my body, and my substance. Will any considerate man say that this is carrying the matter too far? or that anything less is due to him who has given himself for us, than to give him ourselves, all we have, and all we are?'

Wilberforce constantly aspired after holiness, a desire well expressed in his diary in the autumn of 1792: 'I have been praying earnestly to God for his Spirit through Christ to renew my corrupt nature and make me spiritually-minded; what folly is all else! Let me take courage, relying on the sure promises of God in Christ and the powerful operations of the Spirit of grace. Though I am weak he is strong. I must more cherish this heavenly inhabitant.'

REFERENCE: *Private Papers of William Wilberforce* (1897)

'Blessed declarations of mercy'

'Surely goodness and mercy shall follow me all the days of my life: and I will dwell in the house of the LORD *for ever.' Psalm 23:6*
SUGGESTED FURTHER READING: Psalm 23

When I review all my past life, and consider ever since it has been my general desire to live to the glory of God, and in obedience to his laws, what have been my obligations, and what ought to be the amount and effects of my gratitude—what my means and opportunities of usefulness, and what the scantiness of my performances, and with what alloy their motives have been debased—alas, alas! my friend, I have no peace, no rest, but in the assurances of pardon and acceptance to the penitent believer in Christ Jesus; and I adopt the language of the publican, with the blessed declarations of mercy and grace held out to the contrite and broken-hearted. What a blessed truth it is, that it is our duty to be confident in the undeserved bounty and overflowing loving-kindness of our heavenly Father.

FOR MEDITATION: Trust might well-defined as an abiding assurance of what we have been given. 'Undeserved bounty and overflowing loving-kindness' are but other names for grace and mercy. We are assured time and again in God's word that he wishes to bestow grace and mercy upon us. These are to be the constant portion of our faith. As the apostle Paul writes to Timothy in 1 Timothy 1:2—'Unto Timothy, my own son in the faith: Grace, mercy, and peace, from God our Father and Jesus Christ our Lord.'

Much the same words are repeated in 2 Timothy 1:2—'To Timothy, my dearly beloved son: Grace, mercy, and peace, from God the Father and Christ Jesus our Lord.' As believers, grace and mercy will attend our way. We have been given this assurance in God's word.

REFERENCE: *Recollections of William Wilberforce* (1864)

'The most valuable of all possessions'

'Ointment and perfume rejoice the heart: so doth the sweetness of a man's friend by hearty counsel.' Proverbs 27:9
SUGGESTED FURTHER READING: 1 Samuel 18:1–4; 20:1–17

No man has perhaps more cause for gratitude to God than myself. But of all the various instances of his goodness, the greatest of all, excepting only his Heavenly Grace, is the many kind friends with whom a gracious Providence has blessed me. Oh remember, my dearest boy, to form friendships with those only who love and serve God, and when once you have formed them, then preserve them as the most valuable of all possessions.

FOR MEDITATION: Wilberforce knew profoundly what a gift fellowship was, and in particular the blessing of friends who had 'been kind to me beyond a brother's kindness, and I think of it often with wonder as well as with humiliation and gratitude'. These were words he wrote in a letter to James Stephen, which continued: 'Indeed I have long thought that of all the manifold blessings which Providence has heaped on me, the greatest of this world consists of kind and intelligent friends whom he has raised up for my comfort and benefit.'

Mention has already been made of the comfort and encouragement Wilberforce received from his close friends, but he also was able to consult with them on weighty matters, and at times receive constructive criticism from them—for he valued very highly, as they did, friendly reproof when warranted.

We all need friends like this—who will come alongside us in our life's journey. They are friends of the heart, who help us in many ways to chart our course during our earthly pilgrimage. Blessed are those who have such friends in their life.

REFERENCE: *Private Papers of William Wilberforce* (1897)

'Intervals of solitude'

'The wilderness and the solitary place shall be glad for them; and the desert shall rejoice, and blossom as the rose.' Isaiah 35:1
SUGGESTED FURTHER READING: Isaiah 35:1–7

Blessed be God, we serve a gracious Master, a merciful Sovereign. By degrees the humble hope of your having obtained the pardon of your sins and the possession of the divine favour will enable you to look up to God with feelings of filial confidence and love, and to Christ as to an advocate and a friend. The more you do this the better.

My dearest Samuel, take now and then a solitary walk, and in it indulge in these spiritual meditations. This will gradually become a habit of unspeakable value.

'when Isaac, like the solitary saint,
Walks forth to meditate at eventide …'   (William Cowper: *The Task*)

You remember the passage, I doubt not. When I was led into speaking of occasional intervals of solitude, I was mentioning that holy, peaceful, childlike trust in the fatherly love of our God and Saviour which gradually diffuses itself through the soul and takes possession of it, when we are habitually striving to walk by faith under the influence of the Holy Spirit.

FOR MEDITATION: It is a challenge, amidst our often harried lives, to take time for solitary walks and reflection. Wilberforce was incredibly busy. For most of his forty-four years in politics he was MP for the entire County of Yorkshire, and the demands of his constituency were great. Marathon sessions in the House of Commons, mountains of correspondence (handwritten replies!), countless hours of consultation with colleagues and scores of meetings throughout the year for the many charitable societies he supported. Add to this that he and his wife Barbara were the parents of six children.

Wilberforce needed his 'quiet, musing walks'. And we, in an age no less busy than his, need them too. Wherever we are, such walks allow us to unwind. They afford us the chance to remember those feelings of filial confidence and love with which we ought to look up to God, recalling as we do that he is our ever-present Advocate and Friend.

REFERENCE: *Private Papers of William Wilberforce* (1897)

'Keeping God's commandments'

'Let us hear the conclusion of the whole matter: Fear God, and keep his commandments: for this is the whole duty of man.' Ecclesiastes 12:13
SUGGESTED FURTHER READING: Psalm 119:1–12

The best way to promote the right temper of mind will be after earnest prayer to God to bless your endeavours, to try to keep the idea of Jesus Christ and of his sufferings, and of the love which prompted him willingly to undergo them, in your mind continually, and especially when you are about your business. And then recollect that he has declared he will kindly accept as a tribute of gratitude whatever we do to please him, and call to mind all his kindness, all his sacrifices; the glory he left, the humiliation, shame and agony he endured; and then reflect that the only return he, who is at that very moment actually looking upon you, expects from you is that you should remember him and his heavenly Father who sent him, and endeavour to please him. This he tells us is to be done by keeping God's commandments.

Not that we shall be able actually to do this; but then we must wish and desire to do it. And when, from our natural corruption, infirmities do break out we must sincerely lament them, and try to guard against them in future. Thus a true Christian endeavours to have the idea of his Saviour continually present with him. To do his business as the Scripture phrases it, 'unto the Lord and not unto men.' This is the very perfection of religion.

FOR MEDITATION: Wilberforce knew the great hymn writer Charles Wesley, and the story of their first meeting in 1786 is deeply moving. It was just two years before Wesley's death. 'When I came into the room,' Wilberforce wrote, 'Charles Wesley rose from the table … and coming forwards to me, gave me solemnly his blessing. I was scarcely ever more affected. Such was the effect of his manner and appearance, that it altogether overset me, and I burst into tears.' In 1738 Charles Wesley had published a hymn that beautifully complements Wilberforce's words above:

And can it be that I should gain
An interest in the Saviour's blood?
Died he for me, who caused his pain—

For me, who him to death pursued?
Amazing love! How can it be,
That thou, my God, shouldst die for me?

REFERENCE: *Private Papers of William Wilberforce* (1897)

'The produce of the garden of God'

'But that on the good ground are they, which in an honest and good heart, having heard the word, keep it, and bring forth fruit with patience.' Luke 8:15
SUGGESTED FURTHER READING: Matthew 13:1–9

I am anxious to see you manifest those buds and shoots which alone are true indications of a celestial plant, the fruits of which are the produce of the garden of God. My dear Samuel, be honest with yourself; you have enjoyed and still enjoy many advantages for which you are responsible. Use them *honestly;* that is, according to their just intention and fair employment and improvement. Above all things, my dearest boy, cultivate a spirit of prayer. Never hurry over your devotions, still less omit them.

FOR MEDITATION: Of all the wisdom contained in the passage above, the words 'cultivate a spirit of prayer' stand out. If we heed these words, the fruits of the garden of God will be manifest in our lives. So too will we better understand how to make the best use of the advantages God has bestowed upon us. A life of prayer will foster these things within us.

Throughout the course of long life in service to his Lord, Wilberforce's understanding of the importance of cultivating a spirit of prayer—of communing with God—only deepened. His diary makes frequent reference to this. 'How does my experience,' he wrote, 'convince me that true religion is to maintain communion with God.' Elsewhere he stated: 'A Christian's life is hid with Christ in God. He should look for his happiness in fellowship with God, and view with jealousy whatever tends to break in on this communion.'

In his diary, Wilberforce often questioned himself in order that he might preserve the integrity of his spiritual walk. This process of self-examination strengthened his resolve to seek God. 'I seem to want a larger measure of that true faith,' he wrote, 'which realizes unseen things and produces that vigour of the religious affections which, by making communion with God and Christ through the Spirit more fervent and habitual, might render me apt and alert to spiritual things. Therefore let me cultivate the religious affections.'

REFERENCE: *Private Papers of William Wilberforce* (1897)

'The one thing needful'

'Study to shew thyself approved unto God, a workman that needeth not to be ashamed, rightly dividing the word of truth.' 2 Timothy 2:15
SUGGESTED FURTHER READING: Psalm 1; Luke 10:38–42

Above all remember *the one thing needful.* I had far rather that you should be a true Christian than a learned man, but I wish you to become the latter through the influence of the former.

FOR MEDITATION: 'When Mr Wilberforce aimed at giving peculiar force to a sentiment or a maxim,' wrote his friend John Harford, 'the point and terseness of his language could not be surpassed. As an instance of this, the topic of conversation one day being the misery to which Cowper, the poet, was exposed by his extreme sensibility at a public school, "Yes," he exclaimed, "it was a sensitive plant grasped by a hand of iron."'

Wilberforce once observed that 'Pascal is an author who has many "pregnant propositions", as Lord Bacon calls them.' Readers of Pascal's *Pensées* (Thoughts on Religion), of whom Wilberforce was one, know that Pascal had a gift for framing concise phrases about matters of faith that left an indelible impression. At times Wilberforce showed a similar gift.

And so it is with the passage above about the 'one thing needful'—taken from a letter Wilberforce wrote to his third son Samuel. It is a terse, or succinct phrase, but one full of meaning. The Lord Jesus should be the cherished object of our first love. When the integrity of that relationship is as it should be, all else—the pursuit of scholarship or any of the many worthy goals God may give us to pursue—will be conducted aright.

REFERENCE: *Private Papers of William Wilberforce* (1897)

'All may be done through prayer'

'My voice shalt thou hear in the morning, O LORD; *in the morning will I direct my prayer unto thee, and will look up.' Psalm 5:3*
SUGGESTED FURTHER READING: Psalm 5:1–12

All may be done through prayer—almighty prayer, I am ready to say; and why not? for that it is almighty is only through the gracious ordination of the God of love and truth. Oh then, pray, pray, pray, my dearest boy. But then remember to estimate your state on self-examination not by your prayers, but by what you find to be the effects of them on your character, tempers, and life.

FOR MEDITATION: 'O thou that hearest prayer,' the psalmist writes (Psalm 65:2). Thus we know, of a surety, that God hears our petitions. The psalmist also testifies, powerfully, that we serve a God who answers prayer. 'In the day when I cried thou answeredst me, and strengthenedst me with strength in my soul' (Psalm 138:3).

Down through the centuries, the psalms have been a source of unspeakable comfort to God's people. They speak, sometimes with piercing honesty, of the deepest and most troubling of circumstances. And yet we are never beyond the reach of God. Nor do our cries, amidst any circumstances, fall on deaf ears. 'I called upon the Lord in distress: the Lord answered me, and set me in a large place. The Lord is on my side; I will not fear.' (Psalm 118:5–6a).

Such knowledge as this is a tremendous buttress to our faith. When our faith is so strengthened through the office and assurance of prayer, we begin to understand and believe that we can, in the words of the great missionary pioneer William Carey: 'Expect great things from God [and] attempt great things for God.'

REFERENCE: *Private Papers of William Wilberforce* (1897)

'Goodness and mercy'

'For he looked for a city which hath foundations, whose builder and maker is God.' Hebrews 11:10
SUGGESTED FURTHER READING: Hebrews 11:8–10, 13–16

How can I but rejoice rather than lament at a pecuniary loss, which has produced such a result as that of bringing us to dwell under the roofs of our dear children, and witness their enjoyment of a large share of domestic comforts, and their conscientious discharge of the duties of the most important of all professions.

But what causes have I for gratitude—surely no one ought more habitually to feel and adopt the psalmist's language, 'goodness and mercy have followed me all my days.' And now have not we great cause for thankfulness in being moored in our latter days in the peaceful haven which we enjoy under the roofs of our sons in Kent and in the Isle of Wight, relieved from all the worry of family cares, and witnessing the respectability, usefulness, and domestic happiness of those most dear to us. Had not the state of my finances rendered it absolutely necessary however, I fear I should hardly have thought myself warranted in giving up my only residence, but it is really true, speaking unaffectedly, that our heavy loss has led to the solid and great increase of our enjoyments.

FOR MEDITATION: In 1831, a severe financial loss resulted in Wilberforce's having to leave his last and beloved home, Highwood Hill, in the village of Mill Hill. It was a bitter blow, but in the midst of it all he learned anew that 'God is our refuge and strength, a very present help in trouble' (Psalm 46:1). He wrote of this in his diary: 'What gives me repose in all things, is the thought of their being his appointment. I doubt not that the same God who has in mercy ordered so many events for so long a course of time, will never fail to overrule (i.e. oversee or sustain) all things both for my family and myself.'

In the midst of all this, Wilberforce fell victim to a serious illness. When he left Highwood Hill, he weighed only 75 pounds. When he had recovered, it was a source of wonder to him—a blessing beyond measure of a gracious Lord. 'I can scarce understand,' he said, 'why my life is spared so long, except it be to show that a man can be as happy without a fortune, as with one.'

REFERENCE: *The Life of William Wilberforce* (1838)

'The very region of poetry'

'Ye shall have a song, as in the night when a holy solemnity is kept; and gladness of heart, as when one goeth with a pipe to come into the mountain of the LORD, to the mighty One of Israel.' Isaiah 30:29
SUGGESTED FURTHER READING: Psalm 33:1–8

As we were one day talking upon the subject of devotional poetry, Mr Wilberforce said: 'Dr Johnson has passed a very sweeping condemnation upon it, and has given it as his opinion that success in this species of composition is next to impossible; and the reason which he gives for it is, "that all poetry implies exaggeration; but that the objects of religion are so great in themselves, as to be incapable of augmentation".'

'One would think, however,' said Mr Wilberforce, 'that religion ought to be the very region of poetry. It relates to subjects which above all others agitate the hopes and fears of mankind—it embodies everything that can melt by its tenderness or elevate by its sublimity—and it has a natural tendency to call forth in the highest degree feelings of gratitude and thankfulness for inestimable mercies.'

FOR MEDITATION: Wilberforce knew well of what he spoke when he said 'religion ought to be the very region of poetry'. His favorite poet was William Cowper, the co-author with John Newton of the celebrated *Olney Hymns* (1779). 'What a happy art, both of conceiving and expressing, he possesses!' Wilberforce once remarked.

Wilberforce loved *Olney Hymns*, particularly Cowper's. One of them amply demonstrates why he felt religion ought to be 'the very region of poetry':

God moves in a mysterious way
His wonders to perform;
He plants his footsteps in the sea
And rides upon the storm.

Deep in unfathomable mines
Of never failing skill
He treasures up his bright designs
And works his sovereign will.

REFERENCE: *Recollections of William Wilberforce* (1864)

'Oh that God may give me grace'

'God is our refuge and strength, a very present help in trouble.' Psalm 46:1
SUGGESTED FURTHER READING: Psalm 46

This (Sunday) morning, I felt the comfort of sober, religious self-conversation. Yet true Christianity lies not in frames and feelings, but in diligently doing the work of God. I am now about to enter upon a trying scene. Oh that God may give me grace, that I may not dishonour but adorn his cause; that I may watch and pray more earnestly and seriously.

FOR MEDITATION: Our hearts can and often do deceive us. 'The heart is deceitful above all things,' wrote the prophet Jeremiah, 'and desperately wicked: who can know it?' (Jeremiah 17:9). Frames and feelings, to use Wilberforce's words, may mislead. Our hearts may cause us misgivings for any number of reasons. But the truths and assurances given us in God's word do not change. Jesus Christ is the Word made flesh (John 1:14), and of him it has been written: 'Jesus Christ the same yesterday, and to day, and for ever' (Hebrews 13:8).

No matter what life brings, we may trust entirely in the never-changing nature of our Saviour and the Scriptures. The apostle Paul wrote of this when he said: 'For the Son of God, Jesus Christ, who was preached among you by us ... was not yea and nay, but in him was yea. For all the promises of God in him are yea, and in him Amen' (2 Corinthians 1:19–20).

If we seek to keep a humble and diligent heart, as Wilberforce described above, God will help us to do it. What is more, we have this assurance for those who seek to be 'clothed with humility'. God, we are told in 1 Peter 5:5, 'giveth grace to the humble'. By placing our trust in the Giver of grace, we can 'adorn his cause' in our lives.

REFERENCE: *The Life of William Wilberforce* (1838)

'The praises of God arising from every nation'

'God made the world and all things therein ... and hath made of one blood all nations of men for to dwell on all the face of the earth.' Acts 17:24a, 26a
SUGGESTED FURTHER READING: Psalm 85:1–3, 7–13

Whilst I was taking a contemplative walk this morning, my mind was led to consider the providential dispensations of that almighty Being, whose infinitely complicated plan embraces all his creatures, and who especially leads, and directs, and supports all those who in their different walks through this multifarious maze of life, are pursuing in his faith and fear the objects which he has respectively assigned them. Here they often know little of each other, but they are all members of the same community, and at length they shall be all collected into one family; and peace, and love, and joy, and perfect unalloyed friendship, shall reign without intermission or abatement.

'The holy church throughout all the world doth acknowledge thee.' It always presents to my mind a most august idea: the praises of God arising from every nation where his name is known and blending as they rise into one note and body of harmony. How much ought this to stimulate us to enlarge the bounds of our Redeemer's kingdom!

FOR MEDITATION: 'The holy church throughout all the world doth acknowledge thee.' Here Wilberforce is quoting line 10 of *Te Deum Laudamus*, a hymn attributed to Niceta of Remisiana (4th century). This ancient line recalls the verses of Samuel Stone (1866):

The Church's one foundation
Is Jesus Christ her Lord,
She is his new creation
By water and the Word.
From heaven he came and sought her
To be his holy bride;
With his own blood he bought her
And for her life he died.

Elect from every nation,
Yet one o'er all the earth;
Her charter of salvation,
One Lord, one faith, one birth;
One holy Name she blesses,
Partakes one holy food,
And to one hope she presses,
With every grace endued.

REFERENCE: *The Life of William Wilberforce* (1838)

'A Sunday in solitude'

'For thus saith the Lord GOD, the Holy One of Israel; In returning and rest shall ye be saved; in quietness and in confidence shall be your strength ...' Isaiah 30:15
SUGGESTED FURTHER READING: Romans 12:1–18

Occasional retirement Mr Wilberforce found of especial service in maintaining the simplicity of his spirit. 'Often in my visits to [Pitt's estate at] Holwood,' he said, 'when I heard one or another speak of this man's place, or that man's peerage, I felt a rising inclination to pursue the same objects; but a Sunday in solitude never failed to restore me to myself.'

FOR MEDITATION: Moments of solitude allow us the opportunity to think soberly about ourselves. The Sabbath or Lord's Day is especially rich in such opportunities. Wilberforce's habit of observing part of the Lord's Day in this fashion kept him grounded as he sought to live out his faith in public life. His habits of the heart in this regard recall verses penned by the renaissance poet Sir John Davies (1569–1626):

If aught can teach us aught, affliction's looks,
Making us look into ourselves so near,
Teach us to know ourselves beyond all books,
Or all the learned schools that ever were.
This mistress lately plucked me by the ear,
And many a golden lesson hath me taught;
Hath made my senses quick and reason clear,
Reformed my will and rectified my thought.

REFERENCE: *The Life of William Wilberforce* (1838)

'The smiles of his goodness'

'Consider the lilies of the field, how they grow; they toil not, neither do they spin: And yet I say unto you, That even Solomon in all his glory was not arrayed like one of these.' Matthew 6:28b–29
SUGGESTED FURTHER READING: Isaiah 58:8–14

This was most true of Mr Wilberforce's hour of daily exercise. Who that ever joined him in it cannot see him as he walked round his garden at Highwood? Now in animated and even playful conversation, and then drawing from his copious pockets a Psalter, a Horace, a Shakespeare, or Cowper, and reading, and reciting, or refreshing passages; and then catching at long-stored flower leaves as the wind blew them from the pages, or standing before a favourite gum cistus to repair the loss. Then he would point out the harmony of the tints, the beauty of the pencilling, the perfection of the colouring, and run up all into those ascriptions of praise to the Almighty which were ever welling forth from his grateful heart. He loved flowers with all the simple delight of childhood. He would hover from bed to bed over his favourites; and when he came in, even from his shortest walk, deposited a few that he had gathered, safely in his room before he joined the breakfast table.

Often would he say as he enjoyed their fragrance, 'How good is God to us! What should we think of a friend who had furnished us with a magnificent house and all we needed, and then coming in to see that all had been provided according to his wishes, should be hurt to find that no scents had been placed in the rooms? Yet so has God dealt with us. Surely flowers are the smiles of his goodness.'

FOR MEDITATION: Psalm 89:15 states: *'Blessed is the people that know the joyful sound: they shall walk, O LORD, in the light of thy countenance.'* Wilberforce knew what it was to 'join with all nature in manifold witness' to God's 'great faithfulness, mercy and love.' He knew what it was to revel in the simple wonder of an intricately-shaped and finely-coloured flower. If we would see God's handiwork, and know a similar joy, we must allow ourselves time to linger over parts of his creation.

REFERENCE: *The Life of William Wilberforce* (1838)

'What God has done for me'

'And thou shalt remember all the way which the LORD *thy God led thee these forty years in the wilderness, to humble thee, and to prove thee, to know what was in thine heart, whether thou wouldest keep his commandments, or no.' Deuteronomy 8:2*
SUGGESTED FURTHER READING: Deuteronomy 30:15–20

Surely when I look over in detail the last forty years the course of my heart and life; when I call to mind who I have been, and what God has done for me, and by me; when I sum up all together, and recollect that consideration which should never be forgotten, that all the past, present, and to come, are under the view of God in lively colours, I am lost in astonishment, and can only exclaim 'Thy ways are not as our ways, nor thy thoughts as our thoughts.'

I will try to look back through my past life, and to affect my heart, as by the review it ought to be, with humility, love, and confidence, mixed with reverential fear; and adopt the words of Ezekiel 16:63, 'That thou mayest remember, and be confounded, and never open thy mouth any more because of thy shame, when I am pacified toward thee for all that thou hast done, saith the Lord GOD.'

FOR MEDITATION: We ought always to remember what the Lord has done for us. One of the ways we can do this is by reading stories of the conversion of others.

Wilberforce's reference above (Ezekiel 16:63) concerns Newton's *Authentic Narrative* (1764). Passages from this classic conversion narrative struck Wilberforce forcibly, as they have many Christians over the years. Newton wrote the timeless hymn *Amazing Grace*, and one passage from the *Authentic Narrative* shows how profoundly Newton had experienced the grace that 'saved a wretch like me.' He wrote:

'In love to my soul, he delivered me from the pit of corruption, and cast all my aggravated sins behind his back. He brought my feet into the paths of peace. This is, indeed, the chief article, but it is not the whole. When he made me acceptable to himself in the Beloved, he gave me favour in the sight of others. He raised me new friends, protected and guided me through a long series of dangers, and crowned every day with repeated mercies.'

REFERENCE: *The Life of William Wilberforce* (1838)

'I may be called to sharp trials'

'That the trial of your faith, being much more precious than of gold that perisheth, though it be tried with fire, might be found unto praise and honour and glory at the appearing of Jesus Christ.' 1 Peter 1:7
SUGGESTED FURTHER READING: John 16:21–33

The resolutions with which Mr Wilberforce had begun this busy season were 'to redeem time more; to keep God more in view, and Christ, and all he has suffered for us; and the unseen world, where Christ is now sitting at the right hand of God interceding for his people. I would grow in love and tender solicitude for my fellow-creatures' happiness, in preparedness for any events which may befall me in this uncertain state. I may be called to sharp trials, but Christ is able to strengthen me for the event, be it what it may.'

FOR MEDITATION: Wilberforce wrote this in his journal on 8 March 1797, a Fast Day. On 17 April, there was a mutiny at Portsmouth. Britain was also in the midst of a bank crisis. Both of these crises rocked the nation. But the most vexing and grievous situation that confronted Wilberforce at this time was an accusation that he was trying to foment mutiny.

A clergyman named Williams had been recommended to Wilberforce as a deserving recipient of his charity. Though Williams had been reduced to dire financial straits through immoral excess and possible mental imbalance, he was now thought penitent. Wilberforce began to help him. However, Williams had not changed at all. During one interview, he spat in Wilberforce's face, and grew so violent that a Bow Street warrant had to be sworn out against him to restrain him. Finding him truly incorrigible, Wilberforce had written to refuse him any further aid.

Williams, however, filled with spite and resentment, took Wilberforce's letter to the London army barracks. There, before the illiterate soldiers, he pretended to read a seditious message from Wilberforce, after which he showed the genuine Wilberforce signature. Several trying days were to unfold—and Wilberforce received not a few anxious letters from his close friend Prime Minister Pitt—before the mutinous seeds sown by Williams were thoroughly and finally quashed. Wilberforce had indeed been 'called to sharp trials,' but at his point of greatest extremity he found God to be his refuge, strength and deliverer.

REFERENCE: *The Life of William Wilberforce* (1838)

'The same style of friendly reproof'

'A friend loveth at all times, and a brother is born for adversity.'
Proverbs 17:17
SUGGESTED FURTHER READING: Proverbs 10:16–21

My dear Sir, The strong claim on my esteem and gratitude which you established by your first letter is much augmented and confirmed by your last. I speak the real sentiments of my heart, when I assure you that I feel deeply indebted to you. How much do I wish that you had been long ere now in the habit of occasionally addressing me in the same style of friendly, and I will add, Christian, animadversion (criticism), and also, when needed of reproof! Such communications are unspeakably valuable to any public man, who wishes, on the one hand, to do his duty, and who, on the other, is sufficiently aware of the difficulty of his task, and of his own various imperfections.

FOR MEDITATION: The letter above was written by Wilberforce to Samuel Roberts, one of Wilberforce's constituents in Yorkshire. It shows the extent to which Wilberforce had a teachable heart—a trait often commended in the Scriptures. Isaiah 57:15 expresses this well: 'For thus saith the high and lofty One that inhabiteth eternity, whose name is Holy; I dwell in the high and holy place, with him also that is of a contrite and humble spirit.'

Roberts had in his initial letter reproved Wilberforce for being stretched too thin because of over-commitments. Roberts had done this thoughtfully and kindly—from this commenced a correspondence and friendship of great benefit to both men. 'It is really extraordinary,' Wilberforce wrote early on, 'but I find myself opening to you with all the unreservedness of an old friend, and entering with the same confidence of friendly sympathy into my private circumstances and feelings. Frankness begets frankness.'

When Wilberforce was similarly remonstrated with very directly by his brother-in-law James Stephen, he responded in much the same way he had with Roberts. 'Go on my dear Sir,' he told Stephen, 'and welcome.' May we all be given a similar spirit, always accepting constructive criticism.

REFERENCE: *The Life of William Wilberforce* (1838)

'That true honour which cometh from God'

'The fear of the Lord is the instruction of wisdom; and before honour is humility.' Proverbs 15:33
SUGGESTED FURTHER READING: Proverbs 15:29–33

But after all, it is of little real importance what judgment is formed of us by our fellow-creatures. To obtain the approbation of the man within the breast, as conscience has been well called, should be our object, and to seek for that true honour which cometh from God.

FOR MEDITATION: There have been many eloquent descriptions of the word 'conscience' down through the centuries. Not a few of them complement Wilberforce's words about 'the man within the breast.' Of these many descriptions, it might well be said that St Augustine has penned the most eloquent—certainly one of the most Christ-centred. 'A good conscience,' he said, 'is the palace of Christ; the temple of the Holy Ghost ... the standing Sabbath of the saints.'

Many things can be said about Augustine's description, but one that stands out is the notion of the conscience being a standing Sabbath or place of rest for God's people. When we seek the true honour that comes from God through living our lives by the light and leading God gives, we will know the place of blessing—a place of rest, contentment and peace.

'Pray for us,' said the writer of the Book of Hebrews, 'for we trust we have a good conscience, in all things willing to live honestly.' These last seven words might be the best of all summaries of what the word 'conscience' means. May it be our continual prayer that God will help us in all things to live honestly.

REFERENCE: *The Life of William Wilberforce* (1838)

'How good is God to us'

'Better is a dinner of herbs where love is, than a stalled ox and hatred therewith.' Proverbs 15:17
SUGGESTED FURTHER READING: Psalm 127

'During the parliamentary session,' wrote Wilberforce's sons, 'Mr Wilberforce was so busy, and so much from home, that he could see little of them through the week; but Sunday was his own, and he spent it in the midst of his family. His children, after meeting him at prayers, went with him to the house of God; repeating to him in the carriage hymns or verses, or passages from his favourite [poet] Cowper.

'Then they walked with him in the garden, and each had the valued privilege of bringing him a Sunday nosegay, for which the flowers of their little gardens had been hoarded all the week. Then all dined together at an early hour.

'One of his Sunday commonplaces was: "'Better,' says the wise man, 'is a dinner of herbs where love is, than a stalled ox and hatred therewith;' but, my children, how good is God to us! He gives us the stalled ox and love too."'

FOR MEDITATION: Ephesians 3:20 tells us that we serve a God who 'is able to do exceeding abundantly above all that we ask or think.' In John's gospel, the Lord Jesus said to those who will place their faith in him: 'I am come that they might have life, and that they might have it more abundantly.'

To have a strong sense of the Lord's blessing upon our lives is to have a very great deal indeed. Sundays, our weekly day of rest, can bring this truth home to us in ways that sustain us throughout the week to come. Sundays are our own, to paraphrase Wilberforce's sons. It is there that we can say:

And now he takes me to his heart as son,
He asks me not to fill a servant's place;
The 'Far-off country' wanderings all are done,
wide open are the arms of grace.

Such love—such wondrous love
Such love—such wondrous love,
That God should have a sinner such as I,
How wonderful is love like this!

Robert Harkness, © 1928

REFERENCE: *The Life of William Wilberforce* (1838)

'May he daily renew me'

'Create in me a clean heart, O God; and renew a right spirit within me.'
Psalm 51:10
SUGGESTED FURTHER READING: Isaiah 57:15

I am just returned from receiving communion. I was enabled to be earnest in prayer, and to be contrite and humble under a sense of my unworthiness, and of the infinite mercy of God in Christ. I hope that I desire from my heart to lead henceforth a life more worthy of the Christian profession. May it be my meat and drink to do the will of God, my Father. May he daily renew me by his Holy Spirit, and may I walk before him in a frame made up of fear, and gratitude, and humble trust, and assurance of his fatherly kindness and constant concern for me.

FOR MEDITATION: This is one of the many prayers Wilberforce penned in his diary—a prayer that did indeed foster within him the assurance of God's fatherly kindness and constant concern.

William Cowper, Wilberforce's favourite poet, was also one of Britain's most celebrated letter-writers. He spoke of prayer in words that Wilberforce might well have read. Certainly, he would have said a heartfelt 'Amen' to them. 'How happy it is to believe,' Cowper wrote, 'with a steadfast assurance, that our petitions are heard even while we are making them; and how delightful to meet with a proof of it in the effectual and actual grant of them.'

Hannah More, one of Wilberforce's cherished friends and fellow reformers, wrote these lines about prayer:

Fountain of mercy! whose pervading eye
Can look within and read what passes there,
Accept my thoughts for thanks; I have no words,
My soul o'erfraught with gratitude, rejects
The aid of language—Lord!—behold my heart.

REFERENCE: *The Life of William Wilberforce* (1838)

'An entire and habitual dependence upon him'

'I am the vine, ye are the branches: he that abideth in me, and I in him, the same bringeth forth much fruit: for without me ye can do nothing.'
John 15:5
SUGGESTED FURTHER READING: John 15:1–11

It was by careful study, which no press of business ever interrupted, and which continued daily through Mr Wilberforce's life, that he obtained an acquaintance with Holy Scripture unusual even in professed theologians. This may be traced in the altered tone of his most private entries; they abounded in that deep humiliation with which they who have looked closely into the perfect law of liberty must ever contemplate their own fulfilment of its demands.

'Though utterly *unworthy*,' he said, 'I thank God for having enabled me to pray with earnestness. Oh that this may not be as the morning cloud and as the early dew! By his grace I will persevere with more earnestness than ever, labouring to work out my own salvation in an entire and habitual dependence upon him.'

'If you have truly learned to feel the insufficiency of your own powers,' wrote the Dean of Carlisle, to whom he had poured forth his earnest desires after a more rapid growth in holiness, 'you have made more progress than you think of; and if you can support that feeling and act upon it for any time together, your advance is very considerable.'

FOR MEDITATION: Do we long for the Lord? Do we earnestly desire a deeper knowledge of his ways that we might better serve him? Is the cry of our heart like that of the psalmist in Psalm 63:1? Wilberforce knew and treasured these lines from William Cowper, in many ways an eighteenth-century psalmist:

Acquaint thyself with God, if thou would'st taste
His works. Admitted once to his embrace,
Thou shalt perceive that thou wast blind before:
Thine eye shall be instructed; and thine heart
Made pure shall relish with divine delight
Till then unfelt, what hands divine have wrought.

William Cowper, *The Task*

REFERENCE: *The Life of William Wilberforce* (1838)

'Give me a new heart'

'That he would grant you, according to the riches of his glory, to be strengthened with might by his Spirit in the inner man.' Ephesians 3:16
SUGGESTED FURTHER READING: Ephesians 3:14–21

A Christian's life is hid with Christ in God. He ought to have more satisfaction in offering the little sacrifices God requires, as the willing tribute of a grateful heart, than in gratifying fleshly appetites; and that he should look for his happiness in fellowship with God, and view with jealousy whatever tends to break in on this communion. I am apt to be thinking it enough to spend so many hours in reading, religious service, study and so on. What a sad sign is this! How different from that delight in the law and service of God in the inner man, which St Paul speaks of, and which was so eminent in David! O my God, for the sake of thy beloved Son, our propitiation, through whom we may have access to the throne of grace, give me a new heart—give me a real desire and earnest longing for one.

FOR MEDITATION: Psalm 33:21 declares: 'For our heart shall rejoice in him, because we have trusted in his holy name.' Do we live our lives as though we were offering the willing tribute of a grateful heart? Such a tribute lies not in the performance of deeds, so much as it lies in seeking the true happiness that flows from fellowship with him.

The pen of William Cowper has captured what the cry of our grateful hearts should be:

But, O thou bounteous Giver of all good,
Thou art of all thy gifts thyself the crown!
Give what thou canst, without thee we are poor;
And with thee rich, take what thou wilt away.   William Cowper, *The Task*

REFERENCE: *The Life of William Wilberforce* (1838)

'Keeping the Sabbath day holy'

'And the Sabbath of the land shall be meat for you; for thee, and for thy servant, and for thy maid, and for thy hired servant, and for thy stranger that sojourneth with thee.' Leviticus 25:6
SUGGESTED FURTHER READING: Hebrews 4:1–9

O what a blessing is Sunday, interposed between the waves of worldly business like the divine path of the Israelites through Jordan! There is nothing in which I would advise you to be more strictly conscientious than in keeping the Sabbath day holy. I can truly declare that to me the Sabbath has been invaluable.

FOR MEDITATION: The poet George Herbert said: 'On Sunday heaven's gates stand open.' The American poet Henry Wadsworth Longfellow wrote that 'Sunday is the golden clasp that binds together the volume of the week.'

We seldom think of the Sabbath in terms that these poets of an earlier age knew. We are the poorer for it. We rush to stores to purchase that which is easily obtained on any of the other six days of the week. Do we revere the Sabbath as a day in which we can contemplate those things that are beyond price?

By way of renewing a sacred sense of the Sabbath, consider still other descriptions of it by Herbert and Longfellow.

'O day most calm, most bright, the fruit of this, the next world's bud.'—Herbert

'O day of rest! how beautiful, how fair, how welcome to the weary and the old! day of the Lord! and truce of earthly care! day of the Lord, as all our days should be.'—Longfellow

'Sunday observe; think, when the bells do chime, 'tis angels' music: therefore come not too late.'—Herbert

REFERENCE: M BALLOU, *Treasury of Thought*, (BOSTON:1873), P. 456

'A most convenient god'

'For all the gods of the nations are idols: but the Lord *made the heavens.' Psalm 96:5*
SUGGESTED FURTHER READING: Psalm 2

Destiny is also the great principle of the modern infidels. This is that deity whom it has been the labour of philosophers to exalt into the throne of the Almighty; a most convenient god both for the man of reflection who is destitute of all religious principle, for the follower of pleasure who is resolved to riot in licentiousness, for the warrior who is disposed to plunder without mercy, and for the politician who is unbounded in his ambition and not to be restrained in his iniquity.

For destiny has no moral law: it acknowledges neither a heaven nor a hell; it is a god which neither punishes transgressors nor is 'the rewarder of them that diligently seek him': it views with equal eye, the oppressor and the oppressed, the dishonest and the upright, the licentious and the chaste; it encourages no contrition; it suggests no repentance; it regards alike the persevering criminal and the humble penitent.

FOR MEDITATION: Destiny, it might well be said, acknowledges no sovereign. It is devoid of God, and possesses no moral compass. What is more, destiny is a false god—directly at odds with the Lord, who holds our times within his hand (Psalm 31:15). Isaiah 45:11–13 speaks of God as the Author of history, and the One who orders our steps:

Thus saith the Lord, the Holy One of Israel, and his Maker, Ask me of things to come concerning my sons, and concerning the work of my hands command ye me. I have made the earth, and created man upon it: I, even my hands, have stretched out the heavens, and all their host have I commanded. I have raised him up in righteousness, and I will direct all his ways.

REFERENCE: ARTICLE BY WILBERFORCE; *Christian Observer,* NOV. 1803

'The cause of God at large'

'And now I am no more in the world, but these are in the world, and I come to thee. Holy Father, keep through thine own name those whom thou hast given me, that they may be one, as we are.' John 17:11
SUGGESTED FURTHER READING: Ephesians 4:1–6

Though I am an Episcopalian by education and conviction, I yet feel such a oneness and sympathy with the cause of God at large, that nothing would be more delightful than my communing once every year with *every* Church that holds the Head, even Christ.

FOR MEDITATION: On October 19, 1824, Wilberforce wrote in his diary: 'Venerable Rowland Hill dined with me—aged 80.' His regard for this celebrated preacher was high.

Charles Spurgeon felt much the same, and he once described Hill in terms that attested his charitable spirit.

Mr Hill … was glad of a church, and equally delighted with a meeting-house; but the village green, a barn, an assembly room, or a hovel were all used as they were offered. He was not reared in the lap of luxury as a preacher, nor was he surrounded by the society of unmingled aristocracy, so as to be guarded from every whiff of the air of common life. He mingled so thoroughly with the people that he became the people's man, and forever remained so. With all the highmindedness which ought to go with nobility he mingled an unaffected simplicity and benevolence of spirit, which made him dear to persons of all ranks.

Nowhere can Hill's eloquence be better seen than in a brief but powerful statement regarding the bonds of unity that ought to exist among Christians of all traditions. They are a compelling complement to Wilberforce's words in the selection above:

I do not want the walls of separation between different orders of Christians to be destroyed, but only lowered, that we may shake hands a little easier over them.

REFERENCE: *The Autobiography of William Jay* (1854), P. 301–2

'Glad tidings to the poor'

'Blessed are the poor in spirit: for theirs is the kingdom of heaven.'
Matthew 5:3
SUGGESTED FURTHER READING: Matthew 5:1–12

Many of the philosophers spoke out, and professed to keep the lower orders in ignorance for the general good, plainly suggesting that the bulk of mankind was to be considered as almost of an inferior species. Aristotle himself countenanced this opinion. An opposite mode of proceeding naturally belongs to Christianity, which without distinction professes an equal regard for all human beings, and which was characterized by her first promulgator as the messenger of 'glad tidings to the poor'.

FOR MEDITATION: Verses by the poet Oliver Wendell Holmes express that which Wilberforce writes:

Yes, child of suffering, thou mayest well be sure
He who ordained the Sabbath loves the poor.

God's love for those who know poverty is profound. It seeks them out as a father does a beloved child. 'The poor committeth himself unto thee', we read in Psalm 10:14, 'thou art the helper of the fatherless.' This blest assurance is repeated in Psalm 72:12—'For he shall deliver the needy when he crieth; the poor also, and him that hath no helper.' In the New Testament we read that the apostles gave their fellow apostle Paul the following charge: 'Only they would that we should remember the poor; the same which I also was forward to do' (Galatians 2:10).

As followers of Christ in this age, it falls to us to reach out to those in need, as God's ambassadors. We ought to do no less than our heavenly Father—we ought to be helpers of the poor.

REFERENCE: *A Practical View of Christianity* (1797)

'Serving the Lord with all humility'

'The meek will he guide in judgment: and the meek will he teach his way.' Psalm 25:9

SUGGESTED FURTHER READING: 1 Corinthians 2:1–13

Christian beware! There are Antinomians of all classes and descriptions, from the dissipated woman of fashion, who, with a heart absorbed in worldly vanities, reposes an unwarrantable confidence in Christ, and even feels a vain gratitude to that Saviour to whom she trusts for pardon and final happiness; to the self-complacent religionist, who, puffed up with a vain conceit of his superior light and extraordinary proficiency in divine things, fondly flatters himself that he is a favourite of heaven, while his pride, presumption, and indolent self-indulgent censoriousness, betray a state of heart directly opposite to the genuine operations of divine grace. These were exemplified in the character of the meek and lowly Jesus, and in the habits, affections, and language of the apostle [Paul], who, in the midst of labours and sufferings unparalleled, honoured likewise with unequalled disclosures of heavenly glory, was gentle and affectionate (1 Thess 2:7–8), watchful and self-denying (1 Cor 10:27), serving the Lord with all humility of mind, in weakness and fear, and much trembling.

FOR MEDITATION: The great Puritan writer John Flavel once said: 'They that know God will be humble; they that know themselves cannot be proud.' His contemporary Robert Leighton painted a beautiful word picture. He wrote: 'God's sweet dews and showers of grace slide off the mountains of pride, and fall on the valleys of humble hearts, and make them pleasant and fertile.' Wilberforce himself observed: 'The best hope will arise from my bearing about with me a deep impression of my own weakness, and of the urgent need of divine help.'

Would we be God's missionaries, his messengers? If we would, a true and abiding sense of humility should be a hallmark of our Christian profession. It should distinguish us in the eyes of others.

The great missionary pioneer William Carey composed his own epitaph. It speaks volumes about his humbleness of heart. 'A wretched, poor, and helpless worm,' he wrote, 'on thy kind arms I fall.'

REFERENCE: WILBERFORCE, *Christian Observer*, NOV. 1802, P. 637

'The reach of their understandings'

'I applied mine heart to know, and to search, and to seek out wisdom, and the reason of things ...' Ecclesiastes 7:25
SUGGESTED FURTHER READING: Proverbs 2:1–9

There is another class of men, an increasing class, it is to be feared, in this country, that of absolute unbelievers. May the writer, sincerely pitying their melancholy state, be permitted to ask them one plain question? If Christianity be not in their estimation true, yet is there not at least a presumption in its favour sufficient to entitle it to a serious examination; from its having been embraced, and that not blindly and implicitly, but upon full inquiry and deep consideration, by Bacon, and Milton, and Locke, and Newton, and much the greater part of those, who, by the reach of their understandings, or the extent of their knowledge, and by the freedom of their minds, and their daring to combat existing prejudices, have called forth the respect and admiration of mankind.

FOR MEDITATION: Elsewhere in Wilberforce's writings, he observed: 'The faith of immortality gives to every mind that cherishes it a certain firmness of texture.' He cared deeply about that sphere of Christian literature we know as apologetics, which he often referred to as 'the evidences of the Christian religion.' He cared so much about this, in fact, that he wrote a book called *A Practical View of Christianity*, which was published in April 1797.

Wilberforce possessed a keen intellect and great intellectual curiosity. He knew what it was to love God with his mind, and he cherished books. When travelling with Wilberforce, his young friend John Harford noted: 'a large green bag full of books filled a corner of his carriage, and when we stopped at our inn in the evening it was his delight to have this bag into the parlour, and to spread part of its stores over the table. He kindled at the very sight of books.'

It is not surprising, then, to learn that *A Practical View* was a book that touched the lives of readers who possessed great intellectual gifts, among them the celebrated moral philosopher Thomas Chalmers. He wrote to Wilberforce in 1828: 'may that book ... represent you to future generations, and be the instrument of converting many'.

REFERENCE: *A Practical View of Christianity* (1797)

'We little believe how we are loved by him'

'But Jesus called them unto him, and said, Suffer little children to come unto me, and forbid them not: for of such is the kingdom of God.' Luke 18:16
SUGGESTED FURTHER READING: Mark 10:13–16

How little does a child know how much it is loved? It is the same with us and our heavenly Father: we little believe how we are loved by him. I delight in little children: I could spend hours in watching them. How much there is in them that the Saviour loved, when he took a little child and set him in the midst: their simplicity, their confidence in you, the fund of happiness with which their beneficent Creator has endued them; that when intelligence is less developed and so affords less enjoyment, the natural spirits are an inexhaustible fund of infantile pleasure.

FOR MEDITATION: The writer James Hamilton penned thoughts kindred to those of Wilberforce above. 'Bring your little children to the Saviour,' he wrote. 'Place them in his arms. Devote them to his service. Born in his camp, let them wear from the first his colours. Taking advantage of timely opportunities, and with all tenderness of spirit, seek to endear them to the Friend of Sinners, the Good Shepherd of the Lambs, the loving Guardian of the little children.'

Jeremiah 31:3 conveys to us how we are loved by our heavenly Father: 'I have loved thee with an everlasting love: therefore with lovingkindness have I drawn thee.' If we are so loved by our heavenly Father, and by the Saviour who so loved little children, it becomes us, then, to love our children with all that lies within us. If we would draw them to their heavenly Father, if we would bring them to their Saviour, they must first learn love at our knee.

REFERENCE: *The Life of William Wilberforce* (1838)

'True Christians are the best citizens'

'I exhort therefore, that, first of all, supplications, prayers, intercessions, and giving of thanks, be made for all men; for kings, and for all that are in authority; that we may lead a quiet and peaceable life in all godliness and honesty. For this is good and acceptable in the sight of God our Saviour.' 1 Timothy 2:1–3
SUGGESTED FURTHER READING: 1 Peter 2:11–20; Romans 13:1–8

Let true Christians abound in prayers, 'for kings and all that are in authority'; and prove by their orderly, industrious, and contented conduct, that they remember the object, for the attainment of which the apostle directed those prayers to be offered, 'that they may lead a quiet and peaceable life, in all godliness and honesty.'

Let them shun dissipation; let them avoid ostentation and display; let them rather exhibit a degree of Christian sobriety in the enjoyment of the good things in life; and while they use the bounties of heaven with grateful moderation, let them manifest that their hearts are not set upon them, and that they exercise economy and self-denial, the better to enable them to succour the indigent and comfort the wretched.

Thus, by their zeal and piety, by their moderation and sobriety, by their gentleness and humility, by their self-denial and liberality, by their civil, social, and domestic virtues, they will show that true Christians are the best citizens also.

FOR MEDITATION: We have often heard the phrase 'the salt of the earth'. Salt is a preservative, and it adds flavour. In the ancient world it was regarded as a precious commodity and highly valued. Bearing all of these things in mind, the words of the Lord in Matthew 5:13 take on added meaning. 'Ye,' said Jesus, 'are the salt of the earth.'

Immediately after this, the Lord warns us not to let 'the salt (ourselves) lose its savour.' This metaphor reminds us that we are to be salt—and light—wherever we are in God's world. Through acts of service, and the quality of our lives and character, through being trusted friends, through our behaviour in schools and churches within our local community—in all of these ways we can commend our faith. And so we ought to follow the admonition of our Lord, who said forcefully and succinctly in Mark 9:50—'Have salt in yourselves.'

REFERENCE: *A Practical View of Christianity* (1797)

'The continuance of our national blessings'

'If my people, which are called by my name, shall humble themselves, and pray, and seek my face, and turn from their wicked ways; then will I hear from heaven, and will forgive their sin, and will heal their land.'
2 Chronicles 7:14
SUGGESTED FURTHER READING: Psalm 101

No one knows how far his humiliation, of some pious though obscure Christian shall be found to have been the real instrument in prolonging public prosperity, and maintaining the national security, which the politicians of the day had boastingly ascribed to the superior ability and wisdom of their favourite statesman.

Let the meanest and weakest Christian, therefore, labour in his contracted sphere for the promotion of true piety, and pray for the happiness of his native land. Let him pray that our public counsellors may be blest with wisdom, and that all things may be so ordered and settled by their endeavours, on the best and surest foundation, that peace and happiness, truth and justice, religion and piety, may be established among us for all generations.

FOR MEDITATION: The Quaker poet John Greenleaf Whittier wrote movingly of those dedicated to 'making their lives a prayer'. The preacher Rowland Hill said: 'Prayer is the breath of a new-born soul, and there can be no Christian life without it.'

One of the most beautiful descriptions of prayer ever written comes to us from Wilberforce's cherished friend Hannah More:

Prayer is the application of want to him who alone can relieve it, the voice of sin to him who alone can pardon it. It is the urgency of poverty, the prostration of humility, the fervency of penitence, the confidence of trust. It is not eloquence, but earnestness; not figures of speech, but compunction of soul. It is the 'Lord, save us, we perish,' of drowning Peter; the cry of faith to the ear of mercy.

Those who are faithful in the office of prayer, however anonymous or unobserved, perform a holy and magnificent service. They are precious in the sight of God.

REFERENCE: WILBERFORCE, *A Retrospect of the Year 1801* (1802)

The work of the Spirit

'When he, the Spirit of truth, is come, he will guide you into all truth: for he shall not speak of himself; but whatsoever he shall hear, that shall he speak: and he will shew you things to come.' John 16:13
SUGGESTED FURTHER READING: John 14:15–26

But the nature of that happiness which the true Christian seeks to possess, is no other than the restoration of the image of God in his soul: and as to the manner of acquiring it, disclaiming with indignation every idea of attaining it by his own strength, he rests altogether on the operation of God's Holy Spirit, which is promised to all who cordially embrace the gospel. He knows therefore that this holiness is not to precede his reconciliation with God, and be its cause; but to follow it, and be its effect.

FOR MEDITATION: Wilberforce had memorized most of the Letters of Paul. From Ephesians 2:8–10 he gleaned a proper understanding of holiness and its place in the divine economy. Holiness is the fruit of faith, not its foundation. The pursuit of good works—that is to say the manifestation of holiness in our lives—is deeply important. But 'by grace are ye saved through faith', and nothing of our own doing. Faith, Paul writes, 'is the gift of God: not of works, lest any man should boast.' Through faith, and it is vital that we understand this, we are 'created in Christ Jesus unto good works, which God hath before ordained that we should walk in them.' It is as James Aughey said: 'Remember that holiness is not the way to Christ, but Christ is the way to holiness.'

When we understand these things aright, we reflect the image of our Lord. The words of Charles Spurgeon are apposite: 'Holiness is the architectural plan upon which God buildeth up his living temple.'

REFERENCE: *A Practical View of Christianity* (1797)

'As so many instruments to be consecrated'

'I beseech you therefore, brethren, by the mercies of God, that ye present your bodies a living sacrifice, holy, acceptable unto God, which is your reasonable service.' Romans 12:1
SUGGESTED FURTHER READING: Matthew 22:34–40

Christians should yield themselves without reserve to the reasonable service of their rightful Sovereign. 'They are not their own': their bodily and mental faculties, their natural and acquired endowments, their substance, their authority, their time, their influence; all these, they consider as belonging to them, not for their own gratification, but as so many instruments to be consecrated to the honour and employed in the service of God.

This must be the master principle to which every other must be subordinate. Whatever may have been their ruling passion or their leading pursuit, whether sensual, or intellectual, of science, of taste, of fancy, or of feeling, it must now possess but a secondary place; or rather (to speak more correctly) it must exist only at the pleasure, and be put altogether under the control of, our Lord.

FOR MEDITATION: The dictionary tells us that if something is consecrated, it is 'solemnly dedicated to or set apart for a high purpose'. For the Christian, consecration implies a dedication of ourselves and all that we are to the service of our Lord and Sovereign. He is the King who is to reign in our hearts. There is no higher purpose or pursuit we can undertake than that of consecration.

The Puritan writer John Flavel commended the practice of consecration to his readers by saying: 'See that you receive Christ with all your heart. As there is nothing in Christ that may be refused, so there is nothing in you from which he must be excluded.' To seek to be consecrated in our journey of faith is to sit at the feet of the Lord and say:

Teach us, Master, how to give
All we have and are to thee;
Grant us, Saviour, while we live,
Wholly, only thine to be.

Frances Havergal

REFERENCE: *A Practical View of Christianity* (1797)

'Her natural and proper offices'

'He healeth the broken in heart, and bindeth up their wounds.' Psalm 147:3
SUGGESTED FURTHER READING: Isaiah 40:1–11

Christianity then assumes her true character, no less than she performs her natural and proper offices, when she takes under her protection those poor degraded beings on whom philosophy looks down with disdain, or perhaps with contemptuous condescension. On the very first promulgation of Christianity it was declared by its great Author as 'glad tidings to the poor'; and, ever faithful to her character, Christianity still delights to instruct the ignorant, to succour the needy, to comfort the sorrowful, to visit the forsaken.

FOR MEDITATION: The historian, poet and politician Thomas Babington, Lord Macaulay, who knew Wilberforce well, once said: 'The real security of Christianity is to be found in its benevolent morality ... in the consolation which it bears to every house of mourning, in the light with which it brightens the great mystery of the grave.' Macaulay understood, because he had learned from the faith of Wilberforce and his own father that Christianity 'delights ... to succour the needy, to comfort the sorrowful, to visit the forsaken.'

Macaulay's words are moving and eloquent. But never yet have any words come to compare, nor could they, with the words of our Lord in the Sermon on the Mount (Matthew 5:3–9):

Blessed are the poor in spirit: for theirs is the kingdom of heaven.
Blessed are they that mourn: for they shall be comforted.
Blessed are the meek: for they shall inherit the earth.
Blessed are they which do hunger and thirst after righteousness: for they shall be filled.
Blessed are the merciful: for they shall obtain mercy.
Blessed are the pure in heart: for they shall see God.

REFERENCE: DAVID NEWSOME, *The Parting of Friends*, P. 53

'The duties of the day'

'Now the end of the commandment is charity out of a pure heart, and of a good conscience, and of faith unfeigned.' 1 Timothy 1:5
SUGGESTED FURTHER READING: 1 Corinthians 13:1–13

In truth, how short-sighted is man. How limited does the page of history shew to have been the view of those whose sphere of vision we should conceive to have been the widest and the most extended. How uncertain also are all human projects. What a practical lesson does this read us to follow the plain path which our conscience prescribes to us; to do on the day the duties of the day; and never to be drawn from the strict line of rectitude by any flattering prospects which may tempt us to the deviation.

FOR MEDITATION: 'Act from a pure principle,' Wilberforce wrote in the pages of *A Practical View of Christianity*, 'and leave the event to God.' This is but another way of saying that we should 'follow the plain path which our conscience prescribes to us; to do on the day the duties of the day.'

Hannah More's reflections on duty are ones with which Wilberforce would have heartily agreed. 'We are apt,' she wrote, 'to mistake our vocation by looking out of the way for occasions to exercise great and rare virtues, and by stepping over the ordinary ones that lie directly in the road before us.'

The noted nineteenth-century preacher Robert Hall was another contemporary of Wilberforce's. His observations on the subject of duty serve to bring our thoughts into sharp focus: 'Of an accountable creature, duty is the concern of every moment, since he is every moment pleasing or displeasing God.' Verses written by Martin Luther sound a complementary chord:

Put thou thy trust in God;
In duty's path go on;
Fix on his word thy steadfast eye;
So shall thy work be done.

REFERENCE: WILBERFORCE, *The Dangers and Evils of Party* (1804)

'All human events'

'Humble yourselves therefore under the mighty hand of God, that he may exalt you in due time.' 1 Peter 5:6
SUGGESTED FURTHER READING: Psalm 9:7–11

The Supreme Being can at any moment bring light out of darkness; and if at any time our country should again be visited with similar difficulties and dangers, humbling ourselves under his mighty hand, and putting our trust in his mercy, we should assume a holy fortitude, superior to all the chances and changes of this varying life. Our part in such circumstances is, to do the duty of the present hour without despondency; remembering that all human events are under the direction of a being infinitely wise, powerful, and merciful. We may lawfully supplicate him to deliver our country from impending evils, and use the means of providing for the public safety, which our appointed rulers prescribe to us, relying on the Almighty for their success.

FOR MEDITATION: The heart of Wilberforce's reflection above is this: 'all human events are under the direction of a being infinitely wise, powerful, and merciful.' On another occasion, he observed: 'I am afraid it is too true, that many are much inclined to refer human events to fortune, chance, fate, or destiny, rather than to the over-ruling Providence of that Being, whose character is unfolded to us in Scripture.'

The poet John Greenleaf Whittier, who much admired Wilberforce, said this of God's providence:

I know not where his islands lift
Their fronded palms in air;
I only know I cannot drift
Beyond his love and care.

What a source of comfort—a safe harbour in which to moor our hopes. The poet William Cowper understood this as well:

'Tis Providence alone secures
In every change both mine and yours.

REFERENCE: *A Retrospect of the Year 1801* (1802)

'What we are to believe and what to practice'

'So then faith cometh by hearing, and hearing by the word of God.'
Romans 10:17
SUGGESTED FURTHER READING: 2 Timothy 3:14–17

By the diligent study of the Word of God, that blessed repository of divine truth and consolation we are to learn our obligations and our duty, what we are to believe and what to practise. And, surely, one would think it could not be required to press men to the perusal of the sacred volume. Reason dictates, Revelation commands; 'Faith comes by hearing, and hearing by the word of God'; 'Search the Scriptures'; 'Be ready to give to every one a reason of the hope that is in you.' Such are the declarations and injunctions of the inspired writers; injunctions confirmed by commendations of those who obey the admonition. Yet, is it not undeniable that with the Bible in our houses, we are ignorant of its contents; and that hence, in a great measure, it arises, that the bulk of the Christian world know so little, and mistake so greatly, in what regards the religion which they profess?

FOR MEDITATION: Truly the Bible is the blessed repository of divine truth. The nineteenth-century preacher D.L. Moody rightly understood what ought to flow from a belief that the Bible was indeed such a repository: 'Merely reading the Bible is no use at all without we study it thoroughly, and hunt it through, as it were, for some great truth.'

Commending the reading of the Scriptures was a task Moody frequently undertook. 'I never saw a useful Christian,' he once said, 'who was not a student of the Bible. If a man neglects his Bible, he may pray and ask God to use him in his work; but God cannot make much use of him, for there is not much for the Holy Ghost to work upon.'

Two centuries before Moody, the Puritan John Flavel penned this moving tribute to the Bible: 'The Scriptures teach us the best way of living, the noblest way of suffering, and the most comfortable way of dying.'

REFERENCE: *A Practical View of Christianity* (1797)

'The ultimate giver of all good'

'To bind his princes at his pleasure; and teach his senators wisdom.'
Psalm 105:22
SUGGESTED FURTHER READING: Psalm 147

Has any country flourished in peace, and become by a gradual course of improvement, wealthy, populous, and happy at home, and prosperous, united, and formidable abroad? We find the historian lavish in his praises of the wisdom and spirit of the framers of her constitution, and of the equity of her laws; or ardent in his admiration of that sagacity and vigilance in her governors, by which they discovered and drew forth her latent powers and resources; warm in commending the fostering care with which they cherished her infant institutions, and as the occasions might require, originated or seconded, quickened or restrained the efforts of her industry, and the ardour of her people.

But no mention is made of HIM who awardeth, at his pleasure, prosperity or misfortune, victory or defeat; who when he looks with favour on a nation, blesses her councils with wisdom, and her arms with victory; and when a people has incurred his displeasure, delivers them over to defeat in war; or in peace, to faction and anarchy, or to corruption, to slavery, and ruin.

Let us assign their due merit to human instruments. Let us acknowledge the value of their labours and sacrifices. Let us gratefully commemorate their services, and liberally reward them—but let the Christian Observer look beyond the immediate agent, and pay the tribute of his praises to that Being, who is the ultimate giver of all good.

FOR MEDITATION: 'Great is the Lord, and greatly to be praised; and his greatness is unsearchable,' we read in Psalm 145:3. He is the ultimate giver of all good. The poet William Cowper knew this intimately:

Not to understand a treasure's worth,
Till time has stolen away the slightest good,
Is cause of half the poverty we feel,
And makes the world the wilderness it is.

REFERENCE: *A Retrospect of the Year 1801* (1802)

'The habit of living in Christ'

*'I am the vine, ye are the branches: he that abideth in me, and I in him,
the same bringeth forth much fruit: for without me ye can do nothing.'*
John 15:5
SUGGESTED FURTHER READING: Colossians 3:1–17

The true Christian holds, in obedience to the injunction, 'Whatever you
do in word or deed', that the desire to please his God and Saviour must
be universal. It is thus that the habit of living in Christ, and to Christ, is
to be formed. The difference between real and nominal Christians is
more manifest on smaller occasions than on greater. In the latter, all who
do not disclaim the authority of Christ's commands must obey them, but
in the former only they will apply them who do make religion their grand
business, and pleasing their God and Saviour, and pleasing, instead of
grieving the Spirit, their continual and habitual aim.

FOR MEDITATION: Just before the close of the nineteenth century, the Rev.
Maltbie Babcock was called to the prestigious pastorate of the Brick
Presbyterian Church in New York City. Eighteen months after he had
accepted this call, he travelled to the Holy Land. He died overseas of
brucellosis.

Sadly Babcock, a very gifted writer, published nothing during his life.
However, in the years that followed, his wife Catherine collected and
published many of his writings. One of his poems became the basis of
the hymn *This Is My Father's World* (1901). Among his other writings
was this reflection on what it means to cultivate the habit of living in
Christ:

Thinking, speaking, hoping, planning, dreaming—all are to be in the name of the
Lord Jesus. His love and life are to colour and shape our ambitions and
accomplishments. In him, as a plant in soil, in rain and sunshine, we are to live,
growing up by him and into him. In his name we are to work, to pray, to suffer, to
rejoice, and at last to go home. It is only another way of saying, 'For me to live is
Christ.'

REFERENCE: *Private Papers of William Wilberforce* (1797)

'How are we always in his hands'

'For the LORD *is a great God, and a great King above all gods. In his hand are the deep places of the earth: the strength of the hills is his also. The sea is his, and he made it: and his hands formed the dry land. O come, let us worship and bow down: let us kneel before the* LORD *our maker.'*
Psalm 95:3–6
SUGGESTED FURTHER READING: Romans 8:28–39

In 1803, Wilberforce reported to his friend Lord Muncaster on Napoleon's threatened invasion from Boulogne: 'Well, my friend, it is my only comfort that all human affairs are in higher hands than ours, and we are assured that all things work together for good to them that love God. Be it our care to secure this, and then we may exclaim in the triumphant language of the psalmist—"The Lord of hosts is with us; the God of Jacob is our refuge" (Psalm 46:11). Farewell, my friend, I wish I were with you,—my mouth waters to think of your rocks, and mountains, and shady walks.'

The sentiments expressed in this letter were of a piece with words Wilberforce wrote in his diary after experiencing 'a narrow escape from breaking my leg in an accident' on the eve of his greatest election contest in 1807. We do not know the precise nature of this accident, but we do know this, according to Wilberforce's biographer sons: the accident 'would have been fatal to his hopes just when setting out [for the hustings].' That night Wilberforce sat down at his desk and wrote: 'Thank God—how are we always in his hands!'

FOR MEDITATION: Psalm 121:8 tells us: 'The Lord shall preserve thy going out and thy coming in from this time forth, and even for evermore.' The assurances of God's constant, watchful care over us run through the Old and New Testaments. They are a recurring theme throughout the entire Bible.

REFERENCE: *The Life of William Wilberforce* (1838)

'The formidable dangers of prosperity'

'Be clothed with humility: for God resisteth the proud, and giveth grace to the humble.' 1 Peter 5:5
SUGGESTED FURTHER READING: Luke 1:46–55

As of late, in a season of war, we were called on to exercise the virtues of adversity, and to resist that despondency and dismay which the exigence [urgent need] of affairs might tend to produce in us, so let us now guard against the still more formidable dangers of prosperity, and be diligent in practising the virtues for which it calls. Let us be humble and sober-minded, thankful for the blessings we enjoy, and conscious how little we have deserved them. Let us beware of the too ordinary effects of increasing wealth and luxury, in producing a haughty, profane, inconsiderate spirit, in the highest degree hateful to that God, 'who scatters the proud in the imagination of their hearts.'

FOR MEDITATION: Wilberforce's words above recall the warning given to the children of Israel in Deuteronomy 8:6–9 and 11–14. It is an admonition we must always keep in view.

Therefore thou shalt keep the commandments of the LORD thy God, to walk in his ways, and to fear him. For the LORD thy God bringeth thee into a good land, a land of brooks of water, of fountains and depths that spring out of valleys and hills; a land of wheat, and barley, and vines, and fig trees, and pomegranates; a land of oil olive, and honey; a land wherein thou shalt eat bread without scarceness, thou shalt not lack any thing in it ... Beware that thou forget not the LORD thy God, in not keeping his commandments, and his judgments, and his statutes, which I command thee this day ...Lest when thou hast eaten and art full, and hast built goodly houses, and dwelt therein; and when thy herds and thy flocks multiply, and thy silver and thy gold is multiplied, and all that thou hast is multiplied; then thine heart be lifted up, and thou forget the LORD thy God, which brought thee forth out of the land of Egypt, from the house of bondage.

REFERENCE: *A Retrospect of the Year 1801* (1802)

'May I learn wisdom and watchfulness'

'Bless the LORD, O my soul, and forget not all his benefits.' Psalm 103:2
SUGGESTED FURTHER READING: Psalm 103:1–14

Let me now look back on the past year [1797] and bless God for its many mercies. Oh how wonderful are his ways! An eventful year with me—my book—my marriage—health restored in sickness. How ungrateful have I been, and how often tempting God to withdraw from me! But his mercy endureth for ever; and the vilest, prostrating himself before him with penitence and faith in the blood of Jesus, may obtain remission of his sins, and the Spirit of renewing grace. This is my hope—here I rest my foot.

Friends died this year—Eliot—Dr Clarke—Joseph Milner. I still spared. How strongly do these events teach us that the time is short! Oh! may I learn and be wise. Public events—mutiny terminated—Dutch victory. I will go to pray, and humble myself before God. The lessons I have learned of my defects teach me to strive earnestly against pride; inordinate love of the favour of man; every feeling of malice; selfishness in not judging fairly between others and myself; above all earthly-mindedness, not having my mind raised above the region of storms. May I learn wisdom and watchfulness from past falls, and so grow in grace. Oh what a blessed thing is the Sunday for giving us an opportunity of serious self-examination, retrospect, and drawing water out of the wells of salvation!

FOR MEDITATION: The writer of Proverbs tells us 'Happy is the man that findest wisdom, and the man that getteth understanding … all the things that thou canst desire are not to be compared unto her. Length of days is in her right hand … her ways are ways of pleasantness, and all her paths are peace. She is a tree of life to them that lay hold upon her; and happy is everyone that retaineth her' (Proverbs 3:13–18). The circumstances of our lives are known only to the Lord, but we can know, and we can rest in the place where that wisdom that cometh from God resides. There, so we read in Proverbs 18:4, 'the wellspring of wisdom [is] as a flowing brook.'

REFERENCE: *The Life of William Wilberforce* (1838)

'The first hours in the morning'

'For unto thee will I pray. My voice shalt thou hear in the morning, O Lord; in the morning will I direct my prayer unto thee, and will look up.'
Psalm 5:3
SUGGESTED FURTHER READING: Psalm 63:1–11

There are still many who remember with no little interest Kensington Gore. The house was seldom free from guests when Mr Wilberforce was in it. The first hours in the morning were all that he could strictly call his own, and these were spent in devotional exercises. 'I always find that I have most time for business, and it is best done, when I have most properly observed my private devotions.'

'In the calmness of the morning,' was his common observation, 'before the mind is heated and wearied by the turmoil of the day, you have a season of unusual importance for communing with God and with yourself.'

After this, he joined his assembled household for morning prayer—a service which he conducted himself and with peculiar interest.

FOR MEDITATION: Richard Cecil was a leading Anglican clergyman of the late 18th and early 19th centuries. A gifted writer and speaker, he is perhaps best known today as the biographer of John Newton. He was also a wise and learned Christian, whose writings have much to teach us still. Wilberforce read his writings with much profit and often commended them to others.

One of Cecil's reflections on prayer echoes what Wilberforce has above. 'A Christian,' Cecil said, 'will find his parenthesis for prayer, even through his busiest hours.' These words find a corollary in a statement of the great biblical commentator Matthew Henry, who wrote: 'Let prayer be the key of the morning and the bolt of the evening.'

REFERENCE: *The Life of William Wilberforce* (1838)

'Practice the precepts of Christ'

'Behold, I have longed after thy precepts: quicken me in thy righteousness.' Psalm 119:40
SUGGESTED FURTHER READING: Jeremiah 35:1–19

We expect to be Christians without [any] labour, study, or inquiry. This is the more preposterous, because Christianity, being a revelation from God, and not the invention of man, discovering to us new relations, with their correspondent duties; containing also doctrines, and motives, and practical principles, and rules, peculiar to itself, and almost as new in their nature as supreme in their excellence, we cannot reasonably expect to become proficient in it by the accidental intercourses of life, as one might learn insensibly the maxims of worldly policy, or a scheme of mere morals.

The diligent perusal of the Holy Scriptures would discover to us our past ignorance. We should cease to be deceived by superficial appearances, and to confound the gospel of Christ with the systems of philosophers; we should become impressed with that weighty truth, so much forgotten, and never to be too strongly insisted on, that Christianity calls on us, as we value our immortal souls, not merely in *general,* to be *religious* and *moral,* but *specially* to believe the doctrines, and imbibe the principles, and practise the precepts of Christ.

FOR MEDITATION: The Roman writer Seneca said that 'precepts are the rules by which we ought to square our lives.' Wilberforce would have heartily agreed. Precepts were of deep importance to him, so much so that he memorized a portion of Scripture rich in the discussion of them—Psalm 119—the longest psalm in the Bible.

What does Psalm 119 have to say about precepts? We are to keep them and meditate on them. We are to walk in the way of them and long for them. We are to forsake them not, nor forget them. Through the reading of God's precepts we receive understanding. Ever and always, we are to love and esteem them.

REFERENCE: *A Practical View of Christianity* (1797)

'The Creator and Sustainer of the Universe'

'I remember the days of old; I meditate on all thy works; I muse on the work of thy hands.' Psalm 143:5
SUGGESTED FURTHER READING: Psalm 86:1–17

I have been led to feel deeply how much we are called upon to admire and praise the kind condescension of the Almighty in acquainting us with his character and attributes in the degree which he has done. How embarrassing and anxiously distressing might it have been to our feelings if we had been left to judge of the qualities of the Supreme Being by the mere light of our unassisted reason. How gracious then is it in the Creator and Sustainer of the Universe to have quieted our apprehensions with such considerate kindness—to have soothed our misgivings and animated and assured our hopes by such varied means?

FOR MEDITATION: Ephesians 2:7 tells us that God showed 'the exceeding riches of his grace in his kindness toward us through Christ Jesus'. Romans 2:4 admonishes us not to despise 'the riches of his goodness and forbearance and longsuffering because the goodness of God leadeth thee to repentance.'

  How truly, as Wilberforce writes above, we ought to 'admire and praise the kind condescension of the Almighty in acquainting us with his character and attributes.' God is the Creator and Sustainer of a universe vast beyond imagination. Yet we, though in one sense so small a part of that vast universe, are deeply important to God—so much so that we have the frequent assurances in the Scriptures for God's grace, kindness, goodness, forbearance, and longsuffering. God placed these assurances in his word, no less than he placed the planetary spheres in their places in the night sky. What a comfort to know that even as the planets and stars remain in the night sky, these assurances in his word shall remain and be continual sources of blessing.

REFERENCE: *Recollections of William Wilberforce* (1864)

'A spirit of universal love and concord'

'And now I am no more in the world, but these are in the world, and I come to thee. Holy Father, keep through thine own name those whom thou hast given me, that they may be one, as we are.' John 17:11
SUGGESTED FURTHER READING: 1 John 4:1–15

Let Christians cleave to fundamentals, and be less busied in thinking or talking about any deeper or more subtle points of speculation, than about those grand practical truths in which is contained, if we may so speak, the vital essence of Christianity; which will for ever animate the love, and call forth the praises, of the redeemed in a better world. These great fundamental peculiarities of Christianity he must never relinquish, or keep back, or lose sight of. Let him love to dwell on those great and essential doctrines on which he agrees with his fellow Christians of other parties, who trust in the same redeeming blood and sanctifying spirit; who call themselves children of the same Father; and who hope to live together hereafter in the same blessed society, and to join in the same song of praise for evermore.

If these habits of mind, and this course of conduct, render him who maintains them less eminent as a partisan, they will render him, however, a happier man and better Christian. He will enjoy inward peace, which, if this life only be regarded, is ill exchanged for popularity: and however he may be outshone by others of less scrupulous principles and of more bustling habits than himself, he will be more than compensated by the consciousness that he is endeavouring to tread in the steps of his meek and lowly master, and to obey his great injunction, to cultivate a spirit of universal love and concord.

FOR MEDITATION: The primary meaning of the word 'concord' refers to a harmony or agreement of interests or feelings. 'Concord' also has a musical connotation, in which it refers to a harmonious combination of simultaneously sounded tones.

This last definition provides us with perhaps the most helpful word picture. The different faith traditions within the Christian family may be as so many instruments. But then we ought to see how we can concert or work together in harmony for the sake and furtherance of God's kingdom.

REFERENCE: *The Dangers and Evils of Party* (1804)

'Followers of the meek and lowly Jesus'

'By this shall all men know that ye are my disciples, if ye have love one to another.' John 13:35
SUGGESTED FURTHER READING: James 3:1–18

We behold a party hotly accusing their governors of wantonly and wickedly plunging their country into needless sufferings and dangers, to gratify their own mad ambition. With anger in their eye, and the language of proud defiance in their mouths, they pour out their accusations. Instead of joining cordially to sustain the spirits, and animate the efforts of their countrymen, they rather employ themselves in damping their ardour, and almost thwarting necessary measures, whilst they foretell the ruin which must inevitably and speedily ensue.

On the other hand, we see another party, with almost equal violence, returning rage for rage; contending that all has been wise, spirited, and able in the conduct of public affairs, conceived with prudence and executed with ability; but that it is to the pernicious effects of the mischievous labours of the factious, that all our difficulties and dangers are to be ascribed.

On neither side does there appear that persuasion which ought habitually to be borne in mind by Christians, that the schemes of men will often be alloyed with error … there is a tendency to exalt human wisdom and strength, to trust implicitly in the talents of the political leader to whom we are attached, and to forget the solemn condemnation pronounced against those who put their trust in man, instead of glorying and placing their confidence in the Almighty.

FOR MEDITATION: Wilberforce was often grieved that politics was an arena where partisanship had become idolatrous—an end to the exclusion of all other ends. Nowhere in his writings does he write with greater feeling than when urging his fellow citizens to remember that while parties have their place and perform good services, those who profess the name of Christ have a still higher allegiance. Serve in the party that your convictions lead you to, he is in essence saying, but remember as well that this service should always be marked by traits exhibited by the meek and lowly Jesus. If we are his disciples, then certain things must follow, regardless of the party to which we feel drawn.

REFERENCE: *A Retrospect of the Year 1801* (1802)

'The best things when corrupted'

'But I fear, lest by any means, as the serpent beguiled Eve through his subtilty, so your minds should be corrupted from the simplicity that is in Christ.' 2 Corinthians 11:3
SUGGESTED FURTHER READING: Psalm 4:1–8

That the sacred name of religion has been too often prostituted to the most detestable purposes; that furious bigots and bloody persecutors, and self-interested hypocrites of all types, from the rapacious leader of an army, to the canting oracle of a congregation, have falsely called themselves Christians, are sad truths, which are lamented by those who are most concerned for the honour of Christianity.

All this, however, is only one case where the depravity of man perverts the bounty of God. Why is it here only an argument that there is danger of abuse? So is there also in the case of all the potent and operative principles, whether in the natural or moral world. Take for instance the powers and properties of matter. These were doubtless designed by God for our comfort and well-being; but are often misapplied to trifling purposes, and still more frequently turned into agents of misery and death. On this fact indeed is well founded the well-known maxim, that 'the best things when corrupted become the worst:'[1] which is especially true of religion.

FOR MEDITATION: There have been many sad chapters in the history of Christianity—'instances,' to paraphrase Wilberforce, 'wherein the depravity of man has perverted the bounty of God.' The actions of the Spanish Conquistadors in the Americas, for example, deeply grieved him. Their actions, he told his children, brought abiding shame upon the name of Christ. And of course, great abolitionist that he was, he always considered the existence of slavery in Britain's colonies 'the greatest of her crimes': it brought 'the deepest stain of dishonour.'

But there have been many instances where those who have loved the name of Christ have founded hospitals and schools, visited prisons and fought to secure the freedom of slaves. Wilberforce did all these things, and it speaks to the character of his Christian testimony that he did what he could to put many things right—to honour the Lord in his own day.

REFERENCE: *A Practical View of Christianity* (1797)

'Aim high'

'Give me understanding, and I shall keep thy law; yea, I shall observe it with my whole heart.' Psalm 119:34
<small>SUGGESTED FURTHER READING</small>: Psalm 119:9–16

Aim high ... Strive to be a Christian in the highest sense of that term. How little do you know to what services Providence may call you. If when I was at your age, anyone had pointed to me and said, that youth will in a few years (not above seven or eight) be Member [of Parliament] for the first county in England, it would have been deemed the speech of a madman!

<small>FOR MEDITATION</small>: How little do we know to what services Providence may call us. And we shall discover God's purposes for our lives, as we wait upon him, in his good time. The nineteenth-century poet Robert Browning wrote of this:

In some time, his good time, I shall arrive;
He guides me and the bird
In his good time. Robert Browning, *Paracelsus* (pt. I)

There are many passages of Scripture that underscore God's willingness to guide us in our journey of faith. Psalm 25:9 tells us: 'The meek will he guide in judgment: and the meek will he teach his way.' Psalm 32:8 declares: 'I will instruct thee and teach thee in the way which thou shalt go: I will guide thee with mine eye.' Isaiah 58:11 states beautifully and memorably: 'And the Lord shall guide thee continually, and satisfy thy soul in drought ... thou shalt be like a watered garden, and like a spring of water, whose waters fail not.'

<small>REFERENCE</small>: <small>DAVID NEWSOME</small>, *The Parting of Friends*, P. 55

'As a man knows his friend'

'Let, I pray thee, thy merciful kindness be for my comfort, according to thy word unto thy servant.' Psalm 119:76
SUGGESTED FURTHER READING: Psalm 119:97–104

Mr Wilberforce to his latest day seldom mentioned Mr Pitt's name without some affectionate epithet, and he once said to me: 'I certainly never knew, on the whole, so extraordinary a man.' Occasionally, when thus speaking of him, I have heard him express his deep regret that, owing to Mr Pitt being so entirely absorbed in politics, he had never allowed himself time fairly to turn his attention to religion, or to examine Scripture as the rule of life.

He expressed a similar regret with respect to others of his contemporaries with whom he had mingled much in public life, lamenting, not only in their case, but in that also of many learned theologians, the want of a more experimental acquaintance with the Holy Scriptures, adding: 'I question much whether a large proportion of such men be not very deficient in that intimate knowledge of the Bible which we ought all to cultivate. Many of them may be able to give a good account of disputed passages, or talk well as critics and grammarians; but how different is this from a heartfelt delight in the Bible. They know not the Scriptures as a man knows his friend—as he almost knows by the sound of his voice and the expression of his face what he is about to say. They have not that knowledge of it which transmutes the heart and character, by an assimilating influence, into the image of the principles which it unfolds.'

FOR MEDITATION: An anonymous writer once said of the Bible: 'The Bible has been my guide in perplexity, and my comfort in trouble. It has roused me when declining, and animated me in languor. Other writings may be good, but they want certainty and force. The Bible carries its own credentials along with it, and proves spirit and life to the soul. In other writings I hear the words of a stranger or a servant. In the Bible I hear the language of my Father and my friend. Other books contain only the picture of bread. The Bible presents me with real manna, and feeds me with the bread of life.'

REFERENCE: *Recollections of William Wilberforce* (1864)

'The boundary to the roaring sea'

'Marvellous are thy works; and that my soul knoweth right well.'
Psalm 139:14
SUGGESTED FURTHER READING: Jeremiah 5:22; Isaiah 40:21–26

How wonderful an ordination of providence is it that the sand should be placed as the boundary to the roaring sea. 'Who placed the *sand* for a bound to the sea by a perpetual decree etc.' Here we see the power of omnipotence: had counsel been asked of man, he would have said: 'place the granite rock, the adamant bar to restrain the swelling ocean.' But no, God places the sand, that which would seem the weakest of barriers, that which is proverbial for instability, as the bound to the sea which it cannot pass over.

FOR MEDITATION: Jeremiah 5:22 states 'will ye not tremble at my presence, which have placed the sand for the bound of the sea by a perpetual decree, that it cannot pass it: and though the waves thereof toss themselves, yet can they not prevail; though they roar, yet can they not pass over it?' Psalm 59:16 tells us: 'But I will sing of thy power; yea, I will sing aloud of thy mercy in the morning.'

Power wedded to mercy. The sand as a bound for the sea. These and so many other aspects of our heavenly Father's character or creation have captured the imagination of countless writers down through the centuries—no less than Wilberforce's. It was the Victorian writer John Ruskin who observed:

The Divine mind is as visible in its full energy of operation on every lowly bank and mouldering stone, as in the lifting of the pillars of heaven, and settling the foundation of the earth; and that to the rightly perceiving mind, there is the same infinity, the same majesty, the same power, the same unity, and the same perfection, manifest in the casting of the clay as in the scattering of the cloud, in the mouldering of the dust as in the kindling of the daystar.

REFERENCE: DAVID NEWSOME, *The Parting of Friends*, P. 51

'The affections of the soul'

'Set your affection on things above, not on things on the earth.'
Colossians 3:2
SUGGESTED FURTHER READING: Hebrews 12:1–8

Mankind are in general deplorably ignorant of their true state; and there are few perhaps who have any adequate conception of the real strength of the ties by which they are bound to the several objects of their attachment, or who are aware how small a share of their regard is possessed by those concerns on which it ought to be supremely fixed.

Except the affections of the soul be supremely fixed on God; unless it be *the leading and governing desire and primary pursuit* to possess his favour and promote his glory, we are considered as having transferred our fealty to an usurper, and as being in fact revolters from our lawful sovereign. God requires to set up his throne in the heart, and to reign in it without a rival.

FOR MEDITATION: The singleness of heart that should inform our commitment to God has been beautifully expressed by Richard Cecil, the minister of St John's Chapel, Bedford Row, in the late eighteenth century:

The Christian will sometimes be brought to walk in a solitary path. God seems to cut away his props, that he may reduce him to himself. His religion is to be felt as a personal, particular, appropriate possession. He is to feel that, as there is but one Jehovah to bless, so there seems to him as though there were but one penitent in the universe to be blessed by him.

St Augustine also wrote movingly of why the affections of the soul should be supremely fixed on God. He is our very life: 'As the soul is the life of the body, so God is the life of the soul. As therefore the body perishes when the soul leaves it, so the soul dies when God departs from it.'

REFERENCE: *A Practical View of Christianity* (1797)

'The religion of the affections'

'But I have trusted in thy mercy; my heart shall rejoice in thy salvation.'
Psalm 13:5
SUGGESTED FURTHER READING: Psalm 27:1–14

It is Christianity's peculiar glory, and her main office, to bring all the faculties of our nature into their just subordination and dependence; that so the whole man, complete in all his functions, may be restored to the true ends his being, and be devoted, entire and harmonious, to the service and glory of God. 'My son, give me thine *heart*'; 'Thou shalt love the Lord thy God with all thy *heart*.' Such are the direct and comprehensive claims which are made on us in the Holy Scriptures. We can scarcely indeed look into any part of the sacred volume without meeting abundant proofs, that it is the religion of the affections which God particularly requires.

FOR MEDITATION: It was the great reformer Martin Luther who said: 'The slender capacity of man's heart cannot comprehend, much less utter, that unsearchable depth and burning zeal of God's love towards us.'

Luther's words are arresting, but they fall far short of the matchless declaration in Romans 5:8—'But God commendeth his love toward us, in that, while we were yet sinners, Christ died for us.'

If this then is the love that God has for us, what then ought to be our love for him? The great Puritan writer and divine Francis Quarles (1592–1644) answered this question by saying:

God is Alpha and Omega in the great world: endeavour to make him so in the little world: make him thy evening epilogue and thy morning prologue; practise to make him thy last thought at night when thou sleepest, and thy first thought in the morning when thou awakest; so shall thy fancy be sanctified in the night, and thy understanding rectified in the day; so shall thy rest be peaceful, thy labours prosperous, thy life pious and thy death glorious.

REFERENCE: *A Practical View of Christianity* (1797)

'The children of Christ'

'How excellent is thy lovingkindness, O God! therefore the children of men put their trust under the shadow of thy wings.' Psalm 36:7
SUGGESTED FURTHER READING: Matthew 18:1–4

Our blessed Saviour is not removed far from us. He exhibits not himself to us 'dark with excessive brightness,'[2] but is let down as it were to the possibilities of human converse. We may not think that he is incapable of entering into our little concerns, and sympathizing with them; for we are graciously assured that he is not one 'who cannot be touched with the feeling of our infirmities, having been in all points tempted like as we are.' The figures under which he is represented, are such as convey ideas of the utmost tenderness. 'He shall feed his flock like a shepherd; he shall gather the lambs in his arm, and carry them in his bosom, and shall gently lead those that are with young.' 'They shall not hunger nor thirst, neither shall the heat nor sun smite them; for he that hath mercy on them shall lead them, even by the springs of water shall he guide them.' 'I will not leave you orphans,' was one of his last consolatory declarations. The children of Christ are here separated indeed from the personal view of him; but not from his paternal affection and paternal care.

FOR MEDITATION: The Baptist Church Manual speaks of the paternal affection and care that are ours in Christ: 'having risen from the dead he is now enthroned in heaven; and uniting in his wonderful person the tenderest sympathies with divine perfections, he is every way qualified to be a suitable, a compassionate, and an all-sufficient Saviour.' The poet James Smith (1775–1839) wrote lines that breathe the same spirit:

Christ is the head of all things. Everything lies open before his eye; everything is sustained by his power, and everything is disposed of by his wisdom. Not a sparrow can fall to the ground without his notice and permission. Oh, to see Jesus in all things! Oh, to see everything at the disposal of Jesus! Oh, to see that all things are directed, controlled, and overruled by Christ alone! May this calm my mind, compose my spirit, and produce holy resignation in my soul! If Jesus arranges all, sends all, directs all, overrules all, then all things must work together for good to them that love God.

REFERENCE: *A Practical View of Christianity* (1797)

'Heavenly consolations'

'And others had trial of cruel mockings and scourgings, yea, moreover of bonds and imprisonment. They were stoned, they were sawn asunder, were tempted, were slain with the sword: they wandered about in sheepskins and goatskins; being destitute, afflicted, tormented; (Of whom the world was not worthy:) they wandered in deserts, and in mountains, and in dens and caves of the earth.' Hebrews 11:36–38
SUGGESTED FURTHER READING: Hebrews 11:1–40

But let us now turn our eyes to Christians who have not only assumed the name, but who have possessed the substance, and felt the power of Christianity; who though often shamed and cast down under a sense of their many imperfections, have known in their better seasons, what it was to experience hope, joy, trust, and heavenly consolations. In their hearts, love also towards their Redeemer has glowed; a love not *superficial* and unmeaning, but constant and rational, resulting from a strong impression of the worth of its object, and heightened by an abiding sense of great, unmerited, and continually accumulating obligations; ever manifesting itself in acts of diligent obedience, or of patient suffering. Such was the religion of the holy martyrs of the 16th century, the illustrious ornaments of the English church.

Look to their writings, and you will find that their thoughts and affections had been much exercised in habitual views of the blessed Jesus. Persecution and distress, degradation and contempt, in vain assailed them—and not only did their love feel no diminution or abatement, but it burned with an increase of ardour; and when brought forth at last to a cruel and ignominious death, they repined not at their fate; but rather rejoiced that they were counted worthy to suffer for the name of Christ.

FOR MEDITATION: There is little to add to such a moving description of those who have suffered for Christ, save the passage in Acts 5, which tells us how the apostles suffered. May we ever learn from their example, and from those to whom Wilberforce paid tribute above.

REFERENCE: *A Practical View of Christianity* (1797)

'If we would love him'

'But I have trusted in thy mercy; my heart shall rejoice in thy salvation.'
Psalm 13:5
SUGGESTED FURTHER READING: Psalm 115:1–18

If we would love him affectionately, and rejoice in him as triumphantly as the first Christians did, we must learn like them to repose our entire trust in him and to adopt the language of the apostle [Paul], 'God forbid that I should glory, save in the cross of Jesus Christ.' 'Who of God is made unto us wisdom and righteousness, and sanctification, and redemption.'

FOR MEDITATION: Proverbs 16:20 tells us: 'whoso trusteth in the Lord, happy is he.' The poet Henry Wadsworth Longfellow penned a quatrain that underscores the importance of unreserved trust in God, and how our reading of the Scriptures affords a model for that trust:

O holy trust! O endless source of rest!
Like the beloved John
To lay his head upon the Saviour's breast,
And thus to journey on!

A daughter of Maine, the hymn writer Elizabeth Prentiss (1818–1878) also understood what it meant to repose one's entire trust in Christ and to love him as the first Christians did. In 1856, she wrote the words for which she is best remembered:

More love to thee, O Christ, more love to thee!
Hear thou the prayer I make on bended knee.
This is my earnest plea: More love, O Christ, to thee;
More love to thee, more love to thee!
Then shall my latest breath whisper thy praise;
This be the parting cry my heart shall raise;
This still its prayer shall be: More love, O Christ to thee;
More love to thee, more love to thee!

REFERENCE: *A Practical View of Christianity* (1797)

'The appointed hope'

'For we are saved by hope: but hope that is seen is not hope: for what a man seeth, why doth he yet hope for? But if we hope for that we see not, then do we with patience wait for it.' Romans 8:24–25
SUGGESTED FURTHER READING: Romans 8:1–39

Let us then each for himself solemnly ask ourselves, whether *we* have fled for refuge to the appointed hope? And whether we are habitually looking to it, as to the only source of consolation? 'Other foundation can no man lay:' there is no other ground of dependence, no other plea for pardon; but *here* there *is* hope, even to the uttermost. Let us fall down humbly before the throne of God, imploring pity and pardon in the name of the Son of his love. Let us beseech him to give us a true spirit of repentance, and of hearty undivided faith in the Lord Jesus. Let us not be satisfied till the cordiality of our belief be confirmed to us by that character of the apostle, 'that to as many as believe Christ is precious;' and let us strive to increase daily in *love* towards our blessed Saviour; and pray earnestly that 'we may be filled with *joy* and *peace* in believing, that we may abound in *hope* through the power of the Holy Ghost.' Let us diligently put in practice the directions formerly given for cherishing and cultivating the principle of the love of Christ.

With this view let us labour assiduously to increase in knowledge, that ours may be a deeply rooted and rational affection. By frequent meditation on the incidents of our Saviour's life and death; by often calling to mind the state from which he proposes to rescue us, and the glories of his heavenly kingdom; by continual intercourse with him of prayer and praise, of dependence and confidence in dangers, of hope and joy in our brighter hours, let us endeavour to keep him constantly present in our minds, and to render all our conceptions of him more distinct, lively, and intelligent. The title of Christian is a reproach to us, if we estrange ourselves from him after whom we are named.

FOR MEDITATION: Isaiah 26:3–4 tells us: 'Thou wilt keep him in perfect peace, whose mind is stayed on thee: because he trusteth in thee. Trust ye in the Lord for ever: for in the Lord Jehovah is everlasting strength.' Think on these things.

REFERENCE: *A Practical View of Christianity* (1797)

'The habitual sentiment of our hearts'

'And this I pray, that your love may abound yet more and more in knowledge and in all judgment; that ye may approve things that are excellent; that ye may be sincere and without offence till the day of Christ; being filled with the fruits of righteousness, which are by Jesus Christ, unto the glory and praise of God.' Philippians 1:9–11
SUGGESTED FURTHER READING: Ephesians 1:15–23

Great as was the progress which the apostle Paul had made in all virtue, he declares of himself that he still presses forward, 'forgetting the things which are behind, and reaching forth unto the things which are before.' He prays for his beloved disciples, 'that they may be filled with all the fullness of God;' 'that they may be filled with the fruits of righteousness;' 'that they might walk worthy of the Lord unto all pleasing, being fruitful in every good work.' Nor is it a less pregnant and comprehensive petition, which, from our blessed Saviour's inserting it in the prayer he has given as a model for our imitation, we may infer ought to be the habitual sentiment of our hearts; 'Thy will be done on earth as it is in Heaven.'

FOR MEDITATION: Many is the believer who, down through the centuries, has been stirred by the words of the apostle Paul in Philippians 3:13–14. The eighteenth-century theologian and hymn writer Philip Doddridge (whose treatise The Rise and Progress of Religion in the Soul was instrumental in Wilberforce's 'great change' or embrace of Christianity in 1786) had a heart for God like that of the apostle. He put these feelings into verses still sung today:

Awake, my soul, stretch every nerve,
and press with vigour on;
a heavenly race demands thy zeal,
and an immortal crown.
Blest Saviour, called and led by thee,
have I my race begun;
and crowned with victory, at thy feet
I'll lay mine honours down.

REFERENCE: A Practical View of Christianity (1797)

'The reasonable service of their rightful Sovereign'

'For to me to live is Christ.' Philippians 1:21
SUGGESTED FURTHER READING: 1 Thessalonians 5:23

It is the grand, essential, practical characteristic of true Christians, that, relying on the promises to repenting sinners, of acceptance through the Redeemer, they have renounced and abjured all other masters, and have cordially and unreservedly devoted themselves to God. This is indeed the very figure which baptism daily represents to us: like the father of Hannibal, we there bring our infant to the altar, we consecrate him to the service of *his proper owner* and vow, *in his name,* eternal hostilities against all the enemies of his salvation. After the same manner Christians are become the sworn enemies of sin; they will henceforth hold no parley with it, they will allow it in no shape, they will admit it to no composition; the war they have denounced against it, is universal and irreconcilable.

But this is not all—it is now their determined purpose to yield themselves without reserve to the reasonable service of their rightful Sovereign. 'They are not their own:' their bodily and mental faculties, their natural and acquired endowments, their substance, their authority, their time, their influence; all these, they consider as belonging to them, not for their own gratification, but as so many instruments to be consecrated to the honour and employed in the service of God. This must be the master principle to which every other must be subordinate. Whatever may have been hitherto their ruling passion, or leading pursuit, whether sensual, or intellectual, of science, taste, fancy, or feeling, it must now possess but a secondary place; or rather, it must exist only at the pleasure, and be put altogether under the control and direction of its true and legitimate superior.

FOR MEDITATION: 1 Corinthians 6:20 tells us: 'Ye are not your own ... for ye are bought with a price: therefore glorify God in your body, and in your spirit, which are God's.' Compare these thoughts also with 1 Corinthians 7:23–24.

REFERENCE: *A Practical View of Christianity* (1797)

'The rudiments of all true virtue'

'I am crucified with Christ: nevertheless I live; yet not I, but Christ liveth in me: and the life which I now live in the flesh I live by the faith of the Son of God, who loved me, and gave himself for me.' Galatians 2:20
SUGGESTED FURTHER READING: 1 Thessalonians 5:4–8

It is the prerogative of Christianity 'to bring into captivity *every thought* to the obedience of Christ.' They who really feel its power, are resolved (in the language of Scripture) 'to live no longer to themselves, but to him that died for them:' they know indeed their own infirmities; they know that the way on which they have entered is strait and difficult, but they know too the encouraging assurance, 'They that wait on the Lord shall renew their strength;' and, relying on this animating declaration, they deliberately purpose that, so far as they may be able, the governing maxim of their future lives shall be, '*to do all to the glory of God.*'

Behold here the seminal principle, which contains within it, as in an embryo state, the rudiments of all true virtue; which, striking deep its roots, though feeble perhaps and lowly in its beginnings, silently progressive, and almost insensibly maturing, yet will shortly, even in the bleak and churlish temperature of this world, lift up its head and spread abroad its branches, bearing abundant fruits, precious fruits of refreshment and consolation, of which the boasted products of philosophy are but sickly imitations, void of fragrance and of flavour. At length it shall be transplanted into its native region, and enjoy a more genial climate and a kindlier soil; and, bursting forth into full luxuriance, with unfading beauty and unexhausted odours, shall flourish for ever in the paradise of God.

FOR MEDITATION: The nineteenth-century biblical scholar Roswell D. Hitchcock once said: 'Virtue, for us, is obedience to God in Christ.' William Cowper, Wilberforce's favorite poet, wrote of virtue in ways that greatly resemble Wilberforce's words above. They were, very likely, words that Wilberforce knew: 'The only amaranthine flower on earth is virtue.' Amaranthine is a word that means 'eternally beautiful and unfading; everlasting.' A lovely and apposite image for us to cherish.

REFERENCE: *A Practical View of Christianity* (1797)

'To submit in all things'

'O worship the Lord in the beauty of holiness: fear before him, all the earth.' Psalm 96:9
SUGGESTED FURTHER READING: Romans 6:12–23

They who are actuated in their endeavours to excel in all holiness love it for its own sake. This determination has its foundations indeed in a deep and humiliating sense of God's exalted majesty and infinite power, and of their own extreme inferiority and littleness, attended with a settled conviction of its being their duty as his creatures, to submit in all things to the will of their great Creator.

But these awful impressions are relieved and ennobled by an admiring sense of the infinite perfections and infinite amiableness of the divine character; animated by a confiding though humble hope of his fatherly kindness and protection, and quickened by the grateful recollection of immense and continually increasing obligations. This is the Christian love of God! A love compounded of admiration, of preference, of hope, of trust, of joy; chastised by reverential awe, and wakeful with continual gratitude.

FOR MEDITATION: The poet George Herbert penned verses that evoke the kind of reverential awe of which Wilberforce speaks above. They remind us anew that we serve the King of kings and Lord of lords. May we be enabled to see him as he is—exalted far above the heavens.

When once thy foot enters the church, be bare,
God is more there than thou: for thou art there
Only by his permission. Then beware,
And make thyself all reverence and fear.

REFERENCE: *A Practical View of Christianity* (1797)

'Let us not deceive ourselves'

'And what agreement hath the temple of God with idols? for ye are the temple of the living God; as God hath said, I will dwell in them, and walk in them; and I will be their God, and they shall be my people.'
2 Corinthians 6:16
SUGGESTED FURTHER READING: Joshua 24:1–15

All who have read the Scriptures must confess that idolatry is the crime against which God's highest resentment is expressed, and his severest punishment denounced. But let us not deceive ourselves. It is not in bowing the knee to idols that idolatry consists, so much as in the internal homage of the heart; as in feeling towards them, any of that supreme love, or reverence, or gratitude, which God reserves to himself as his own exclusive prerogative.

On the same principle, whatever else draws off the heart from him, engrosses our prime regard, and holds the chief place in our esteem and affections, *that,* in the estimation of reason, is no less an idol to us than an image of wood or stone would be; before which we should fall down and worship. Think not this a strained analogy; it is the very language and argument of inspiration. The servant of God is commanded not to set up his idol in his *heart*; and sensuality and covetousness are repeatedly termed *idolatry.*

FOR MEDITATION: The nineteenth-century writer John Ruskin had a gift for forceful and arresting prose. His reflections on the pitfalls of idolatry are ones we would do well to remember:

God will put up with a great many things in the human heart, but there is one thing he will not put up with in it—a second place. He who offers God a second place offers him no place.

REFERENCE: *A Practical View of Christianity* (1797)

'The desire of nations'

'I have longed for thy salvation, O LORD …' Psalm 119:174
SUGGESTED FURTHER READING: Luke 2:25–35

Christianity is always represented in Scripture as the grand, the unparalleled instance of God's bounty to mankind. It was graciously held forth in the original promise to our first parents; it was predicted by a long continued series of prophets; the subject of their prayers, inquiries, and longing expectations. In a world which opposed and persecuted them, it was their source of peace, and hope, and consolation. At length it approached—the Desire of all Nations—the long expected Star announced its presence—a multitude of the heavenly host hailed its introduction, and proclaimed its character; 'Glory to God in the highest, on earth peace, good will towards men.' It is every where represented in Scripture by such figures as may most deeply impress on us a sense of its value; it is spoken of as light from darkness, as release from prison, as deliverance from captivity, as life from death.

FOR MEDITATION: The poet and essayist Matthew Arnold penned verses that recall Wilberforce's words above. They are, in their own way, a rendering of the good news given to the shepherds of Bethlehem so long ago:

Now, the whole world hears
Or shall hear,—surely shall hear, at the last,
Though men delay, and doubt, and faint, and fail,—
That promise faithful:—'Fear not, little flock!
It is your Father's will and joy, to give
To you, the Kingdom!'

REFERENCE: *A Practical View of Christianity* (1797)

'An awful and an affecting spectacle'

'Seek ye the LORD while he may be found, call ye upon him while he is near.' Isaiah 55:6
SUGGESTED FURTHER READING: Isaiah 55:1–7

To anyone who is seriously impressed with a sense of the critical state in which we are here placed, a short and uncertain space in which to make our peace with God, and then the last judgment, and an eternity of unspeakable happiness or misery, it is indeed an awful and an affecting spectacle, to see men thus busying themselves in these speculations of arrogant curiosity, and trifling with their dearest, their everlasting interests. It is but a feeble illustration of this exquisite folly, to compare it to the conduct of some convicted rebel, who, brought into the presence of his Sovereign, instead of seizing the occasion to sue for mercy, should even neglect and trifle with the pardon which should be offered to him, and insolently employ himself in prying into his Sovereign's designs and criticizing his counsels. Our case indeed, is in another point of comparison, but too much like that of the convicted rebel. But there is this grand difference—that at the best, his success must be uncertain, ours, if it be not our own fault is sure; and while, on the other hand, our guilt is unspeakably greater than that of any rebel against an earthly monarch; so, on the other, we know that our Sovereign is 'long-suffering, and easy to be entreated'; more ready to grant, than we to ask, forgiveness. Well then may we adopt the language of the poet:

What better can we do, than ... prostrate fall
Before him reverent; and there confess
Humbly our faults, and pardon beg; with tears
Watering the ground, and with our sighs the air
Frequenting, sent from hearts contrite, in sign
Of sorrow unfeign'd, and humiliation meek?   John Milton, *Paradise Lost*

FOR MEDITATION: This solemn subject needs no further comment. May we all 'commune with our own hearts on our beds, and be still' (see Psalm 4:4).

REFERENCE: *A Practical View of Christianity* (1797)

'A far different temper'

'Charity suffereth long, and is kind; charity envieth not; charity vaunteth not itself, is not puffed up, doth not behave itself unseemly, seeketh not her own, is not easily provoked, thinketh no evil.' 1 Corinthians 13:4–5
SUGGESTED FURTHER READING: 1 Corinthians 13

But the Christian's is a far different temper: not a temper of sordid sensuality, or lazy apathy, or dogmatizing pride, or disappointed ambition: more truly independent of worldly estimation than philosophy with all her boasts, it forms a perfect contrast to epicurean selfishness, to stoical pride, and to cynical brutality. It is a temper compounded of firmness, and complacency, and peace, and love; manifesting itself in acts of kindness and of courtesy; a kindness not pretended but genuine; a courtesy, not false and superficial, but cordial and sincere. In the hour of popularity it is not intoxicated, or insolent; in the hour of unpopularity, it is not desponding, or morose; unshaken in constancy, unwearied in benevolence, firm without roughness, and assiduous without servility.

FOR MEDITATION: Wilberforce's reflections about the Christian's temper, or rather, the traits of the Christian temperament, afford a telling contrast to many prevailing attitudes. So too, do the kindred reflections offered by other writers in the eighteenth and nineteenth centuries. The poet Edward Young observed: 'A Christian is the highest style of man.' In America, the orator Daniel Webster said: 'Whatever makes men good Christians, makes them good citizens.'

The theologian Jonathan Edwards offered this bracing assessment: 'A greater absurdity cannot be thought of than a morose, hard-hearted, covetous, proud, malicious Christian.' Many centuries ago, Clement of Alexandria painted a word picture of Christians as they ought to be: 'The purified righteous man has become a coin of the Lord, and has the impress of his King stamped upon him.'

REFERENCE: *A Practical View of Christianity* (1797)

'A work to accomplish'

'For consider him that endured such contradiction of sinners against himself, lest ye be wearied and faint in your minds.' Hebrews 12:3
SUGGESTED FURTHER READING: Psalm 27:13

We have every one of us a work to accomplish, wherein our eternal interests are at stake; a work to which we are naturally indisposed. We live in a world abounding with objects which distract our attention and divert our endeavours; and a deadly enemy is ever at hand to seduce and beguile us. If we persevere indeed, success is certain; but our efforts must know no remission. There is a call on us for vigorous and continual resolution, self-denial, and activity.

FOR MEDITATION: The nineteenth-century American poet Sarah Hale wrote verses that sound a chord in unison with Wilberforce's words above:

Rugged strength and radiant beauty—
These were one in Nature's plan;
Humble toil and heavenward duty—
These will form the perfect man.

Her countryman and contemporary poet, the Quaker John Greenleaf Whittier, concurred—we must be about our Master's business:

Thine to work as well as pray,
Clearing thorny wrongs away;
Plucking up the weeds of sin,
Letting heaven's warm sunshine in.

REFERENCE: *A Practical View of Christianity* (1797)

'Present peace and future glory'

'That at the name of Jesus every knee should bow, of things in heaven, and things in earth, and things under the earth; and that every tongue should confess that Jesus Christ is Lord, to the glory of God the Father.'
Philippians 2:10–11
SUGGESTED FURTHER READING: Philippians 2:5–11

The name of Jesus is to be engraved deeply on the heart, there written by the finger of God himself in everlasting characters. It is our title known and understood to present peace and future glory. The assurance which it conveys of a bright reversion, will lighten the burdens, and alleviate the sorrows of life; and in some happier moments, it will impart to us somewhat of that fulness of joy which is at God's right hand, enabling us to join even here in the heavenly Hosannah, 'Worthy is the Lamb that was slain, to receive power, and riches, and wisdom, and strength, and honour, and glory, and blessing.' 'Blessing, and honour, and glory, and power, be unto him that sitteth upon the throne, and unto the Lamb for ever and ever.' (Revelation 5:12,14)

FOR MEDITATION: Henry Manning was author of many searching and eloquent reflections on the Christian life. His understanding of what the word 'praise' meant forms a fitting complement to Wilberforce's words above. 'Praise,' Manning wrote, 'consists in the love of God, in wonder at the goodness of God, in recognition of the gifts of God, in seeing God in all things he gives us, ay, and even in the things he refuses to us; so as to see our whole life in the light of God: and seeing this, to bless him, adore him, and glorify him.'

John Keble was Manning's contemporary, and his verse often paints a picture of what Wilberforce called a 'heavenly Hosannah':

God, the Lord, a King remaineth,
Robed in his own glorious light;
God hath robed him and he reigneth;
He hath girded him with might.
Alleluia! Alleluia!
God is King in depth and height.

REFERENCE: *A Practical View of Christianity* (1797)

'Thus loaded with mercies'

'Bless the LORD, O my soul, and forget not all his benefits.' Psalm 103:2
SUGGESTED FURTHER READING: Psalm 34

But surely to any who call themselves Christians, it may be justly urged as
an astonishing instance of human depravity, that we ourselves, who enjoy
the full light of revelation, to whom God has vouchsafed such clear
discoveries of what it concerns us to know of his being and attributes;
who profess to believe 'that in him we live, and move, and have our
being;' that to him we owe all the comforts we here enjoy, and the offer of
eternal Glory purchased for us by the atoning blood of his own son
('thanks be to God for his unspeakable gift'); that we, thus loaded with
mercies, should every one of us be continually chargeable with forgetting
his authority, and being ungrateful for his benefits; with slighting his
gracious proposals, or receiving them at best but heartlessly and coldly.

FOR MEDITATION: The words of the psalmist remind us that Christians are
to 'set their hope in God, and not forget the works of God, but keep his
commandments' (Psalm 78:7). The response of our hearts should be as
described by Joseph Addison, whose works Wilberforce knew well:

When all thy mercies, O my God,
my rising soul surveys,
transported with the view, I'm lost
in wonder, love and praise.

To all my weak complaints and cries
thy mercy lent an ear,
ere yet my feeble thoughts had learned
to form themselves in prayer.

Unnumbered comforts to my soul
thy tender care bestowed,
before my infant heart conceived
from whom those comforts flowed.

Thy bounteous hand with worldly bliss
hath made my cup run o'er;
and, in a kind and faithful Friend,
hath doubled all my store.

Ten thousand thousand precious gifts
my daily thanks employ;
nor is the last a cheerful heart
that tastes those gifts with joy.

When worn with sickness, oft hast thou
with health renewed my face;
and, when in sins and sorrows sunk,
revived my soul with grace.

REFERENCE: *A Practical View of Christianity* (1797)

'We must learn to press forward humbly'

'He keepeth the paths of judgment, and preserveth the way of his saints.'
Proverbs 2:8
SUGGESTED FURTHER READING: Proverbs 2:1–22

We are all of us apt to be unreasonable in our expectations of the progress we are to make in the Christian course ere we have well begun our journey. We look on ourselves as at the end of it, and deem it hard if we enjoy not those comforts which are reserved for those only who have borne the burden and heat of the day. In both these respects let us be more moderate, and neither be cast down if we find not our attainments equal to our wishes, nor disgusted if our religious exercises do not afford us all that pleasure which we might hope to derive from them. But then let not this produce in us such an acquiescence in our present state as may terminate in our sitting down contented with it: we must learn to press forward humbly depending on God's help for the success of our labours, and resigned in all respects to his sovereign will: persevere and 'may the God of grace, when you have suffered awhile, comfort, strengthen, stablish, settle you.' I need not suggest to you the benefit of religious contemplation, or how much more than reading it tends to lift the soul beyond the fogs and vapours of this nether atmosphere.

FOR MEDITATION: The seventeenth-century theologian Jeremy Taylor penned a thought-provoking description of meditation. Meditation is what Wilberforce meant by religious contemplation—that which 'tends to lift the soul beyond the fogs and vapours of this nether atmosphere.' Taylor wrote:

Meditation is the tongue of the soul and the language of our spirit; and our wandering thoughts in prayer are but the neglects of meditation and recessions from that duty; and according as we neglect meditation, so are our prayers imperfect, meditation being the soul of prayer and the intention of our spirit.

REFERENCE: *The Correspondence of William Wilberforce* (1840)

'Consider the Lord's Day'

'Remember the Sabbath day, to keep it holy.' Exodus 20:8
SUGGESTED FURTHER READING: Mark 2:15–28

For my own part, I consider the Lord's Day as mainly intended for
strengthening our impression of invisible and eternal things; for
cultivating a spirit of love to God, and to our fellow-creatures; for
devising and promoting plans for the glory of God, and the happiness of
man; and, in short, for securing the great object of our everlasting
welfare, which the Scriptures teach us depends on the use we make of this
probationary state.

FOR MEDITATION: The Scriptures tell us, with wonderful simplicity, that
'the Sabbath was made for man' (Mark 2:27). It is a gift to be treasured,
savoured and kept.

The nineteenth-century poet Robert Browning wrote a couplet that
expresses so much of what the Sabbath, or Lord's Day, ought to mean to
the Christian:

Thou art my single day, God lends to leaven
What were all earth else, with a feel of heaven.

Philip Henry, father of the celebrated biblical commentator Matthew
Henry, conveyed in prose much of what Browning had written in verse:
'The happiness of heaven,' the elder Henry wrote, 'is the constant
keeping of the Sabbath. Heaven is called a Sabbath, to make those who
have Sabbaths long for heaven, and those who long for heaven love
Sabbaths.'

REFERENCE: *The Correspondence of William Wilberforce* (1840)

'Them that are of a broken heart'

'O taste and see that the LORD *is good: blessed is the man that trusteth in him. O fear the* LORD, *ye his saints: for there is no want to them that fear him.' Psalm 34:8–9*
SUGGESTED FURTHER READING: Psalm 34:1–7

We ought always to feel as those who, having been justified through the goodness of God through Christ, are assured that God is reconciled to us if we will but cast ourselves on his mercy, and that he is willing to give us every blessing we can desire. But among these blessings, we ought to remember there are several which may seem likely at the time, at least at first, rather to impair our present comfort than to heighten it. Among these is an increasing tenderness of conscience, an increasing sense of the guilt of sin and of our own sinfulness and weakness. This will, at first, increase our nomination and contrition, and make it rise at times even to self-abhorrence; but, blessed be God! there are promises in abundance, and I am sure I say blessed be God for them, to those who are in this very state of mind: 'The Lord is nigh unto them that are of a broken heart, and will save such as are of a contrite spirit,' etc., etc. Even David was instructed to say this in Psalm 34, but how much more confidently we may speak thus, when we consider the atoning blood of Christ. In this frame and spirit let us cast ourselves at the foot of the Cross, and assure ourselves of the mercy and loving kindness of him who has declared 'Them that come unto me I will in no wise cast out.' Who else are the poor in spirit, the lambs, whom Christ will carry in his bosom, but those who feel in this very way?

FOR MEDITATION: The American clergyman and author Edwin Hubbel Chapin (1814–1880) understood well that the Lord is nigh unto them that are of a broken heart, for he knew well the Lord who had fashioned our hearts. 'What a proof of the Divine tenderness,' he wrote, 'is there in the human heart itself, which is the organ and receptacle of so many sympathies! When we consider how exquisite are those conditions by which it is even made capable of so much suffering—the capabilities of a child's heart, of a mother's heart—what must be the nature of him who fashioned its depths, and strung its chords.'

REFERENCE: *The Correspondence of William Wilberforce* (1840)

'The comfort of Christianity'

'Wherefore comfort one another with these words.' 1 *Thessalonians 4:18*
SUGGESTED FURTHER READING: 1 Thessalonians 5:1–11

May you be enabled to know more of the comfort of Christianity. 'There remaineth a rest for the people of God,' a rest not from labour only and turmoil, but from disquietude and sorrow. Meanwhile endeavour to look more to the Saviour for every blessing and may you be strengthened with might by his Spirit in the inner man, and be more filled by the God of hope with all joy and peace in believing, that you may abound in hope through the power of the Holy Ghost.

FOR MEDITATION: 2 Corinthians 1:5 imparts to us words of profound comfort. There, the apostle Paul wrote: 'For as the sufferings of Christ abound in us, so our consolation also aboundeth by Christ.' In 2 Thessalonians 2:16–17, Paul reveals more of the comforts that are ours in the Lord: 'Now our Lord Jesus Christ himself, and God, even our Father, which hath loved us, and hath given us everlasting consolation and good hope through grace, comfort your hearts, and stablish you in every good word and work.'

The poet and hymn writer John Keble had this to say of the consolations that are imparted to the Christian when most needed:

Sprinkled along the waste of years
Full many a soft green isle appears:
Pause where we may upon the desert road,
Some shelter is in sight, some sacred safe abode.

REFERENCE: *The Correspondence of William Wilberforce* (1840)

'To acquaint ourselves with God'

'O taste and see that the LORD *is good: blessed is the man that trusteth in him.'* Psalm 34:8
SUGGESTED FURTHER READING: Psalm 34:14–19

What an unspeakable blessing is it to be disposed to retire from the crowd, and to acquaint ourselves with God, and be at peace. And it is, we are authorized to say, the work of God! We are even taught and enjoined to regard it in that light. Let us then praise God for the disposition, and be assured that it is only a specimen, and an earnest and pledge of his general inclinations towards us. It is because he loves us, that he has done this for us, and he will do greater things than this.

FOR MEDITATION: 'All things that speak of Heaven speak of peace,' wrote the nineteenth-century poet Philip Bailey. Numberless are the consolations that the Scriptures impart to believers. Perhaps the most famous of them is this: 'Thou wilt keep him in perfect peace whose mind is stayed on thee, because he trusteth in thee' (Isaiah 26:3).

John Bunyan, the author of the timeless allegory *Pilgrim's Progress*, crafted this word picture of peace: 'The pilgrim they laid in a large upper chamber, whose window opened toward the sun-rising; the name of the chamber was Peace, where he slept till break of day, and then he awoke and sang.'

Bishop Patrick's description of the peace believers know is a keepsake in prose: 'Peace is the proper result of the Christian temper. It is the great kindness which our religion doth us, that it brings to us a settledness of mind.'

REFERENCE: *The Correspondence of William Wilberforce* (1840)

'Give me a new heart'

'For a day in thy courts is better than a thousand. I had rather be a doorkeeper in the house of my God, than to dwell in the tents of wickedness.' Psalm 84:10

SUGGESTED FURTHER READING: Psalm 73:21–28

A Christian's life is hid with Christ in God. He should look for his happiness in fellowship with God, and view with jealousy whatever tends to break in on this communion. O my God, for the sake of thy beloved Son, our propitiation, through whom we may have access to the throne of grace, give me a new heart—give me a real desire and earnest longing for one.

FOR MEDITATION: In the Old Testament we read: 'A new heart also will I give you, and a new spirit will I put within you: and I will take away the stony heart out of your flesh, and I will give you an heart of flesh' (Ezekiel 36:26).

Such is the blessing of fellowship with God. John Newton, Wilberforce's cherished spiritual mentor and friend, described what he had come to know of the blessings of fellowship with God in the following lines:

May the grace of Christ our Saviour
and the Father's boundless love
with the Holy Spirit's favour,
rest upon us from above.
Thus may we abide in union
with each other and the Lord,
and possess, in sweet communion,
joys which earth cannot afford.

REFERENCE: *The Life of William Wilberforce* (1838)

'May he daily renew me'

*'Teach me thy way, O L*ORD*; I will walk in thy truth: unite my heart to fear thy name.' Psalm 86:11*
SUGGESTED FURTHER READING: Proverbs 3:1–11

I am just returned from receiving the sacrament. I was enabled to be earnest in prayer, and to be contrite and humble under a sense of my unworthiness, and of the infinite mercy of God in Christ. I hope that I desire from my heart to lead henceforth a life more worthy of the Christian profession. May it be my meat and drink to do the will of God, my Father. May he daily renew me by his Holy Spirit, and may I walk before him in a frame made up of fear, and gratitude, and humble trust, and assurance of his fatherly kindness and constant concern for me.

FOR MEDITATION: In 2 Corinthians 4:16 the apostle Paul conveys the assurance that 'the inward man is renewed day by day.' Colossians 3:10 conveys a kindred assurance—one that ought always to be present to our minds as a cause of thankfulness—that the Christian is 'renewed in knowledge after the image of him that created him.'

We may safely trust in the truth of these verses, and treasure them, when our hearts misgive us, as our hearts so often do. These verses afford a solid ground upon which we may stand and move forward in our journey of faith.

REFERENCE: *The Life of William Wilberforce* (1838)

'The most animating promises'

'For unto whomsoever much is given, of him shall be much required.'
Luke 12:48
SUGGESTED FURTHER READING: Psalm 31:19–24

Scripture everywhere holds forth the most animating promises. 'Ask, and ye shall receive; seek, and ye shall find; knock, and it shall be opened unto you.' 'Ho! everyone that thirsteth, come ye to the waters'; such are the comfortable assurances, such the gracious encouragements to the truly sincere inquirer. How deep will be our guilt, if we slight all these merciful offers. 'How many prophets and kings have desired to hear the things that we hear, and have not heard them.' Great indeed are our opportunities, great also is our responsibility.

FOR MEDITATION: 2 Peter 1:4 states: 'Whereby are given unto us exceeding great and precious promises: that by these ye might be partakers of the divine nature.' Of this passage, the celebrated biblical commentator Matthew Henry observes:

Those who receive the promises of the gospel partake of the divine nature. They are renewed in the spirit of their mind, after the image of God, in knowledge, righteousness, and holiness; their hearts are set for God and his service. They have a divine temper and disposition of soul … Those, in whom the Spirit works the divine nature, are freed from the bondage of corruption. Those who are, by the Spirit of grace, renewed in the spirit of their mind, are translated into the liberty of the children of God.

REFERENCE: *A Practical View of Christianity* (1797)

'The man after God's own heart'

'And we have known and believed the love that God hath to us. God is love; and he that dwelleth in love dwelleth in God, and God in him.'
1 John 4:16
SUGGESTED FURTHER READING: Psalm 5:1–12

It is the prayer of an inspired teacher [Paul] in behalf of those for whom he was most interested 'that their love' (already acknowledged to be great) 'might abound yet more and more.' If we look to the most eminent of the Scripture characters, we shall find them warm, zealous, and affectionate. When engaged in their favourite work of celebrating the goodness of their Supreme Benefactor, their souls appear to burn within them, their hearts kindle into rapture; the powers of language are made inadequate to the expression of their transports; and they call on all nature to swell the chorus, and to unite with them in hallelujahs of gratitude, and joy, and praise. The man after God's own heart most of all abounds in these glowing effusions; and his compositions appear to have been given us in order to set the tone, as it were, to all succeeding generations.

FOR MEDITATION: 'All is holy where devotion kneels,' wrote the nineteenth-century American poet Oliver Wendell Holmes. Devotion kneels within the heart, that place where the religious affections grow. Though of course it is always true that out of the abundance of the heart the mouth speaks (Matthew 12:34), there are times when the deepest yearnings of our hearts for God are unspoken. The nineteenth-century poet Thomas Moore understood this:

As down in the sunless retreats of the ocean
Sweet flowers are springing no mortal can see,
So deep in my soul the still prayer of devotion,
Unheard by the world, rises silent to thee.
As still to the star of its worship, though clouded,
The needle points faithfully o'er the dim sea,
So dark when I roam in this wintry world shrouded,
The hope of my spirit turns trembling to thee.

REFERENCE: *A Practical View of Christianity* (1797)

'To bring their hearts'

'Give unto the LORD *the glory due unto his name; worship the* LORD *in the beauty of holiness.' Psalm 29:2*
SUGGESTED FURTHER READING: Psalm 95:1–11

The worship and service of the glorified spirits in Heaven is not represented to us as a cold intellectual investigation, but as the worship and service of gratitude and love. And surely it will not be disputed, that it should be even here the humble endeavour of those, who are promised while here on earth 'to be made meet to be partakers of the inheritance of the saints in light,' to bring their hearts into capacity for joining in those everlasting praises.

FOR MEDITATION: The seventeenth-century poet John Milton was one whom Wilberforce often quoted. In *Paradise Lost*, Milton envisioned this picture of the praises that all creation ought to offer up to God:

Join voices, all ye living souls: ye birds,
That singing up to heaven-gate ascend,
Bear on your wings and in your notes his praise.

The nineteenth-century clergyman William Samways Oke described how a continuing spirit of praise and worship should inform the life of the Christian:

Lord, let us to thy gates repair
To hear the gladdening sound,
That we may find salvation there,
While yet it may be found …
And so increase our love for thee,
That all our future days
May one continued Sabbath be
Of gratitude and praise.

REFERENCE: *A Practical View of Christianity* (1797)

'That honour which cometh from God'

*'How can ye believe, which receive honour one of another, and seek not
the honour that cometh from God only?' John 5:44*
SUGGESTED FURTHER READING: Proverbs 4:20–27

The Christian too is well aware that the excessive desire of human
approbation is a passion of so subtle a nature, that there is nothing into
which it cannot penetrate. To those who wish to conform themselves to
the injunctions of the word of God, we must advise a laborious
watchfulness, a jealous guard, a close and frequent scrutiny of their own
hearts, that they may not mistake their real character, and too late find
themselves to have been mistaken, as to what they had conceived to be
their governing motives.

Above all, let them labour, with humble prayers for the Divine
assistance, to fix in themselves a deep, habitual, and practical sense of the
excellence of 'that honour which cometh from God,' and of the
comparative worthlessness of all earthly estimation and pre-eminence. In
truth, unless the affections of the soul be thus predominantly engaged on
the side of heavenly in preference to that of human honour, though we
may have relinquished the pursuit of fame, we shall not have acquired
that firm contexture of mind, which can bear disgrace and shame
without yielding to the pressure.

FOR MEDITATION: The writer of Hebrews tells us that Christians ought to
'desire a better country, that is, an heavenly' (Hebrews 11:16). The
apostle Paul, in 1 Corinthians 7:31, admonishes us to remember that 'the
fashion of this world passeth away.'

Many are the writers that have urged Christians to make sure of where
their ultimate allegiances lie. The eighteenth-century clergyman Richard
Cecil gave this charge to his readers: 'Keep thyself unspotted from the
world.' The eighteenth-century poet and royal chaplain Edward Young
stated: 'What is this world? thy school, O misery!'

Since we began with Scripture, it would be well to end with it. Mark
8:36 contains perhaps the most famous passage on this subject of all: 'For
what shall it profit a man, if he shall gain the whole world, and lose his
own soul?'

REFERENCE: *A Practical View of Christianity* (1797)

'The worst of our case'

'We should live soberly, righteously, and godly, in this present world.'
Titus 2:12
SUGGESTED FURTHER READING: 1 Peter 1:10–16

Above all, let us guard against the temptation to which we shall certainly
be exposed, of lowering down our views to our state, instead of
endeavouring to rise to the level of our views. Let us rather determine to
know the worst of our case, and strive to be suitably affected with it; not
forward to speak peace to ourselves, but patiently carrying about with us
a deep conviction of our backwardness and inaptitude to religious duties,
and a just sense of our great weakness and numerous infirmities. This
cannot be an unbecoming temper in those who are commanded to 'work
out their salvation with fear and trembling.' It prompts to constant and
earnest prayer. It produces that sobriety, and lowliness and tenderness of
mind, that meekness of demeanour and circumspection in conduct,
which are such eminent characteristics of the true Christian.

FOR MEDITATION: Wilberforce writes above concerning the need for the
Christian to exhibit circumspection in conduct. In this, he is
paraphrasing the apostle Paul, who wrote in Ephesians 5:15: 'See then
that ye walk circumspectly, not as fools, but as wise.'

And what is the beginning of wisdom? Proverbs 9:10 tells us: 'The fear
of the Lord is the beginning of wisdom: and the knowledge of the holy is
understanding.' Bearing this in mind, we should always remember the
promise of Proverbs 2:10–11: 'When wisdom entereth into thine heart,
and knowledge is pleasant unto thy soul; discretion shall preserve thee,
understanding shall keep thee.'

REFERENCE: *A Practical View of Christianity* (1797)

'We are to be created anew'

'But ye are a chosen generation, a royal priesthood, an holy nation, a peculiar people; that ye should shew forth the praises of him who hath called you out of darkness into his marvellous light.' 1 Peter 2:9
SUGGESTED FURTHER READING: Psalm 33:10–22

In the language of Scripture, Christianity is not a geographical, but a moral term. It is not the being a native of a Christian country: it is *a condition, a state;* the possession of a *peculiar nature,* with the qualities and properties which belong to it.

Farther than this; it is a state into which we are not *born,* but into which we must be *translated;* a nature which we do not *inherit,* but into which we are to be *created anew.* To the undeserved grace of God, which is promised on our use of the appointed means, we must be indebted for the attainment of this nature; and, to acquire and make sure of it, is that great 'work of our salvation' which we are commanded to 'work out with fear and trembling.' We are everywhere reminded, that this is a matter of labour and difficulty, requiring continual watchfulness, and unceasing effort, and unwearied patience. Even to the very last, towards the close of a long life consumed in active service, or in cheerful suffering, we find Paul himself declaring that he conceived bodily self-denial and mental discipline to be indispensably necessary to his very safety. Christians, who are really worthy of the name, are represented as being 'made meet for the inheritance of the saints in light'; as 'waiting for the coming of our Lord Jesus Christ,' as 'looking for and hasting unto the coming of the day of God.' It is stated as being enough to make them happy, that 'Christ should receive them to himself'; and the songs of the blessed spirits in Heaven are described to be the same as those in which the servants of God on earth pour forth their gratitude and adoration.

FOR MEDITATION: The seventeenth-century divine Thomas Fuller described the traits that ought to distinguish a Christian: 'Christians are called saints, for their holiness; believers, for their faith; brethren, for their love; disciples, for their knowledge.' It is by the pursuit of such that we become, to use Wilberforce's phrase, 'Christians who are really worthy of the name.'

REFERENCE: *A Practical View of Christianity* (1797)

'The indispensable necessity'

'Every valley shall be exalted, and every mountain and hill shall be made low: and the crooked shall be made straight, and the rough places plain.'
Isaiah 40:4
SUGGESTED FURTHER READING: John 9:1–41 (noting v.4)

Conscious of the indispensable necessity, and of the arduous nature of the service in which he is engaged, the true Christian sets himself to the work with vigour, and prosecutes it with diligence; his motto is that of the painter:

'Nullus dies sine linea.'
not a day without a line

Fled as it were from a country in which the plague is raging, he thinks it not enough just to pass the boundary line, but would put out of doubt his escape beyond the limits of infection. Prepared to meet with difficulties, he is not discouraged when they occur; warned of his numerous adversaries, he is not alarmed on their approach, or unprovided for encountering them. He knows that the beginning of every new course may be expected to be rough and painful; but he is assured that the paths on which he is entering will ere long seem smoother, and become indeed 'paths of pleasantness and peace.'

FOR MEDITATION: Psalm 119 is one of the most beautiful psalms in the Bible. Inasmuch as Wilberforce writes above concerning Christians embarking on a new course, it is well to consider how the psalmist writes of the places in which a pilgrim sojourns in Psalm 119:54–55. 'Thy statutes,' this passage begins, 'have been my songs in the house of my pilgrimage. I have remembered thy name, O LORD, in the night, and have kept thy law.'

REFERENCE: *A Practical View of Christianity* (1797)

'This desire of pleasing God'

'She looketh well to the ways of her household, and eateth not the bread of idleness.' Proverbs 31:27
SUGGESTED FURTHER READING: Colossians 1:9–17

But it belongs to this desire of pleasing God, that we should be continually solicitous to discover the path of duty; that we should not indolently wait, satisfied with not refusing occasions of glorifying God, when they are forced upon us, but that we should pray to God for wisdom and spiritual understanding, that we may be acute in discerning opportunities of serving him in the world. Guard indeed against the distraction of worldly cares, and cultivate heavenly mindedness, and a spirit of continual prayer, and neglect not to watch incessantly over the workings of your deceitful heart; but be active also, and useful. Let not your precious time be wasted 'in shapeless idleness:'[3] an admonition which, in our days, is rendered but too necessary by the relaxed habits of persons even of real piety; but wisely husband and improve this fleeting treasure. Never be satisfied with your present attainments; and run the race that is set before you without flagging in your course.

FOR MEDITATION: 'Without flagging in your course.' Wilberforce loved the poems and hymns of Isaac Watts, specially one of his *Songs for Children* called 'Summer's Evening,' which speaks movingly of the course an aged Christian has run:

How fine has the day been! how bright was the sun!
How lovely and joyful the course that he run;
Though he rose in a mist when his race he begun,
And there followed some droppings of rain:
But now the fair traveller's come to the west,
His rays are all gold, and his beauties are best;
He paints the skies gay as he sinks to his rest,
And foretells a bright rising again.

REFERENCE: *A Practical View of Christianity* (1797)

'Love to God and man'

'We know that we have passed from death unto life, because we love the brethren. He that loveth not his brother abideth in death.' 1 John 3:14
SUGGESTED FURTHER READING: John 13:31–35

Above all, measure your progress by your improvement in love to God and man. 'God is Love.' This is the sacred principle which warms and enlightens the heavenly world, that blessed seat of God's visible presence. There it shines with unclouded radiance. Some scattered beams are graciously lent to us on earth, or we had been benighted and lost in darkness and misery; but a larger portion of it is infused into the hearts of the servants of God, who thus 'are renewed in the divine likeness,' and even here exhibit some faint traces of the image of their heavenly Father. It is the principle of love which disposes them to yield themselves up without reserve to the service of him, 'who has bought them with the price of his own blood.'

FOR MEDITATION: No better complement for Wilberforce's reflections above can be found than in lines the eighteenth-century poet Edward Young wrote:

Thou, my all!
My theme! my inspiration! my crown!
My strength in age—my rise in low estate!
My soul's ambition, pleasure, wealth!—my world!
My light in darkness! and my life in death!
My boast through time! bliss through eternity!
Eternity, too short to speak thy praise!
Or fathom thy profound of love to man!   *Night Thoughts*

REFERENCE: *A Practical View of Christianity* (1797)

'The debt of gratitude'

'bringing into captivity every thought to the obedience of Christ.'
2 Corinthians 10:5
SUGGESTED FURTHER READING: Ephesians 6:7

Servile, and base, and mercenary, is the notion of Christian practice among the bulk of nominal Christians. They give no more than they *dare* not withhold; they abstain from nothing but what they *must* not practice. When you state to them the doubtful quality of any action, and the consequent obligation to desist from it, they reply to you in the very spirit of Shylock, 'they cannot find it in the bond.'[4]

In short, they know Christianity only as a system of restraints. She is despoiled of every liberal and generous principle: she is rendered almost unfit for the social intercourses of life, and is only suited to the gloomy walls of that cloister, in which they would confine her. But *true Christians* consider themselves not as satisfying some rigorous creditor, but as discharging a debt of gratitude. Theirs is accordingly not the stinted return of a constrained obedience, but the large and liberal measure of a voluntary service.

FOR MEDITATION: Psalm 100:2 tells us that we ought to 'Serve the Lord with gladness,' and 'come before his presence with singing.'

What else can we learn from the Scriptures about how we ought to serve God? In Psalm 119:124–25 we learn that we are to pray that God will teach us his ways, in order that we might better serve him: 'Deal with thy servant according unto thy mercy,' the psalmist asks, 'and teach me thy statutes. I am thy servant; give me understanding, that I may know thy testimonies.'

REFERENCE: *A Practical View of Christianity* (1797)

'Mercies so dearly bought'

'The Lord is good to all: and his tender mercies are over all his works.'
Psalm 145:9
SUGGESTED FURTHER READING: Romans 11:30–36

The greatest possible services of man to man must appear contemptible, when compared with 'the unspeakable mercies of Christ': mercies so dearly bought, the gift of 'a crown of glory, that fadeth not away.'

True love is an ardent, and active principle. When these generous affections really exist in vigour, are we not ever fond of dwelling on the value and enumerating the merits of our benefactor? How are we moved when anything is asserted to his disparagement! How do we delight to tell of his kindness! With what pious care do we preserve any memorial of him, which we may happen to possess! How gladly do we seize any opportunity of rendering to him, or to those who are dear to him, any little good offices, which, though in themselves of small intrinsic worth, may testify the sincerity of our thankfulness! The very mention of his name will cheer the heart, and light up the countenance!

FOR MEDITATION: The eighteenth-century poet and essayist Joseph Addison wrote these lines in speaking of the mercies of God:

When all thy mercies, O my God,
My rising soul surveys,
Transported with the view I'm lost,
In wonder, love and praise.

In the nineteenth century, thoughts of God's mercy came powerfully to the poet William Wordsworth while he was standing on the banks of the River Nith in Scotland:

Sweet Mercy! to the gates of Heaven
This minstrel lead, his sins forgiven;
The rueful conflict, the heart riven
With vain endeavour,
And memory of earth's bitter leaven
Effaced forever.

REFERENCE: *A Practical View of Christianity* (1797)

'Is it no cause of joy?'

'To whom God would make known what is the riches of the glory of this mystery among the Gentiles; which is Christ in you, the hope of glory.' Colossians 1:27

SUGGESTED FURTHER READING: Colossians 1:9–29

Is it no obligation, that he who 'thought it not robbery to be equal with God,' should yet, for our sakes, 'make himself of no reputation, and take upon him the form of a servant, and be made in the likeness of men; and humble himself, and become obedient unto death, even the death of the cross'! Is it no cause of *joy,* 'that to us is born a Saviour,' by whom we may 'be delivered from the power of darkness; and be made meet to be partakers of the inheritance of the saints in light?' Can there be a '*hope* comparable to that of our calling,' 'which is Christ in us, the hope of glory?' Can there be a *trust* to be preferred to the reliance on 'Christ Jesus; who is the same yesterday, to-day, and for ever?'

FOR MEDITATION: The apostle Paul said in 1 Corinthians 13, 'now abideth faith, hope and charity—these three.' Words that he wrote about charity might well then be applied to the hope that belongs to the Christian. Hope 'beareth all things, believeth all things, hopeth all things, endureth all things. [Hope] never faileth.'

The eighteenth-century poet Oliver Goldsmith wrote of hope in a similar strain:

Hope, like the gleaming taper's light,
Adorns and cheers our way;
And still, as darker grows the night,
Emits a brighter ray.

REFERENCE: *A Practical View of Christianity* (1797)

'Miracles of mercy'

'*But as for me, I will come into thy house in the multitude of thy mercy: and in thy fear will I worship toward thy holy temple.*' Psalm 5:7
SUGGESTED FURTHER READING: Psalm 13:1–5

When from reading that our Saviour was 'the brightness of his Father's glory, and the express image of his person, upholding all things by the word of his power,' we go on to consider the purpose for which he came to earth, and all that he did and suffered for us; surely if we have a spark of ingenuousness left within us we shall condemn ourselves as guilty of the blackest ingratitude, in rarely noticing, or coldly turning away, on whatever shallow pretences, from the contemplation of these miracles of mercy.

FOR MEDITATION: The seventeenth-century Puritan Thomas Brooks (1608–1680) understood well the feelings the realization of God's mercy towards us ought to produce: 'Nothing humbles and breaks the heart of a sinner like mercy and love. Souls that converse much with sin and wrath, may be much terrified; but souls that converse much with grace and mercy, will be much humbled.'

In Christ, we are the beneficiaries of God's enduring miracle of mercy. When the eyes of our heart look upon all that our Lord did and suffered for us, we say with the psalmist: 'To him who alone doeth great wonders: for his mercy endureth for ever' (Psalm 136:4).

REFERENCE: *A Practical View of Christianity* (1797)

'The great, and the wise, and the learned'

'him that hath an high look and a proud heart will not I suffer.' Psalm 101:5
SUGGESTED FURTHER READING: 1 Peter 5:1–11

The same God who declares—'My glory I will not give to another, neither my praise *to graven images*,' declares also—'Let not the wise man glory in his wisdom, neither let the mighty man *glory* in his might; let not the rich man *glory* in his riches.' 'No flesh may *glory* in his presence'; 'he that *glorieth*, let him glory in the Lord.' The sudden vengeance by which the vainglorious ostentation of Herod was punished, when, acquiescing in the servile adulation of an admiring multitude, 'he gave not God the *glory*,' is a dreadful comment on these injunctions.

These awful declarations, it is to be feared, are little regarded. Let the Great, and the Wise, and the Learned, and the Successful lay them seriously to heart, and labour habitually to consider their superiority, whether derived from nature, or study, or fortune, as the unmerited bounty of God. This reflection will naturally tend to produce a disposition, instead of that proud self-complacency so apt to grow upon the human heart, in all respects opposite to it; a disposition honourable to God, and useful to man; a temper composed of reverence, humility, and gratitude, and delighting to be engaged in the praises, and employed in the benevolent service of the universal Benefactor.

FOR MEDITATION: Psalm 30:4 tells us 'Sing unto the Lord, O ye saints of his, and give thanks at the remembrance of his holiness.'

The Psalms are as so many doxologies—that is to say expressions of praise to God, or short hymns. When we think of the glory of God, especially in the ways in which Wilberforce writes above, Ephesians 1:18–23 seems especially appropriate. These verses are a kind of doxology, and well worth our careful and prayerful study.

REFERENCE: *A Practical View of Christianity* (1797)

'All human events'

'My times are in thy hand.' Psalm 31:15
SUGGESTED FURTHER READING: Psalm 31:1–24

The Supreme Being can at any moment bring light out of darkness; and if at any time our country should again be visited with similar difficulties and dangers, humbling ourselves under his mighty hand, and putting our trust in his mercy, we should assume a holy fortitude, superior to all the chances and changes of this varying life. Our part in such circumstances is, to do the duty of the present hour without despondency; remembering that all human events are under the direction of a being infinitely wise, powerful, and merciful.

FOR MEDITATION: Hebrews 1:3 tells us: 'Who being the brightness of his glory, and the express image of his person, and *upholding all things by the word of his power*, when he had by himself purged our sins, sat down on the right hand of the Majesty on high.'

Jesus upholds all things by his power. What a blest assurance. And Hebrews 7:25 states a wonderfully kindred thought: 'Therefore he is able also to save them to the uttermost that come unto God by him, seeing he ever liveth to make intercession for them.' Christ upholds all things. He saves to the uttermost. He ever lives to make intercession for us. Our Lord is superior to all the chances and changes of this varying life.

The nineteenth-century poet Thomas Haynes Bayly wrote a couplet that speaks of the trust and confidence we can have because of Christ and his providence:

Fear not, but trust in Providence,
Wherever thou may'st be.

REFERENCE: WILBERFORCE, *A Retrospect of the Year 1801*

'Ever remember'

'That Christ may dwell in your hearts by faith; that ye, being rooted and grounded in love, may be able to comprehend with all saints what is the breadth, and length, and depth, and height; and to know the love of Christ, which passeth knowledge, that ye might be filled with all the fulness of God.' Ephesians 3:17–19
SUGGESTED FURTHER READING: Romans 8:37–39

What a comfort it is to know that our Heavenly Father is ever ready to receive all who call upon him. He delighteth in mercy, and ever remember that as you have heard me say, mercy is kindness to the guilty, to those who deserve punishment. What a delightful consideration it is that our Saviour loves his people better than we love each other, than an earthly parent loves his child.

FOR MEDITATION: How can we begin to fathom the depths of God's love? It transcends any comparisons we might make, for God himself is transcendent. And yet the Scriptures are replete with declarations of the love and mercy God has for us and has shown towards us. Here are but some of the most precious assurances we have been given.

Psalm 86:5 tells us 'For thou, LORD, art good, and ready to forgive; and plenteous in mercy unto all them that call upon thee.' Psalm 145:9 affirms 'The LORD is good to all: and his tender mercies are over all his works.' Psalm 103:4 declares that we serve a God 'who redeemeth thy life from destruction; who crowneth thee with lovingkindness and tender mercies.' Psalm 130:7 reads: 'with the LORD there is mercy, and with him is plenteous redemption.' Psalm 25:10 teaches us that 'All the paths of the LORD are mercy and truth unto such as keep his covenant and his testimonies.' 2 Corinthians 1:3 offers this note of praise: 'Blessed be God, even the Father of our Lord Jesus Christ, the Father of mercies, and the God of all comfort.'

REFERENCE: *Private Papers of William Wilberforce* (1897)

'The Christian's hope'

'In hope of eternal life, which God, that cannot lie, promised before the world began.' Titus 1:2
SUGGESTED FURTHER READING: Titus 3:4–7

The Christian's hope is founded, not on the speculations or the strength of man, but on the declaration of him who cannot lie, on the power of Omnipotence.

FOR MEDITATION: 'Marvellous are thy works,' we read in Psalm 139:14, 'and that my soul knoweth right well.' Revelation 19:6 declares: 'I heard as it were the voice of a great multitude, and as the voice of many waters, and as the voice of mighty thunderings, saying, Alleluia: for the Lord God omnipotent reigneth.'

The last six words of this verse are part of one of the most famous refrains in all sacred music: Handel's *Hallelujah Chorus*. Wilberforce loved this oratorio, and it deeply moved him. So we find his biographer sons writing of him in the year 1827 as follows: 'His love for music was as strong as ever. This very year he speaks of himself as "quite overpowered by the Hallelujah Chorus in the *Messiah*, a flood of tears ensued, and the impression on my mind remained through the day."'

How many a soul has been stirred during a performance of the *Messiah* by the sound of many voices singing 'for the Lord God omnipotent reigneth'? And if our souls are stirred by a performance, how much more should they be stirred by the reality of God's word: the Christian's hope is founded, not on the speculations or the strength of man, but on the declaration of him who cannot lie, on the power of Omnipotence.

REFERENCE: *A Practical View of Christianity* (1797)

'The door of mercy'

'I am the door: by me if any man enter in, he shall be saved.' John 10:9
SUGGESTED FURTHER READING: John 14:1–14

Christianity is a scheme 'for justifying *the ungodly*,' by Christ's dying for them *'while yet sinners:'* a scheme 'for reconciling us to God—*when enemies.'* In short, it opens freely the door of mercy, to the greatest and vilest of penitent sinners; who obeying the blessed impulse of the grace of God, whereby they had been awakened from the sleep of death, and moved to seek for pardon, may enter in, and, through the regenerating influence of the Holy Spirit, might be enabled to bring forth the fruits of Righteousness.

FOR MEDITATION: The seventeenth-century poet John Milton declared, famously, 'But infinite in pardon is my Judge.' In the Scriptures, we have many declarations of God's constancy and willingness to pardon our offences. Nehemiah 9:17 states: 'but thou art a God ready to pardon, gracious and merciful, slow to anger, and of great kindness.' Micah 7:18 reminds us, powerfully: 'Who is a God like unto thee, that pardoneth iniquity … he retaineth not his anger for ever, because he delighteth in mercy.' Jeremiah 33:8 affirms: 'And I will cleanse them from all their iniquity, whereby they have sinned against me; and I will pardon all their iniquities.'

REFERENCE: *A Practical View of Christianity* (1797)

'The reality of meekness and gentleness'

'But the fruit of the Spirit is love, joy, peace, longsuffering, gentleness, goodness, faith, meekness, temperance: against such there is no law.'
Galatians 5:22–23
SUGGESTED FURTHER READING: Romans 12:3

Christianity teaches us not to prize human estimation at a very high rate, and thereby provides for the practice of her injunction, to love from the heart those who, justly or unjustly, may have attacked our reputation, and wounded our character. She commands not the show but the reality of meekness and gentleness; and by thus taking away the aliment of anger and the fomenters of discord, she provides for the maintenance of peace, and the restoration of good temper among men, when it may have sustained a temporary interruption.

FOR MEDITATION: In 1 Thessalonians 2:7, the apostle Paul tells the Thessalonians: 'But we were gentle among you, even as a nurse cherisheth her children.' If such was the way in which the apostles treated fellow believers, how ought we to treat one another? Consider these passages of Scripture.

In 2 Corinthians 10:1 Paul writes of 'the meekness and gentleness of Christ'. In 2 Timothy 2:24–25 the apostle admonishes his young protégé Timothy: 'And the servant of the Lord must not strive; but be gentle unto all men, apt to teach, patient, in meekness instructing those that oppose themselves; if God peradventure will give them repentance to the acknowledging of the truth.' In Galatians 5:22–23 Paul teaches that the fruits of the Spirit in our lives are to be: 'love, joy, peace, longsuffering, gentleness, goodness, faith, meekness [and] temperance.' Lastly, the apostle James urges his readers to remember that 'the wisdom that is from above is first pure, then peaceable, gentle, and easy to be intreated, full of mercy and good fruits, without partiality, and without hypocrisy' (James 3:17). May God grant us the grace, the conviction and the resolve to live our lives as these passages dictate.

REFERENCE: *A Practical View of Christianity* (1797)

'The prevalence of real religion'

'But the path of the just is as the shining light, that shineth more and more unto the perfect day.' Proverbs 4:18
SUGGESTED FURTHER READING: Psalm 25:1–10

But in fact, so far is it from being true that the prevalence of real religion would produce a stagnation in life, it would infallibly produce the very reverse: a man, whatever might be his employment or pursuit, would be furnished with a new motive to prosecute it with alacrity, a motive far more constant and vigorous than any which merely human prospects can supply: at the same time, his solicitude being not so much to succeed in whatever he might be engaged in, as to act from a pure principle, and leave the event to God, he would not be liable to the same disappointments, as men who are active and laborious from a desire of worldly gain or of human estimation. Thus he would possess the true secret of a life at the same time useful and happy. Following peace also with all men, and looking upon them as members of the same family, entitled not only to the debts of justice, but to the less definite and more liberal claims of fraternal kindness; he would naturally be respected and beloved by others, and be in himself free from the annoyance of those bad passions, by which those who are actuated by worldly principles are so commonly corroded.

FOR MEDITATION: The sixteenth-century essayist Francis Bacon was a writer who had a profound influence upon Wilberforce. All his life Wilberforce read and often memorized portions of Bacon's writings. He quoted from Bacon in his own published works. In his essay, 'Of Goodness', Bacon had this to say of Christianity: 'There was never law, or set, or opinion did so much magnify goodness, as the Christian religion doth.'

REFERENCE: *A Practical View of Christianity* (1797)

'An unfailing and abundant source'

'I will open rivers in high places, and fountains in the midst of the valleys: I will make the wilderness a pool of water, and the dry land springs of water.' Isaiah 41:18
SUGGESTED FURTHER READING: Psalm 107:33

But true Christian benevolence is always occupied in producing happiness to the utmost of its power, and according to the extent of its sphere, be it larger or more limited; it contracts itself to the measure of the smallest; it can expand itself to the amplitude of the largest. It resembles majestic rivers, which are poured from an unfailing and abundant source. Silent and peaceful in their course, they begin with dispensing beauty and comfort to every cottage by which they pass. In their further progress they fertilize provinces and enrich kingdoms. At length they pour themselves into the ocean, where, changing their names, but not their nature, they visit distant nations and other hemispheres, and spread throughout the world the expansive tide of their beneficence.

FOR MEDITATION: Many are the writers who, like Wilberforce, have understood how the Christian faith fosters beneficence. The seventeenth-century American divine Cotton Mather declared: 'Our opportunities to do good are our talents.' His near contemporary in Britain, the poet John Milton, said: 'Good, the more communicated, more abundant grows.'

The nineteenth-century moral philosopher and theologian Thomas Chalmers, who came to faith through his reading of Wilberforce's *A Practical View of Christianity*, said this of benevolence, the sister of beneficence:

Benevolence is not in word and in tongue, but in deed and in truth ... It is a duty which you must perform at the call of principle; though there be no voice of eloquence to give splendour to your exertions ... You must go to the poor man's cottage, though no verdure flourish around it, and no rivulet be nigh to delight you by the gentleness of its murmurs. If you look for the romantic simplicity of fiction you will be disappointed; but it is your duty to persevere in spite of every discouragement. Benevolence is not merely a feeling but a principle; not a dream of rapture for the fancy to indulge in, but a business for the hand to execute.

REFERENCE: *A Practical View of Christianity* (1797)

'The wisest, and the best, and the ablest of men'

'Whoso is wise, and will observe these things, even they shall understand the lovingkindness of the LORD.*' Psalm 107:43*
SUGGESTED FURTHER READING: Daniel 2:19–23

The various arguments for the truth of our holy religion have been sufficient to satisfy the wisest, and the best, and the ablest of men.

FOR MEDITATION: The seventeenth-century essayist Joseph Addison, whom Wilberforce read avidly all his life, crafted a phrase that complements Wilberforce's words above: 'It happened very providentially, to the honour of the Christian religion, that it did not take its rise in the dark illiterate ages of the world, but at a time when arts and sciences were at their height.'

The New Dictionary of National Biography has declared that Samuel Johnson, another of Wilberforce's favourite writers, was 'arguably the most distinguished man of letters in English history.' This only serves to underscore the importance of what Johnson said on behalf of the arguments for the truth of Christianity:

As to the Christian religion, besides the strong evidence which we have for it, there is a balance in its favour from the number of great men who have been convinced of its truth after a serious consideration of the question. Grotius was an acute man, a lawyer, a man accustomed to examine evidence, and he was convinced. Grotius was not a recluse, but a man of the world, who certainly had no bias on the side of religion. Sir Isaac Newton set out an infidel, and came to be a very firm believer.

REFERENCE: *A Practical View of Christianity* (1797)

'Enlighten our understandings'

'But grow in grace, and in the knowledge of our Lord and Saviour Jesus Christ. To him be glory both now and for ever. Amen.' 2 Peter 3:18
SUGGESTED FURTHER READING: Ephesians 1:15–23

We are directed to pray for the influence of the Holy Spirit to enlighten our understandings, to dissipate our prejudices, to purify our corrupt minds, and renew us after the image of our heavenly Father. It is this influence which is represented as originally awakening us from slumber, as enlightening us in darkness, as 'quickening us when dead,' as 'delivering us from the power of the devil,' as drawing us to God, as 'translating us into the kingdom of his dear Son,' as 'creating us anew in Christ Jesus,' as 'dwelling in us, and walking in us;' so that 'putting off the old man with his deeds,' we are to consider ourselves as 'having put on the new man, which is renewed in knowledge after the image of him that created him;' and as those who are to be 'an habitation of God through the Spirit.' It is by this Divine assistance only that we grow in Grace, and improve in all Holiness.

FOR MEDITATION: 'Holiness,' declared Charles Haddon Spurgeon, 'is the architectural plan upon which God buildeth up his living temple.' How then, do we obtain the divine assistance we need to follow through on God's architectural plan for our lives?

Prayerful reliance upon the Lord is the key. In this we take our cue spiritually from the apostle Paul, who wrote to the Philippians: 'Always in every prayer of mine for you all making request with joy, for your fellowship in the gospel from the first day until now; being confident of this very thing, that *he which hath begun a good work in you will perform it until the day of Jesus Christ*' (Philippians 1:4–6). Daily we are to pray that God will produce in our lives the fruit of holiness. And as we do, we can rest in the assurance that God's good work in our lives will be done.

REFERENCE: *A Practical View of Christianity* (1797)

'Christianity has been too often disgraced'

'They shall put you out of the synagogues: yea, the time cometh, that whosoever killeth you will think that he doeth God service. And these things will they do unto you, because they have not known the Father, nor me.' John 16:2–3
SUGGESTED FURTHER READING: Matthew 5:38–48

Christianity itself has been too often disgraced. The gospel of peace has been turned into an engine of cruelty, and amidst the bitterness of persecution, every trace has disappeared of the mild and beneficent spirit of the religion of Jesus. In what degree must the taint have worked itself into the frame, and have corrupted the habit, when the most wholesome nutriment can be thus converted into the deadliest poison?

FOR MEDITATION: In October 1822 Wilberforce wrote to the then Foreign Minister (and future Prime Minister), George Canning, 'entreating his good offices for the Waldenses, of whose depressed and almost persecuted situation I heard from a gentleman who had resided in their country.'

This was one instance when Wilberforce's faith led him to champion the cause of the persecuted. The supreme example of this was his opposition to slavery, of which he wrote in the spring of 1817: 'surely the cause we are engaged in is the cause of God—endeavouring ... to succour the wretched and right the injured and oppressed.'

In this Wilberforce was acting on the precepts of Scripture. The following citation from Wilberforce's writings is used elsewhere in this collection of readings, but it warrants insertion here: 'In the Scriptures,' he wrote, 'no national crime is condemned so frequently, and few so strongly, as oppression and cruelty, and the not using our best endeavours to deliver our fellow-creatures from them. See Jeremiah 6:6; "This is a city (Jerusalem) to be visited; she is wholly oppression in the midst of her," also Ezekiel 16:49, of Sodom's crimes: "Neither did she strengthen the hands of the poor and needy."'

REFERENCE: *A Practical View of Christianity* (1797)

'Pardon, and grace, and strength'

'But not as the offence, so also is the free gift. For if through the offence of one many be dead, much more the grace of God, and the gift by grace, which is by one man, Jesus Christ, hath abounded unto many.'
Romans 5:15
SUGGESTED FURTHER READING: Ephesians 2:1–10

If our natural condition be depraved and weak, our temptations numerous, the offers to penitent sinners of pardon, and grace, and strength, are universal and unlimited. Let it also be remembered, that if in Christianity some things are difficult, that which it most concerns us to know, is plain and obvious. To this it is true wisdom to attach ourselves.

FOR MEDITATION: How good it is to know that the assurances we most desire from the Lord, those things which it most concerns us to know, are near at hand. 'But verily God hath heard me,' we read in Psalm 66:19, 'he hath attended to the voice of my prayer.'

Psalm 103:17 tells us: 'But the mercy of the Lord is from everlasting to everlasting upon them that fear him, and his righteousness unto children's children.' Concerning grace, the apostle Paul writes in Romans 5:17— 'For if by one man's offence [Adam's], death reigned by one; much more they which receive abundance of grace and of the gift of righteousness shall reign in life by one, Jesus Christ.' And in 2 Corinthians, Paul affirms that he has set forth the gospel in words that are easy to understand: 'Seeing then that we have such hope, we use great plainness of speech' (2 Corinthians 3:12). Lastly, the psalmist declares this good and gracious saying: 'LORD, thou hast heard the desire of the humble: thou wilt prepare their heart, thou wilt cause thine ear to hear' (Psalm 10:17).

REFERENCE: *A Practical View of Christianity* (1797)

'Events and circumstances'

'For this cause we also, since the day we heard it, do not cease to pray for you, and to desire that ye might be filled with the knowledge of his will in all wisdom and spiritual understanding.' Colossians 1:9
SUGGESTED FURTHER READING: Psalm 16:1–11

Christ—as is stated in Revelation 3—'stands at the door and knocks,' that is, he uses particular events and circumstances of our lives, for impressing us with the importance of spiritual things.

FOR MEDITATION: 'The meek,' we read in Psalm 25:9, 'will he guide in judgment: and the meek will he teach his way.' Psalm 32:8 declares: 'I will instruct thee and teach thee in the way which thou shalt go: I will guide thee with mine eye.'

Given this, we can understand why the psalmist offers this prayer: 'So teach us to number our days, that we may apply our hearts unto wisdom' (Psalm 90:12). And so we ought to pray this prayer with the psalmist, bearing in mind as we do, words written in the Book of Isaiah: 'Thus saith the LORD, thy Redeemer, the Holy One of Israel; I am the LORD thy God which teacheth thee to profit, which leadeth thee by the way that thou shouldest go' (Isaiah 48:17).

The writer of Proverbs adds one further component as to how we may apply our hearts to wisdom: diligent seeking. 'Get wisdom,' he writes, 'get understanding: forget it not; neither decline from the words of my mouth. Forsake her not, and she shall preserve thee: love her, and she shall keep thee. Wisdom is the principal thing; therefore get wisdom: and with all thy getting get understanding' (Proverbs 4:5–7).

REFERENCE: *Private Papers of William Wilberforce* (1897)

'Solitariness of spirit'

'For the LORD *hath comforted his people, and will have mercy upon his afflicted.'* Isaiah 49:13
SUGGESTED FURTHER READING: John 14:26

Meanwhile let me advise you, dear child, whenever you do feel anything of that solitariness of spirit of which you speak, to endeavour to find an antidote for it in prayer.

FOR MEDITATION: Wilberforce wrote these words in July 1830 to his beloved daughter Elizabeth, or, as he called her, Lizzy. His words recall those of an anonymous writer:

Doubt not but God who sits on high,
Thy secret prayers can hear.

Psalm 27:5 contains one of the loveliest and most comforting promises for those who have known solitariness of spirit: 'For in the time of trouble he shall hide me in his pavilion: in the secret of his tabernacle shall he hide me.' The apostle Paul told the Christians at Rome that they were 'beloved of God.' So too are we. In our times of trouble, God hears our secret prayers. It is then, under the shadow of his wings, he tells us we are his beloved. This abiding comfort and assurance the psalmist had known. 'I will be glad and rejoice in thy mercy,' he wrote, 'for thou hast considered my trouble; thou hast known my soul in adversities' (Psalm 31:7).

REFERENCE: *Private Papers of William Wilberforce* (1897)

'Whatever we do to please him'

'That ye might walk worthy of the Lord unto all pleasing, being fruitful in every good work, and increasing in the knowledge of God.' Colossians 1:10
SUGGESTED FURTHER READING: 2 Peter 1:5–7

The best way to promote the right temper of mind will be after earnest prayer to God to bless your endeavours, to try to keep the idea of Jesus Christ and of his sufferings, and of the love which prompted him willingly to undergo them, in your mind continually, and especially when you are going to do, occasionally when you are doing, your business. And then recollect that he has declared he will kindly accept as a tribute of gratitude whatever we do to please him.

FOR MEDITATION: Wilberforce wrote these words in November 1820 to his third son Samuel. Samuel was then fifteen years old. Wilberforce wrote over 600 letters to his son, each of which was carefully numbered and treasured.

Wilberforce invested himself in the life of his son, and his was the joy of seeing his son thrive and flourish under the lessons he had been taught by his father in the school of Christ. The picture here is not unlike that we find in Psalm 92:12–14: 'The righteous shall flourish like the palm tree: he shall grow like a cedar in Lebanon. Those that be planted in the house of the Lord shall flourish in the courts of our God. They shall still bring forth fruit in old age.' Samuel Wilberforce became one of the greatest prelates the Church of England has ever known. God had answered the prayers of a father who longed for his son to become a man of God.

REFERENCE: *Private Papers of William Wilberforce* (1897)

'Communication with heaven'

'For our conversation is in heaven; from whence also we look for the Saviour, the Lord Jesus Christ.' Philippians 3:20
SUGGESTED FURTHER READING: Hebrews 11:1–10

Prayer is the grand means of maintaining our communication with heaven, and the life of religion in the soul, claiming all possible attention.

FOR MEDITATION: 'Prayer begins where human capacity ends,' said the great African-American singer Marian Anderson. And so we have been given this blest assurance in Matthew 7:7–8: 'Ask, and it shall be given you; seek, and ye shall find; knock, and it shall be opened unto you: for every one that asketh receiveth; and he that seeketh findeth; and to him that knocketh it shall be opened.'

The seventeenth-century biblical commentator Matthew Henry said of prayer: 'The design of the Christian religion is to promote prayer; and the disciples of Christ must be praying people ... In our prayers we are to have a generous concern for others as well as for ourselves; we are to pray for all men, and to give thanks for all men; and must not confine our prayers nor thanksgiving to our own persons or families. Prayer consists of various parts, of supplications, intercessions, and thanksgivings; for we must pray for the mercies we want, as well as be thankful for mercies already received ... Prayer is not to be confined to any one particular house of prayer, but men must pray everywhere: no place is amiss for prayer, no place more acceptable to God than another. Pray everywhere. We must pray in our closets, pray in our families, pray at our meals, pray when we are on journeys, and pray in the solemn assemblies.'

REFERENCE: *Private Papers of William Wilberforce* (1897)

'Let your religion consist much in prayer'

'Let my prayer be set forth before thee as incense; and the lifting up of my hands as the evening sacrifice.' Psalm 141:2
SUGGESTED FURTHER READING: Psalm 22:22–31

Prayer, prayer, my dear Samuel; let your religion consist much in prayer. May you be enabled more and more to walk by faith and not by sight, to feel habitually as well as to recognize in all your more deliberate calculations and plans, that the things that are seen are temporal, but the things that are not seen are eternal. Then you will live above the world, as one who is waiting for the coming of the Lord Jesus Christ.

FOR MEDITATION: Prayer is the life-blood of the church and of individual believers. In the place of prayer we commune with God, learning the importance of seeking forgiveness and the necessity of praying for wisdom. From prayer we receive strength according to the day, and in prayer we offer thanks for the blessing of the day.

It has been said that the church marches forward on her knees. Sure enough it is that we shall make no progress in the Christian life if our lives are devoid of prayer. For prayer is fellowship with God. And if we do not pray to him, how shall we be able to fix our eyes upon him? How shall that trust in him be cultivated wherewith we place our very lives in his hands? We must abide in Christ, else our spiritual life shall wither. We must abide in the place of prayer, that we may know him in whom we have believed. And he longs for us to know him.

REFERENCE: *Private Papers of William Wilberforce* (1897)

'The duty of constant prayer'

'by manifestation of the truth commending ourselves to every man's conscience in the sight of God.' 2 Corinthians 4:2
SUGGESTED FURTHER READING: 1 Thessalonians 5:16–24

To your young friend again I need not suggest the duty of constant prayer for his nearest relatives. By degrees they will become softened, and he will probably enjoy the delight of finding them come over to the blessed path he is himself pursuing. He will also find that self-denial, and a disposition to subject himself to any trouble or annoyance in order to promote his friends' comfort, or exemption from some grievance, will have a very powerful effect in conciliating his friends.

FOR MEDITATION: How many a beloved son or daughter has come to faith only to find that for long years they had been pursued by the prayers of a loving parent? How many have had a cherished friend testify to a blessed surrender to God, only have that friend learn upon the occasion that during all the years when this friend wanted nothing of God, prayers were offered for them continually in the watches of the night?
Prayer renders the hopeless hopeful. And though we cannot see all ends that are known to God, there are those times when, with hindsight, it shall be given us to see that our prayers have been instrumental in some end that has been a desire of the heart.
The eighteenth-century poet William Cowper wrote:

And Satan trembles when he sees
The weakest saint upon his knees.

Our prayers, however halting or humbly voiced, are never for nothing. God hears and answers prayer. We should go to him. He is waiting. He is there, as he always been, at our point of greatest need.

REFERENCE: *Private Papers of William Wilberforce* (1897)

'Occupy till I come'

'As every man hath received the gift, even so minister the same one to another, as good stewards of the manifold grace of God.' 1 Peter 4:10
SUGGESTED FURTHER READING: 1 Corinthians 4:1–5

So little sense of responsibility seems attached to the possession of high rank, or splendid abilities, or affluent fortunes, or other means or instruments of usefulness. The instructive admonitions, 'give an account of thy stewardship,'—'Occupy till I come,' are forgotten.

FOR MEDITATION: The great seventeenth-century biblical commentator Matthew Henry said this of stewardship: 'we must so lay out what we have in works of piety and charity as that we may meet it again with comfort on the other side of death and the grave. If we would act wisely, we must be diligent and industrious to employ our riches in the acts of piety and charity ... We are but stewards. Whatever we have, the property of it is God's; we have only the use of it, and that according to the direction of our great Lord, and for his honour. Rabbi Kimchi, quoted by Dr Lightfoot, says, "This world is a house; heaven the roof; the stars the lights; the earth, with its fruits, a table spread; the Master of the house is the holy and blessed God; man is the steward, into whose hands the goods of this house are delivered; if he behave himself well, he shall find favour in the eyes of his Lord."'

In 1874 the hymn writer Frances Havergal published verses that speak to the heart of true, biblical stewardship:

Take my life, and let it be consecrated, Lord, to thee.
Take my moments and my days; let them flow in ceaseless praise.
Take my hands, and let them move at the impulse of thy love.
Take my feet, and let them be swift and beautiful for thee.

REFERENCE: *A Practical View of Christianity* (1797)

'The aid of some faithful friend'

'Ointment and perfume rejoice the heart: so doth the sweetness of a man's friend by hearty counsel.' Proverbs 27:9
SUGGESTED FURTHER READING: Proverbs 11:1–15

Where there is so much room for self-deceit, call in the aid of some faithful friend and, unbosoming yourself to him without concealment, ask his impartial and unreserved opinion of your behaviour and condition. Our unwillingness to do this often betrays to others, indeed it not seldom discovers to ourselves, that we entertain a secret distrust of our own character and conduct.

FOR MEDITATION: Proverbs 11:14 tells us: 'where no counsel is, the people fall: but in the multitude of counsellors there is safety.' The writer Robert Burton (1576–1640) penned his own proverb; wise as it is concise: 'He loves who advises.'

'Good counsels observed are chains of grace,' wrote the seventeenth-century divine Thomas Fuller. The sixteenth-century writer Francis Bacon wrote in a similar strain: 'The best receipt—best to work and best to take—is the admonition of a friend.'

In 1 Thessalonians, the apostle Paul instructed them saying: 'And we beseech you, brethren, to know them which labour among you, and are over you in the Lord, and admonish you; and to esteem them very highly in love for their work's sake' (1 Thessalonians 5:12–13). Do we have faithful friends, or know of wise and experienced counsellors who have been placed in positions of authority? When they offer counsel, they are entitled to our esteem, respect and attention.

REFERENCE: *A Practical View of Christianity* (1797)

'Patterns of mercy'

'but the righteous sheweth mercy, and giveth.' Psalm 37:21
SUGGESTED FURTHER READING: Psalm 85:7–13

Rough and churlish tempers are a direct contrast to the 'meekness and gentleness of Christ.' Christians are strongly and repeatedly enjoined to copy after their great Model in these particulars, and to be themselves patterns of 'mercy and kindness, and humbleness of mind, and meekness, and long-suffering.' They are to 'put away all bitterness, and wrath, and anger, and clamour, and evil-speaking;' not only 'being ready to every good work, but being *gentle* unto *all* men;' 'showing *all* meekness unto *all* men;' 'forbearing, forgiving,' tenderhearted. Remember the apostle's declaration, that 'if any man bridleth not his tongue, he only seemeth to be religious, and deceiveth his own heart;' and that it is one of the characters of that love, without which all pretensions to the name of Christian are but vain, that 'it doth not behave itself unseemly.' Consider how much these acrimonious tempers must break in upon the peace, and destroy the comfort, of those around you. Remember also that the honour of your Christian profession is at stake, and be solicitous not to discredit it: justly dreading lest you should disgust those whom you ought to conciliate, and thus conveying an unfavourable impression of your principles and character.

FOR MEDITATION: 'Be at peace among yourselves,' we read in 1 Thessalonians 5:13. As this apostolic admonition is short, so it is important and binding. Are we careful to practise conciliation?

Wilberforce wrote often about conciliation. 'I ought to do,' he said, 'as I would be done by.' Conciliation in his mind was not solely for fellow Christians. To those seeking to commend their faith, he wrote that the Christian 'will studiously and diligently use any degree of worldly credit he may enjoy, in removing or lessening prejudices; in conciliating good-will, and thereby making way for the less obstructed progress of truth.'

The dictionary tells us that the hallmarks of conciliation are (1) a willingness to overcome distrust or animosity; and (2) a commitment to regain or to try to regain friendship through considerate behaviour.

REFERENCE: *A Practical View of Christianity* (1797)

'Intimations conveyed to us'

'In my Father's house are many mansions: if it were not so, I would have told you. I go to prepare a place for you.' John 14:2
SUGGESTED FURTHER READING: Revelation 21:1–22:7

Although we should use great modesty in speculating on the invisible and eternal world, yet we may reasonably presume from intimations conveyed to us in the Holy Scriptures, and from inferences which they fairly suggest, that we shall retain of our earthly character and feelings in that which is not sinful, and therefore we may expect (this, I think, is very clear), to know each other, and to think and talk over the various circumstances of our lives, our several hopes and fears and plans and speculations; and you and I, if it please God, may talk over the incidents of our respective lives, and connected with them, those of our nearest and dearest relatives.

FOR MEDITATION: 'But as it is written,' we read in 1 Corinthians 2:9, 'Eye hath not seen, nor ear heard, neither have entered into the heart of man, the things which God hath prepared for them that love him.'
    There is no picture more beautiful in all of Scripture than the description of heaven we find in Revelation 21:1–5:

And I saw a new heaven and a new earth: for the first heaven and the first earth were passed away; and there was no more sea. And I John saw the holy city, new Jerusalem, coming down from God out of heaven, prepared as a bride adorned for her husband. And I heard a great voice out of heaven saying, 'Behold, the tabernacle of God is with men, and he will dwell with them, and they shall be his people, and God himself shall be with them, and be their God. And God shall wipe away all tears from their eyes; and there shall be no more death, neither sorrow, nor crying, neither shall there be any more pain: for the former things are passed away.' And he that sat upon the throne said, 'Behold, I make all things new.' And he said unto me, 'Write: for these words are true and faithful.'

REFERENCE: *Private Papers of William Wilberforce* (1897)

'The privilege of friendship'

'Confess your faults one to another, and pray one for another, that ye may be healed.' James 5:16
SUGGESTED FURTHER READING: Galatians 6:1–10

Speaking of the privileges and responsibilities of friendship, Wilberforce wrote to his daughter Elizabeth in November 1816: 'You will never find telling [your brother] Robert of any fault offend him, if you do it when you are *tête-à-tête,* and when he sees from your manner and from the circumstances that you can only have his happiness at heart.'

FOR MEDITATION: The seventeenth-century poet John Dryden described friendship in ways that add meaningfully to Wilberforce's words above:

For friendship, of itself a holy tie,
Is made more sacred by adversity.

Proverbs 17:17 provides the biblical foundation for enduring friendship. It states: 'A friend loveth at all times, and a brother is born for adversity.' For those friends who possess a pure heart and gracious spirit Proverbs 22:11 has this to say: 'He that loveth pureness of heart, for the grace of his lips the king shall be his friend.'
True friends weather the seasons of life, and they know when to speak a word in season—be it a hard truth or words of solace. Such friends are the gift of God.

REFERENCE: *Private Papers of William Wilberforce* (1897)

'Teach us to know ourselves'

'Teach us to number our days, that we may apply our hearts unto wisdom.' Psalm 90:12

SUGGESTED FURTHER READING: Proverbs 4:5–27

But if I am to exercise this best prerogative, this most sacred and indispensable duty of friendship, ... I must declare to you, that it will be necessary for my dear girl to guard herself with the utmost watchfulness, and, still more, to *prepare herself* with conscientious care. This is what St Paul terms 'herein do I exercise myself, to have always a conscience void of offence toward God, and toward men': what the Book of Proverbs styles, 'keeping the heart *with all diligence:*' for unless we have accustomed ourselves to *self-suspicion,* if I may use such a phrase, we never benefit as we might from the friendly reproofs of a real friend. We may receive his remarks with civility, and even give him credit for his kind intentions, but we shall be almost sure to let it appear to any acute observer at least, that we rather tolerate his frankness out of principle, or put up with it in consideration of the friendly motives by which it has been prompted, than that we listen to it with a sincere desire of profiting from it, still less that we welcome it as one of the most valuable services that could be rendered to us.

The grand preparation that is needed is humility; that sense of our own infirmities and our own weakness, which is felt by every true, at least by every flourishing Christian. We read in the Scripture that 'our hearts are deceitful above all things:' by which is meant, that we are all prone to flatter ourselves. Now it is the first office of the Holy Spirit to teach us to know ourselves, and immediately to *suspect* ourselves as the first effect of that knowledge. I know how difficult it is in practice from my own experience; and because it is so difficult, it is here that we need the special aid of the Holy Spirit, and should earnestly pray for his blessed influence to teach us to know ourselves.

FOR MEDITATION: Psalm 39:4 provides perhaps the best biblical reference for what Wilberforce has stated above: 'Lord, make me to know mine end, and the measure of my days, what it is; that I may know how frail I am.'

REFERENCE: *Private Papers of William Wilberforce* (1897)

'A gracious and tender Saviour'

'I will both lay me down in peace, and sleep: for thou, LORD, *only makest me dwell in safety.' Psalm 4:8*
SUGGESTED FURTHER READING: Psalm 121

It is a delightful consideration, my dearest child, that there is a gracious and tender Saviour who, in our sleeping as well as waking hours, is watching over us for good, if we are of the number of those who look to him habitually for consolation and peace, and such I trust will be more and more the case of my dear Elizabeth.

FOR MEDITATION: Psalm 119:156 declares: 'Great are thy tender mercies, O Lord.' Lamentations 3 also contains verses that afford continuing consolation and peace: But 'this I recall to my mind, therefore have I hope'. 'The steadfast love of the Lord never ceases, his mercies never come to an end; they are new every morning; great is thy faithfulness.' 'The LORD is my portion, saith my soul, therefore will I hope in him. The LORD is good unto them that wait for him, to the soul that seeketh him.'
    The nineteenth-century American poet John Greenleaf Whittier framed a lovely couplet to convey the peace imparted by our gracious God:

As on the Sea of Galilee,
The Christ is whispering 'Peace.'

REFERENCE: *Private Papers of William Wilberforce* (1897)

'Their first song of exultation'

'*O death, where is thy sting? O grave, where is thy victory?*'
1 Corinthians 15:55
SUGGESTED FURTHER READING: 1 Corinthians 15:25–28; 50–57

'Early in the winter of 1815,' wrote John Harford, 'I received a letter from Mr Wilberforce, alluding to the decease of my honoured father, of which the following is an extract:'

I did not till a short time ago hear that your long course of solicitude had terminated in the death of your beloved parent.

Even by those who feel concerning the events of this chequered life as real Christians, such an incident as the death of a parent, or even of a near and dear friend, will be felt severely; and, indeed, it ought to be so felt, for here, as in so many other instances, it is the glorious privilege of Christianity, and the evidence of its superior excellence, that it does not, like the systems of human fabrication, strive to extinguish our natural feelings, from a consciousness that it is only by lessening them that it can deal with them—if I may so express myself—and enable us to bear the misfortune as we ought; but it so softens, and sweetens, and increases the ability of our hearts and tempers as to make us love our friends better, and feel more keenly the loss for the whole of this life of our former delightful intercourse with them.

Yet it, at the same time so spiritualizes and elevates our minds as to cheer us amidst all our sorrows, and enabling us on these as on other occasions to walk by faith and live by the spirit, it raises us to the level of our ascended friends, till we hear almost their first song of exultation, and would not even wish to interrupt it, while we rather indulge the humble hope of one day joining in the chorus.

FOR MEDITATION: 'And I heard a great voice out of heaven saying, "Behold, the tabernacle of God is with men, and he will dwell with them, and they shall be his people, and God himself shall be with them, and be their God"' (Revelation 21:3).

REFERENCE: *Recollections of William Wilberforce* (1864)

'An inheritance of eternal glory'

'The Spirit itself beareth witness with our spirit, that we are the children of God: And if children, then heirs; heirs of God, and joint-heirs with Christ.' Romans 8:16–17
SUGGESTED FURTHER READING: 1 Peter 1:3–9

It is by faith in Christ only that the Christian is to be justified in the sight of God: to be delivered from the condition of a child of wrath and a slave of Satan; to be adopted into the family of God; to become an heir of God, and a joint heir with Christ, entitled to all the privileges which belong to this high relation; here, to the spirit of grace, and a partial renewal after the image of his Creator; hereafter, to the more perfect possession of the Divine likeness, and an inheritance of eternal glory.

FOR MEDITATION: Romans 6:23 tells us: 'For the wages of sin is death; but the gift of God is eternal life through Jesus Christ our Lord.' John 3:16–17 tells us yet more about the salvation that is ours through Jesus Christ—and the hope of eternity held out to us: 'For God so loved the world, that he gave his only begotten Son, that whosoever believeth in him should not perish, but have everlasting life. For God sent not his Son into the world to condemn the world; but that the world through him might be saved.'
  The seventeenth-century poet John Milton has written of

That golden key
That opes the palace of eternity.

For the Christian, that golden key is nothing more and nothing less than this: 'that whosoever believeth in him should not perish, but have everlasting life.' Those who have placed their faith in Christ will someday see what the nineteenth-century poet Matthew Arnold called

the glimmering verge of heaven, and there
The columns of the heavenly palaces.

All blessing be to our great God and our Saviour Jesus Christ, 'who gave himself for us, that he might redeem us from all iniquity' (Titus 2:14).

REFERENCE: *A Practical View of Christianity* (1797)

'A measure of the heavenly happiness'

'He maketh peace in thy borders.' Psalm 147:14
SUGGESTED FURTHER READING: Philippians 4:1–9

'Sunday,' wrote John Harford, 'turned all Mr Wilberforce's feelings into a new channel. His letters were put aside, and all thoughts of business banished. To the closest observer of his private hours he seemed throughout the day as free from all the feelings of a politician as if he had never mixed in the busy scenes of public life. In pursuance of objects like these, it may well be said, using his own expressive words:

Surely an entire day should not seem long amidst these various employments. It might well be deemed a privilege thus to spend it, in this more immediate presence of our Heavenly Father, in the exercises of humble admiration and grateful homage; of the benevolent, and domestic, and social feelings, and of all the best affections of our nature, prompted by their true motives, conversant about their proper objects, and directed to their noblest end; all sorrows mitigated, all cares suspended, all fears repressed, every angry emotion softened, every envious or revengeful or malignant passion expelled; and the bosom, thus quieted, purified, enlarged, ennobled, partaking almost of a measure of the heavenly happiness, and become for a while the seat of love, and joy, and confidence, and harmony.

FOR MEDITATION: Wilberforce closed a letter to Lady Waldegrave in February 1806 with words written in a similar strain to those above: 'May God bless and support your heart, my dear Lady W. and cheer you under every trial; giving you in proportion to your temporal trials, a more than compensating taste of that peace which passeth all understanding, and that "joy with which a stranger intermeddles not," the peace and joy in believing through the power of the Holy Ghost. O blessed words, "The rest that remaineth for the people of God."'

REFERENCE: *Recollections of William Wilberforce* (1864)

'The cordials graciously administered to us'

'Who comforteth us in all our tribulation, that we may be able to comfort them which are in any trouble, by the comfort wherewith we ourselves are comforted of God.' 1 Corinthians 1:4
SUGGESTED FURTHER READING: Psalm 94:14–22

Blessed be God, in proportion as the trial became sharper the cordials graciously administered to us by Providence became greater; and towards the last especially, the spirituality, the resignation, the patience, the humility combined with faith in the mercies of God, through the Redeemer and Intercessor, were delightful evidences of the state of mind of her who had been 'made meet to be a partaker of the inheritance of the saints in light.'

FOR MEDITATION: Cordials of grace. What a lovely image. The letters of the apostle Paul in the New Testament speak often of being refreshed, more than once of a refreshing of one's spirit. This is an image that also comes to mind in Wilberforce's words above.

In Acts 3:19 the apostle Peter also speaks of a refreshing. 'Times of refreshing,' he said, 'shall come from the presence of the Lord.' The Sabbath, or Lord's Day, is an earnest of the refreshing that God imparts to his people, as we read in Exodus 31:17—'It is a sign between me and the children of Israel for ever: for in six days the LORD made heaven and earth, and on the seventh day he rested, and was refreshed.'

So too are words that refresh, as with the verse in Proverbs 25 that tells us: 'As the cold of snow in the time of harvest, so is a faithful messenger to them that send him: for he refresheth the soul of his masters' (Proverbs 25:13). Lastly, there is a refreshing that comes from fellowship, as when Paul writes in Romans 15:32—'That I may come unto you with joy by the will of God, and may with you be refreshed.' Cordials of grace—gifts from a loving God.

REFERENCE: *Recollections of William Wilberforce* (1864)

'Religion dispenses the choicest cordials'

'How sweet are thy words unto my taste! yea, sweeter than honey to my mouth!' Psalm 119:103
SUGGESTED FURTHER READING: Proverbs 16:20–24

What striking lessons have *we* had of the precarious tenure of all sublunary possessions. Wealth, and power, and prosperity, how peculiarly transitory and uncertain! But religion dispenses the choicest cordials in the seasons of exigence, in poverty, in exile, in sickness, and in death. The essential superiority of that support which is derived from religion is less felt, at least it is less apparent, when the Christian is in full possession of riches, and splendour, and rank, and all the gifts of nature and fortune. But when all these are swept away by the rude hand of time, or the rough blasts of adversity, the true Christian stands, like the glory of the forest.

FOR MEDITATION: Wilberforce wrote often of 'heavenly cordials.' At times, he wrote of faith in God as the source of celestial comforts, for those who possessed such faith were 'not as those who are without hope, but as those sustained by the most efficacious of all cordials.'

Perhaps Wilberforce's most moving description of heavenly cordials concerned the Scriptures themselves—the words of God which imparted 'consolation in affliction [and] hope in death.' These are things, he stated, 'which the blessed word of God offers to all who will embrace it.' He rejoiced with other Christians who worked with him to distribute Bibles throughout the world. He and they, he said, had been 'permitted to be the honoured instruments of the Almighty, in diffusing such a cordial as this through a dying world. How could I but rejoice in being allowed to join with you in endeavouring to circulate these imperishable blessings?'

REFERENCE: *A Practical View of Christianity* (1797)

'What cause have we for thankfulness'

'Whom having not seen, ye love; in whom, though now ye see him not, yet believing, ye rejoice with joy unspeakable and full of glory.' 1 Peter 1:8
SUGGESTED FURTHER READING: Micah 7:8–20

O my friend, what cause have we for thankfulness who know thus where to go for pardon and for peace, as well as for grace and strength. May I be enabled to spend any remainder of life that may be spared me more profitably—more according the measure of the rich abundance of mercies and blessings for which my utmost services, as well as warmest gratitude are due.

FOR MEDITATION: Ephesians 2:4–6 tells us: 'But God, who is rich in mercy, for his great love wherewith he loved us, even when we were dead in sins, hath quickened us together with Christ, (by grace ye are saved;) and hath raised us up together, and made us sit together in heavenly places in Christ Jesus.'
Psalm 33:18 presents an Old Testament view of the mercy God has shown us: 'Behold, the eye of the LORD is upon them that fear him, upon them that hope in his mercy.'
It has been said, many times in many ways, that God watches over his people. This verse is a source of particular comfort. Those who hope in the mercy of the Lord are always under his watchful eye. The serve a gracious Lord who 'neither slumbers nor sleeps' (Psalm 121:4).

REFERENCE: *Recollections of William Wilberforce* (1864)

'The everlasting possession'

'*Now our Lord Jesus Christ himself, and God, even our Father, which hath loved us, and hath given us everlasting consolation and good hope through grace.*' 2 Thessalonians 2:16
SUGGESTED FURTHER READING: Psalm 100:1–5

Never forget that Christ Jesus is to be made unto his people wisdom and righteousness and sanctification and redemption—were we ever to bear this in view and act on it how much more wise and upright and holy should we be! It is pride and self-dependence that ruin us: whereas, were we to look with stedfast eye to the author and finisher of our faith we should learn to despise both the pleasures and the griefs of this life and long for that blessed day which, disencumbering the people of God from their fleshly impediments, shall introduce them into that state of glory of which Christ died to purchase for them the everlasting possession.

FOR MEDITATION: Romans 6:23 tells us: 'the gift of God is eternal life through Jesus Christ our Lord.' This is our everlasting possession.

And this everlasting possession has been imparted to us by him who is himself everlasting. Psalm 90:2 tells us: 'Before the mountains were brought forth, or ever thou hadst formed the earth and the world, even from everlasting to everlasting, thou art God.' Our gift, therefore, is everlasting because he who is the giver of it is everlasting.

Have we felt the weight of grief or sorrow? There is a 'balm in Gilead' (Jeremiah 46:11), and we may do as the psalmist tells us in Psalm 55:22—'Cast thy burden upon the LORD, and he shall sustain thee: he shall never suffer the righteous to be moved.' He is the everlasting God. He is always there to care for us. He is the Giver of the everlasting possession.

REFERENCE: *The Correspondence of William Wilberforce* (1840)

'The dispensations of the Almighty'

'That the trial of your faith, being much more precious than of gold that perisheth, though it be tried with fire, might be found unto praise and honour and glory at the appearing of Jesus Christ.' 1 Peter 1:7
SUGGESTED FURTHER READING: Psalm 132:1–18

We are expressly told in the Scriptures that the dispensations of the Almighty are designed with the gracious purpose of improving our moral condition, we ought, on all such occasions, to make it our deliberate care and earnest endeavour, that the intentions of Heaven, if I may so express myself, are not disappointed, but that they may produce the intended effects.

FOR MEDITATION: Once, as we read in Romans 6, we 'were the servants of sin.' Having been made free from sin through the placing of our faith in Christ, the apostle Paul writes, we 'became the servants of righteousness.' And, even as we once were 'servants to uncleanness and to iniquity unto iniquity,' so now we are to be 'servants to righteousness unto holiness' (Romans 6:17–19).

This is the pursuit of holiness or, to use Wilberforce's words above, making 'it our deliberate care and earnest endeavour' to cultivate purity of moral behaviour. But—and this is deeply important—even as we make it our deliberate care and earnest endeavour to pursue holiness, we must earnestly ask for God's help to do this. We cannot do it in and of ourselves. The wonder and the blessing is that when we do ask this of God, ours is the assurance that he will send the Holy Spirit, of whom we read in John 16:13 'he will guide you into all truth.' God will guide our steps aright. If we long for holiness, he will walk with us in the way.

REFERENCE: *The Correspondence of William Wilberforce* (1840)

'That great change'

'And that ye put on the new man, which after God is created in righteousness and true holiness.' Ephesians 4:24
SUGGESTED FURTHER READING: 2 Corinthians 5:17

People too often think they only need improvement, when in reality they want a radical reform. They require the completion of that great change of which our Saviour and his apostles speak so often and so forcibly, under the expressions of putting off the old and putting on the new man—of becoming a new creature, etc., etc.

FOR MEDITATION: The great seventeenth-century biblical commentator Matthew Henry had this to say of Ephesians 4:24: 'The principles, habits, and dispositions of the soul must be changed, before there can be a saving change of the life. The old man must be put off. The corrupt nature is called a man, because, like the human body, it consists of divers parts, mutually supporting and strengthening one another. Sinful inclinations and desires are deceitful lusts: they promise men happiness, but render them more miserable, and if not subdued and mortified betray them into destruction. These therefore must be put off as an old garment that we should be ashamed to be seen in: they must be subdued and mortified.

'The new man must be put on. It is not enough to shake off corrupt principles, but we must be actuated by gracious ones. We must embrace them, espouse them, and get them written on our hearts: it is not enough to cease to do evil, but we must learn to do well.

'By the new man is meant the new nature, the new creature, which is actuated by a new principle, even regenerating grace, enabling a man to lead a new life, that life of righteousness and holiness which Christianity requires. This new man is created, or produced out of confusion and emptiness, by God's almighty power, whose workmanship it is, truly excellent and beautiful. We are said to put on this new man when, in the use of all God's appointed means, we are endeavouring after this divine nature, this new creature. This is the more general exhortation to purity and holiness of heart and life.'

REFERENCE: *The Correspondence of William Wilberforce* (1840)

'To perfect faith'

'But whoso keepeth his word, in him verily is the love of God perfected: hereby know we that we are in him.' 1 John 2:5
SUGGESTED FURTHER READING: 2 Corinthians 7:1–12

I am too easily contented with a general impression of religion, and do not labour to perfect faith by habituating myself to act upon a principle of love. I scarcely dare resolve, after so many defeats; but I trust I shall do better, relying entirely for success upon the assistance of that Holy Spirit which we are promised.

FOR MEDITATION: Romans 8:26 tells us: 'Likewise the Spirit also helpeth our infirmities.' Our reliance for the pursuit of holiness or, 'to perfect faith' in our lives (as Wilberforce states above) must be placed solely upon the Holy Spirit.

This was something of which the American nineteenth-century evangelist D. L. Moody was intensely aware: 'I firmly believe that the moment our hearts are emptied of pride and selfishness and ambition and self-seeking and everything that is contrary to God's law, the Holy Ghost will come and fill every corner of our hearts; but if we are full of pride and conceit and ambition and self-seeking and pleasure and the world, there is no room for the Spirit of God; and I believe many a man is praying for God to fill him when he is already full of something else.'

Moody also spoke movingly of the work of the Spirit in the believer's life. 'The work of the Spirit is to impart life, to implant hope, to give liberty, to testify of Christ, to guide us into all truth, to teach us all things, to comfort the believer, and to convict the world of sin.'

REFERENCE: *The Life of William Wilberforce* (1838)

'Not trusting in myself'

'It is God that girdeth me with strength, and maketh my way perfect.'
Psalm 18:32
SUGGESTED FURTHER READING: Hebrews 6:9–20

Let me therefore make a spirited effort, not trusting in myself, but in the strength of the Lord God. Let me labour to live a life of faith, and prayer, and humility, and self-denial, and heavenly-mindedness, and sobriety, and diligence. Oh that the blessed day may come, when in the words of St Paul, I may assert of myself that my conversation is in heaven; that the life I now lead in the flesh, I live by faith in the Son of God, who loved me and gave himself for me!

FOR MEDITATION: Wilberforce is quoting Galatians 2:20 above: 'I am crucified with Christ: nevertheless I live; yet not I, but Christ liveth in me: and the life which I now live in the flesh I live by the faith of the Son of God, who loved me, and gave himself for me.'

Christ lives in the heart of the believer. This being so we may trust to his strength throughout the duration of our journey of faith here on earth. If we ask it of him, he will help us 'to live a life of faith, and prayer, and humility, and self-denial, and heavenly-mindedness, and sobriety, and diligence.' As Paul wrote to the Philippians: 'I can do all things through Christ which strengtheneth me' (4:13).

We should also bear in mind words written by the great reformer Martin Luther, who said this of the Holy Ghost, the third person of the Trinity who also dwells within us: 'The believing man hath the Holy Ghost; and where the Holy Ghost dwelleth, he will not suffer a man to be idle, but stirreth him up to all exercises of piety and godliness, and of true religion, to the love of God, to the patient suffering of afflictions, to prayer, to thanksgiving, and the exercise of charity toward all men.'

REFERENCE: *The Life of William Wilberforce* (1838)

'Continuing constant in prayer'

'Therefore, my beloved brethren, be ye stedfast, unmoveable, always abounding in the work of the Lord, forasmuch as ye know that your labour is not in vain in the Lord.' 1 Corinthians 15:58
SUGGESTED FURTHER READING: Hebrews 6:19

Let me as often as possible retire up into the mountain, and come down only on errands of usefulness and love. Oh may God enable me to fix my affections mainly on him, and to desire to glorify him, whether in life or death; looking unto Jesus, and continuing constant in prayer.

FOR MEDITATION: Colossians 4:2 tells us: 'Continue in prayer, and watch in the same with thanksgiving.' Romans 12:12 states that Christians are to be a people who are 'rejoicing in hope; patient in tribulation; continuing instant in prayer.' Both of these admonitions were written by the apostle Paul, who also wrote to the church at Thessalonica: 'pray without ceasing. In every thing give thanks: for this is the will of God in Christ Jesus concerning you' (1 Thessalonians 5:17–18).

Nothing is more central or essential to the life of the believer than prayer. Study the gospels, see how often our Lord prayed. If we would follow him who is our Lord, we must be faithful in the place of prayer, students of the practice of prayer, and people who commend others and our requests to God through prayer.

REFERENCE: *The Life of William Wilberforce* (1838)

'The important work of self-examination'

'Examine yourselves, whether ye be in the faith; prove your own selves.'
2 Corinthians 13:5
SUGGESTED FURTHER READING: Psalm 26:1–12

It pleased God to give me this morning an affecting sense of my own sinfulness, and a determination to live henceforth, by his grace, more to his glory. I was cold at first, yet moved afterwards by a sense of heavenly things, and determined to go to the important work of self-examination, and to set about a thorough change. Henceforth I purpose, by God's grace, to employ my faculties and powers more to his glory; to live a godly, diligent, useful, self-denying life. I know my own weakness, and I trust to God alone for strength.

FOR MEDITATION: Two among Britain's greatest writers of verse reflected on the practice of self-examination and its place before God. Isaac Watts wrote:

Let not soft slumber close your eyes,
Before you've collected thrice
The train of action through the day!
Where have my feet chose out their way?
What have I learnt, where'er I've been,
From all I've heard, from all I've seen?
What have I more that's worth the knowing?
What have I done that's worth the doing?
What have I sought that I should shun?
What duty have I left undone,
Or into what new follies run?
These self-inquiries are the road
That lead to virtue and to God.

While Edward Young penned these three lines:

'Tis greatly wise to talk with our past hours;
And ask them what report they bore to heaven:
And how they might have borne more welcome news.

REFERENCE: *The Life of William Wilberforce* (1838)

'Firmly relying upon him'

'O taste and see that the LORD *is good: blessed is the man that trusteth in him.' Psalm 34:8*
SUGGESTED FURTHER READING: Jeremiah 17:5–14

Let me strive more against my corruptions, and particularly not straiten prayer. I find myself confiding in my resolutions; let me universally distrust myself, but let me throw myself at the feet of Christ as an undone creature, distrusting yea despairing of myself, but firmly relying upon him. 'Him that cometh unto me I will no wise cast out.' 'They that wait on the Lord shall renew their strength.'

FOR MEDITATION: In Second Corinthians 12:9 the apostle Paul wrote words that have become proverbial: 'And he said unto me, "My grace is sufficient for thee: for *my strength is made perfect in weakness.* Most gladly therefore will I rather glory in my infirmities, that the power of Christ may rest upon me."'

These words, and the utter reliance upon God that they convey, ought to be ever present to our minds. We are very weakness—sinful and full of faults. Before coming to faith in Christ, we needed redemption and forgiveness. Both were given us in Christ.

So too do we need God's grace to live for him as Christians. None of us can do this on our own, we can only do so through the power God supplies. Paul so often had the gift of an arresting phrase. It is no different here in the verse above. We must learn, as he did, what it is to glory in our infirmities, or weaknesses, so that the power of Christ may rest upon us. May we so learn Christ (Ephesians 4:20–24).

REFERENCE: *The Life of William Wilberforce* (1838)

'We must indeed live the life'

'For whether we live, we live unto the Lord; and whether we die, we die unto the Lord: whether we live therefore, or die, we are the Lord's.'
Romans 14:8
SUGGESTED FURTHER READING: Galatians 5:16–26

When I seem to you at any time to be intoxicated as it were by the hurry, the business, or the dissipation of life, spare not the best offices of friendship; recall me to that sobriety and seriousness of mind, which become those who know not when they may be called away: place before me the solemn triumphs of which you have been a spectator, and animate me to press forward in emulation of so glorious an example. To die the death, we must indeed live the life, of Christians. We must fix our affections on things above, not on things on the earth. We must endeavour habitually to preserve that frame of mind, and that course of conduct, with which we may be justly said to be waiting for the appearance of the Lord Jesus Christ. I know not any description of a Christian which impresses itself so forcibly as this on my mind.

FOR MEDITATION: In Matthew 25, we read the following: 'After a long time the lord of those servants cometh, and reckoneth with them. And so he that had received five talents came and brought other five talents, saying, "Lord, thou deliveredst unto me five talents: behold, I have gained beside them five talents more." His lord said unto him, "Well done, thou good and faithful servant"' (Matthew 25:19–21).

Samuel Johnson, whose writings Wilberforce much admired, wrote this couplet concerning the ways in which we ought to use the talents given us:

And sure th' Eternal Master found
His single talent well employ'd.

How we wait for the coming of our Lord, the anticipation—as it were—with which we serve him, says everything about the nature of our commitment to him. May God grant us the grace to be found waiting, and about our Master's business.

REFERENCE: *The Life of William Wilberforce* (1838)

'The mercies of God in Christ'

'Blessed be God, even the Father of our Lord Jesus Christ, the Father of mercies, and the God of all comfort.' 2 Corinthians 1:3
SUGGESTED FURTHER READING: Psalm 25:1–14

I throw myself on the mercies of God in Christ; I resolve to venture all on this foundation; and relying on that help which is promised to them that ask it, I determine to struggle with all my corruptions, and to employ what is left to me of life, and talents, and influence, in the way which shall appear to me most pleasing to my heavenly Father. Oh with what humiliation have I to look back on the years wherein all these were so grossly wasted; and what reason have I to rejoice that I was not then snatched away!

FOR MEDITATION: In Ephesians 3:8, the apostle Paul wrote this: 'Unto me, who am less than the least of all saints, is this grace given, that I should preach among the Gentiles the unsearchable riches of Christ.' Paul understood profoundly what he had been, and he knew beyond knowing what God had done in his life.

Wilberforce wrote in similar terms: I have lately been led to think of that part of my life wherein I lived without God in the world, wasting and even abusing all the faculties he had given me for his glory. Surely when I think of the way in which I went on for many years, from about sixteen to 1785–6, I can only fall down with astonishment as well as humiliation before the throne of grace, and adore with wonder, no less than remorse and gratitude, that infinite mercy of God which did not cast me off, but on the contrary guiding me by a way which I knew not, led me to those from whom I was to receive the knowledge of salvation (not more manifestly his work was St Paul's instruction by Ananias), softened my hard heart, and has enabled me to continue until this day. Praise the Lord, O my soul!

REFERENCE: *The Life of William Wilberforce* (1838)

'And may I fear alway'

'But shewing all good fidelity; that they may adorn the doctrine of God our Saviour in all things.' Titus 2:10
SUGGESTED FURTHER READING: 2 Thessalonians 3:1–5

'The beginning of a long recess draws near,' Wilberforce wrote in 1792, 'and I will endeavour to consecrate it to God by a day of solemn prayer and fasting. I will labour to lay aside every weight, and the sin which doth so easily beset me, and to adorn the doctrine of God my Saviour; to follow peace with all men, and above all to love the Lord my God with all my heart. O strengthen me, Lord, by thy grace, for I am very weakness. Cleanse me, for I am all corruption. May I be clothed with humility, and may I fear alway.'

FOR MEDITATION: In 2 Corinthians 12:9 the apostle Paul wrote of the utter reliance he reposed in God: 'And he said unto me, My grace is sufficient for thee: for my strength is made perfect in weakness. Most gladly therefore will I rather glory in my infirmities, that the power of Christ may rest upon me.'

Wilberforce, for his part, had come to understand early on in his Christian walk that 'it is the grace of God, however, only that can teach.' One is struck in reading Wilberforce's words above how rich they are in biblical allusions. He meditated continually upon the Scriptures, often committing to memory long portions, including most of the letters of Paul in fact, and the entire 119th Psalm. He invested much time in seeking to have 'the mind of Christ' (1 Corinthians 2:16)—cultivating a deep and searching knowledge of the Scriptures. But he also surrounded such studies and exercises with much prayer, asking that God would, by his grace, make of him a man of God.

REFERENCE: *The Life of William Wilberforce* (1838)

'To seek in all things to please him'

'Furthermore then we beseech you, brethren, and exhort you by the Lord Jesus, that as ye have received of us how ye ought to walk and to please God, so ye would abound more and more.' 1 Thessalonians 4:1
SUGGESTED FURTHER READING: 2 Timothy 2:15–26

I mean to set aside a day this week for fasting and religious exercises; for seeking God and praying for political direction, for a blessing on my parliamentary labours, on my country, and on those who have specially desired my prayers. May God for Christ's sake enable me to seek in all things to please him, and submit to his will—to repress vanity, cultivate humility, constant self-examination—think of death—of saints in past times.

FOR MEDITATION: The seventeenth-century poet George Herbert understood the value of spiritual exercises like fasting and self-examination. Of the last, he wrote:

Summe up at night what thou hast done by day;
And in the morning what thou hast to do.
Dresse and undresse thy soul; mark the decay
And growth of it; if, with thy watch, that too
Be down then winde up both; since we shall be
Most surely judg'd, make thy accounts agree.

In 2 Corinthians 6:4–6 the apostle Paul wrote of the spiritual exercises and acts of devotion that characterized his ministry, commending these things to the Corinthians: 'But in all things approving ourselves as the ministers of God, in much patience, in afflictions, in necessities, in distresses, in stripes, in imprisonments, in tumults, in labours, in watchings, in fastings; by pureness, by knowledge, by longsuffering, by kindness, by the Holy Ghost, by love unfeigned.' May we be so devoted to our Lord and Saviour.

REFERENCE: *The Life of William Wilberforce* (1838)

'What can be too much for him'

'With my whole heart have I sought thee: O let me not wander from thy commandments.' Psalm 119:10
SUGGESTED FURTHER READING: Psalm 119:25–40

This morning I have been much affected—I fasted, and received the sacrament. Oh may I be renewed in the spirit of my mind. May this little recess from the hurry of life enable me seriously to look into my heart, plan of life, and general conduct, and to turn unto the Lord with my whole soul; what can be too much for him, who bought us so dearly—I go to prayer.

FOR MEDITATION: The seventeenth-century Puritan divine John Flavel authored many writings which reveal a deep understanding of many elements of the Christian life. This was certainly true of consecration, of which Flavel wrote: 'See that you receive Christ with all your heart. As there is nothing in Christ that may be refused, so there is nothing in you from which he must be excluded.'

The nineteenth-century hymn writer Frances Havergal wrote often of consecration. Four of the best lines she ever wrote on the subject were these:

Teach us, Master, how to give
All we have and are to thee;
Grant us, Saviour, while we live,
Wholly, only thine to be.

Consecration—to give ourselves wholly to God and to be wholly dependent upon God.

May we always strive for this.

REFERENCE: *The Life of William Wilberforce* (1838)

'The fulness which is in Jesus'

'And of his fulness have all we received, and grace for grace.' John 1:16
SUGGESTED FURTHER READING: Ephesians 3:14–21

Easter Sunday 1795. What a blessing it is to be permitted to retire from the bustle of the world, and to be furnished with so many helps for realizing unseen things! I seem to myself to day to be in some degree under the power of real Christianity; conscious, deeply conscious of corruption and unprofitableness; yet to such a one, repenting and confessing his sins, and looking to the cross of Christ, pardon and reconciliation are held forth, and the promise of the Holy Spirit, to renew the mind, and enable him to conquer his spiritual enemies, and get the better of his corruption. Be not then cast down, O my soul, but ask for grace from the fulness which is in Jesus.

FOR MEDITATION: The seventeenth-century poet John Dryden said this of grace: 'Let grace and goodness be the principal loadstone of thy affections.' Two centuries later Charles Spurgeon wrote: 'The grace of the spirit comes only from heaven, and lights up the whole bodily presence.'

The fulness which is in Jesus. It is there that strengthening grace is to be found.

Grace and truth shall mark the way
Where the Lord his own will lead,
If his Word they still obey
And his testimonies heed.

The Psalter, 1912

REFERENCE: *The Life of William Wilberforce* (1838)

'Wait, watch and pray'

'Watch ye, stand fast in the faith, quit you like men, be strong.'
1 Corinthians 16:13
SUGGESTED FURTHER READING: Psalm 119:145–152

Jesus came not to call the righteous, but sinners. He was the friend of sinners. Look therefore unto him, and plead his promises, and firmly resolve through the strength derived from him, to struggle with thy sins; with all of them, allowing none of them in any degree; and to endeavour to devote all thy faculties to his glory. My frame of mind at this time seems to me compounded of humiliation and hope; a kind of sober determination to throw myself upon the promises of the gospel, as my only confidence, and a composure of mind, resulting from a reliance on the mercy and truth of God. Still I perceive vanity and other evils working; but Christ is made unto us sanctification, and our heavenly Father will give his Holy Spirit to them that ask him. Wait therefore on the Lord. Wait, watch and pray, and wait.

FOR MEDITATION: The American hymn writer Fanny Crosby knew what it was to wait upon the Lord. In 1898, she rendered her reflections into verse:

Wait on the Lord, wait patiently,
And thou shalt in him be blest;
After the storm, a holy calm,
And after thy labour rest.
Wait on the Lord, for whom hast thou
On earth or in heaven but he?
Over thy soul a watch he keeps,
Wherever thy path may be.

REFERENCE: *The Life of William Wilberforce* (1838)

'He is truth as well as love'

'All the paths of the LORD *are mercy and truth unto such as keep his covenant and his testimonies.' Psalm 25:10*
SUGGESTED FURTHER READING: 3 John 1–14

But what a solid satisfaction is it to reflect that our ascended Lord views us with a pitying and sympathetic eye; that he knows what it is to have a feeling of our infirmities, that he promises, and he is truth as well as love, that they who wait on him shall renew their strength!

FOR MEDITATION: On 8 October 1786, Wilberforce wrote: 'Recollect that Christ, who was also tempted, sympathizes with thy weakness, and that he stands ready to support thee, if thou wilt sincerely call on him for help.'

What a moving reminder of Christ's love and mercy. Psalm 34:18 reminds us beautifully of the nearness of God in our times of trouble: 'The Lord is nigh unto them that are of a broken heart; and saveth such as be of a contrite spirit.'

Many circumstances in life serve only to show us the extent of our weakness and human frailty. And yet, in the midst of sobering thoughts, we have many sources of solace in the Scriptures.

In Psalm 39, the psalmist writes: 'LORD, make me to know mine end, and the measure of my days, what it is; that I may know how frail I am.' Then follows a dialogue about the vanities of life and sobering limitations of humanity. The psalmist then concludes with a question that expresses the heart of the matter. 'And now, Lord, what wait I for? my hope is in thee.'

REFERENCE: *The Life of William Wilberforce* (1838)

'A day of secret prayer'

'Yet the LORD *will command his lovingkindness in the daytime, and in the night his song shall be with me, and my prayer unto the God of my life.' Psalm 42:8*
SUGGESTED FURTHER READING: Psalm 66:13–20

My chief reasons for a day of secret prayer are, 1st, That the state of public affairs is very critical, and calls for earnest deprecation of the Divine displeasure. 2ndly, My station in life is a very difficult one, wherein I am at a loss to know how to act. Direction therefore should be specially sought from time to time. Thirdly, I have been graciously supported in difficult situations of a public nature.

FOR MEDITATION: Words by an unknown author inscribed on the walls of Gloucester Cathedral say this about prayer:

Doubt not but God who sits on high,
Thy secret prayers can hear

Psalm 44:21 says this of God: 'he knoweth the secrets of the heart.' God also dwells in secret places, the Scriptures tell us. When we seek him there, we have this assurance: 'He that dwelleth in the secret place of the Most High shall abide under the shadow of the Almighty' (Psalm 91:1). Those who are righteous in heart also have this good and blessed word: 'his secret is with the righteous' (Proverbs 3:32).

REFERENCE: *The Life of William Wilberforce* (1838)

'To work whilst it is day'

'The righteous shall be glad in the LORD, *and shall trust in him; and all the upright in heart shall glory.'* Psalm 64:10
SUGGESTED FURTHER READING: Psalm 79:5–13

How little has my heart joined in the prayers of the day! How little am I impressed as I ought to be with a sense of heavenly things! and yet I hope I am labouring after them, and striving to raise my mind. I go to prayer, to bless God for his mercies. I will pray to him for my country, and for wisdom for myself, to teach me how to act. Oh may the resolution to live for his glory be uppermost in my soul, and may I learn a holy resignation to his will; endeavouring to work whilst it is day.

FOR MEDITATION: Our Lord states in John 9:4 'I must work the works of him that sent me, while it is day: the night cometh, when no man can work'. We must follow in the steps of our Lord, and so we too must work while it is day. As citizens of our respective countries, we must also show those around us that our ultimate citizenship is in heaven. We must serve the Lord and, in so doing, serve others.

As Wilberforce wrote in *A Practical View of Christianity* (1797): 'if by patriotism be understood that quality which, without shutting up our philanthropy in the narrow bounds of a single kingdom, yet attaches us in particular to the country to which we belong; of this true patriotism, Christianity is the most copious source, and the surest preservative.' To this he added: 'that circumstance wherein the principle of patriotism chiefly consists, whereby the duty of patriotism is best practised, and the happiest effect to the general weal produced, is, that it should be the desire and aim of every individual to fill well his own proper circle, as a part and member of the whole, with a view to the production of general happiness.'

REFERENCE: *The Life of William Wilberforce* (1838)

'To walk worthy'

'The meek will he guide in judgment: and the meek will he teach his way.' Psalm 25:9
SUGGESTED FURTHER READING: Psalm 78:50–55

O Lord, I would resolutely endeavour to walk worthy of my high and holy calling. O enlighten my ignorance, purify my corruptions, warm my coldness, and fix my volatility.

FOR MEDITATION: The seventeenth-century biblical commentator Matthew Henry had this to say of the calling that is ours in Christ: 'God has called us with a holy calling, called us to holiness. Christianity is a calling, a holy calling; it is the calling wherewith we are called, the calling to which we are called, to labour in it. Wherever the call of the gospel is an effectual call, it is found to be a holy call, making those holy who are effectually called. The origin of it is the free grace and eternal purpose of God in Christ Jesus. This grace is said to be given us before the world began, that is, in the purpose and designs of God from all eternity.'

Isaiah 57:15 tells us this about the eternal God and his purposes towards us: 'For thus saith the high and lofty One that inhabiteth eternity, whose name is Holy; I dwell in the high and holy place, with him also that is of a contrite and humble spirit, to revive the spirit of the humble, and to revive the heart of the contrite ones.'

Paul wrote to the Ephesians concerning the gift of the gospel and the purposes of God: 'Unto me, who am less than the least of all saints, is this grace given, that I should preach among the Gentiles the unsearchable riches of Christ; and to make all men see what is the fellowship of the mystery, which from the beginning of the world hath been hid in God, who created all things by Jesus Christ: according to the eternal purpose which he purposed in Christ Jesus our Lord' (Ephesians 3:8–9,11).

REFERENCE: *The Life of William Wilberforce* (1838)

'We know not what times are coming on'

'My times are in thy hand.' Psalm 31:15
SUGGESTED FURTHER READING: Psalm 9:1–11

We know not what times are coming on, but if God be for us, who can be against us? Oh may I therefore lay up treasure in heaven, and wait upon the Lord. Now that he seems about to try his people, what cause have I to pray, and gird up the loins of my mind! May I grow in grace, and become more 'meet for the inheritance of the saints in light.'

FOR MEDITATION: God is the Author of history; and he knows the ends of all things. He inhabits eternity. He is all-wise and all-powerful. He is everywhere. And the God of whom all this is true is the God of whom we read in John's gospel: 'God so loved the world that he gave his only begotten Son, that whosoever believeth in him should not perish, but have everlasting life.'

This is a matchless source of comfort and hope—a strong tower to which we may repair whenever we need to. The hope born of all these things was such that the apostle Paul wrote: 'I know whom I have believed, and am persuaded that he is able to keep that which I have committed unto him against that day' (2 Timothy 1:12).

No, we do not know what times are coming on, but we do know the God who never changes and of whom all the things said above are true. In this we may safely trust. This is our stay.

REFERENCE: *The Life of William Wilberforce* (1838)

'Give me a single heart and a single eye'

'The light of the body is the eye: therefore when thine eye is single, thy whole body also is full of light.' Luke 11:34
SUGGESTED FURTHER READING: Matthew 6:19–22

I know that all external means are nothing without the quickening Spirit: but the Scripture enjoins constant prayer, and the writings and example of all good men suggest and enforce the necessity of a considerable proportion of meditation and other religious exercises, for maintaining the spiritual life vigorous and flourishing. Let me therefore make the effort in humble reliance on Divine grace. God, if he will, can turn the hearts of men, and give me favourable opportunities, and enable me to use them, and more than compensate for all the hours taken from study, business, or civility, and devoted to him. O God, give me a single heart and a single eye, fixed on thy favours, and resolutely determined to live to thy glory, careless whether I succeed or not in worldly concerns, leaving all my human interests and objects to thee, and beseeching thee to enable me to set my affections on things above; and walking by faith, to wait on Christ, and live on him day by day here.

FOR MEDITATION: Psalm 119:10 presents us with one of the most godly passages of the Old Testament: 'With my whole heart have I sought thee: O let me not wander from thy commandments.' The psalmist here exhibits total devotion to the Lord.

In the New Testament, the apostle Paul writes in the same spirit in 1 Corinthians 10:31 when he declares: 'whatsoever ye do, do all to the glory of God.'

Wilberforce, student of the Scriptures that he was, understood this and sought to live his life accordingly. And so we find him writing in *A Practical View of Christianity* that 'the prevalence of real religion' in a person's life—that is, a true commitment to Christ—fosters within them a solicitude 'to act from a pure principle and leave the event to God'.

This is telling. We cannot know how things we strive for will turn out. But if our motives and desires flow from a heart set upon seeking God, we can leave the outcomes of events to him, and trust that all will be well.

REFERENCE: *The Life of William Wilberforce* (1838)

Looking with humble hope

'Be of good courage, and he shall strengthen your heart, all ye that hope in the LORD.*' Psalm 31:24*
SUGGESTED FURTHER READING: Psalm 34:1–22

O my soul, praise the Lord, and forget not all his mercies. God is love, and his promises are sure. What though I have been sadly wanting to myself, yet we are assured that those that come unto him he will in no wise cast out. I therefore look to him with humble hope, I disclaim every other plea than that of the publican, offered up through the Redeemer; but I would animate my hopes, trusting in him that he will perfect, stablish, strengthen, settle me.

FOR MEDITATION: There is, within the pages of *A Practical View of Christianity*, a passage that reads like a doxology. Rich in biblical allusions, it strikes a perfect note of accord with what Wilberforce has written above: 'God so loved the world, as of his tender mercy to give his only Son Jesus Christ for our redemption. Our blessed Lord willingly left the glory of the Father, and was made man. He was despised and rejected of men; a man of sorrows, and acquainted with grief. He was wounded for our transgressions; and bruised for our iniquities. The Lord laid on him the iniquity of us all. At length he humbled himself—even to the death of the Cross, for us miserable sinners; to the end that all who with hearty repentance and true faith, should come to him, might not perish, but have everlasting life. He is now at the right hand of God, making intercession for his people. Being reconciled to God by the death of his Son, we may come boldly unto the throne of grace, to obtain mercy and find grace to help in time of need. Our heavenly Father will surely give his Holy Spirit to them that ask him. By this divine influence we are to be renewed in knowledge after the image of him who created us, and to be filled with the fruits of righteousness, to the praise of the glory of his grace.'

REFERENCE: *The Life of William Wilberforce* (1838)

'Constant prayer and watchfulness'

'Be ye therefore sober, and watch unto prayer.' 1 Peter 4:7
SUGGESTED FURTHER READING: Matthew 26:26–36

I fear that I have not studied the Scriptures enough. Surely in the summer recess I ought to read Scripture an hour or two every day, besides prayer, devotional reading, and meditation. God will prosper me better if I wait on him. The experience of all good men shows, that without constant prayer and watchfulness the life of God in the soul stagnates. Philip Doddridge's morning and evening devotions were serious matters. Colonel Gardiner always spent hours in prayer in the morning before he came forth. James Bonnell practised private devotions largely morning and evening, and repeated Psalms to raise his mind to heavenly things. I would look up to God to make the means effectual, but let me use them with humble thankfulness, and bless God for the almost unequalled advantages and privileges I enjoy.

FOR MEDITATION: In the pages of *A Practical View of Christianity* Wilberforce paid tribute to the Moravian Christians of his day in a way that says much about his understanding of constancy in service to God. The Moravians, he wrote, 'have perhaps excelled all mankind in solid and unequivocal proofs of the love of Christ, and of the most ardent, and active, and patient zeal in his service. It is a zeal tempered with prudence, softened with meekness, soberly aiming at great ends ... supported by a courage which no danger can intimidate, and a quiet constancy which no hardships can exhaust.'

REFERENCE: *The Life of William Wilberforce* (1838)

'That infinite mercy of God'

'For thou, LORD, art good, and ready to forgive; and plenteous in mercy unto all them that call upon thee.' Psalm 86:5
SUGGESTED FURTHER READING: Psalm 108:4

I have lately been led to think of that part of my life wherein I lived without God in the world, wasting and even abusing all the faculties he had given me for his glory. Surely when I think of the way in which I went on for many years, from about sixteen to 1785–6, I can only fall down with astonishment as well as humiliation before the throne of grace, and adore with wonder, no less than remorse and gratitude, that infinite mercy of God which did not cast me off, but on the contrary guiding me by a way which I knew not, led me to those from whom I was to receive the knowledge of salvation (not more manifestly his work was St Paul's instruction by Ananias), softened my hard heart, and has enabled me to continue until this day. Praise the Lord, O my soul!

FOR MEDITATION: Some Christians know the blessing of being able to say that they came to faith so early in life as to almost not be able to remember a time when they didn't love God as their Lord and Saviour. Others, many others, can look back on many years when God was not the Lord of their lives—many years before they came to faith.

For those who are of this last description, can we say that we keep in close remembrance who we were and what our actions were before our redemption? Does that memory prompt within us an abiding sense of the grace and mercy God bestowed upon us? May we never lose sight of the days when God led us to the throne of grace. Without him, where would we be?

REFERENCE: *The Life of William Wilberforce* (1838)

'The frame of a real Christian'

'The LORD *is my strength and my shield; my heart trusted in him, and I am helped: therefore my heart greatly rejoiceth; and with my song will I praise him.' Psalm 28:7*
SUGGESTED FURTHER READING: Psalm 46:1–11

How many and great corruptions does the House of Commons discover to me in myself! What love of worldly estimation, vanity, earthly-mindedness! How different should be the frame of a real Christian, who, poor in spirit, and feeling himself a stranger and a pilgrim on earth, is looking for the coming of his Lord and Saviour. I know that this world is passing away, and that the favour of God, and a share in the blessings of the Redeemer's purchase, are alone worthy of the pursuit of a rational being: but alas! alas! I scarcely dare say I love God and his ways. Let me not acquiesce then in my sinful state. Thanks be to God, who giveth us the victory through our Lord Jesus Christ. Yes, we may, I may, become holy. Press forward then, O my soul. Strive more vigorously. God and Christ will not refuse their help. And may the emotions I have been now experiencing, be the gracious motions of the divine Spirit, quickening my dead heart.

FOR MEDITATION: In Colossians 1:9–10 the apostle Paul writes: 'we do not cease to pray for you, and to desire that ye might be filled with the knowledge of his will in all wisdom and spiritual understanding; that ye might walk worthy of the Lord unto all pleasing, being fruitful in every good work, and increasing in the knowledge of God.'

Paul's prayer expresses the belief that indeed the Colossians will come to that place in their lives where they are 'being fruitful in every good work, and increasing in the knowledge of God.' How good it is to have this passage of Scripture to call to our remembrance as we pray that God will help us to live for him.

REFERENCE: *The Life of William Wilberforce* (1838)

'The sense of Divine things'

'My hands also will I lift up unto thy commandments, which I have loved; and I will meditate in thy statutes.' Psalm 119:48
SUGGESTED FURTHER READING: Psalm 77:1–12

Without watchfulness, humiliation, and prayer, the sense of Divine things must languish, as much as the grass withers for want of refreshing rains and dews. The word of God and the lives of good men give us reason to believe, that without these there can be no lively exercise of Christian graces. Trifle not then, O my soul, with thy immortal interests. Heaven is not to be won without labour. Oh then press forward: whatever else is neglected, let this one thing needful be attended to; then will God bless.

FOR MEDITATION: 'As the grass withers for want of refreshing rains and dews.' How like the Psalms or Proverbs this sounds. Indeed, we read in Proverbs 3:19–24:

The LORD by wisdom hath founded the earth; by understanding hath he established the heavens. By his knowledge the depths are broken up, and the clouds drop down the dew. My son, let not them depart from thine eyes: keep sound wisdom and discretion: so shall they be life unto thy soul, and grace to thy neck. Then shalt thou walk in thy way safely, and thy foot shall not stumble. When thou liest down, thou shalt not be afraid: yea, thou shalt lie down, and thy sleep shall be sweet.

REFERENCE: *The Life of William Wilberforce* (1838)

'Warmed with heavenly fire'

'He spread a cloud for a covering; and fire to give light in the night.'
Psalm 105:39
SUGGESTED FURTHER READING: Luke 5:16

I will try to retire at nine or half-past, and every evening give half an hour, or an hour, to secret exercises, endeavouring to raise my mind more, and that it may be more warmed with heavenly fire. Help me, O Lord—without thee I can do nothing. Let me strive to maintain a uniform frame of gratitude, veneration, love, and humility, not unelevated with holy confidence, and trembling hope in the mercies of that God, whose ways are not as our ways, nor his thoughts as our thoughts. Strive, O my soul, to maintain and keep alive impressions, first, of the constant presence of a holy, omniscient, omnipotent, but infinitely merciful and gracious God, of Christ our Almighty Shepherd and of the Holy Spirit.

FOR MEDITATION: 'Without thee I can do nothing.' Such a truth, rooted in Scripture, is sobering. But then we are given to know—as Wilberforce knew based upon his reading of Scripture—that we serve a God who is 'holy, omniscient, omnipotent, but infinitely merciful and gracious.' What is more, Christ is our Almighty Shepherd, and the Holy Spirit is present in our lives to guide us into all truth. These are things which ought to warm our hearts with heavenly fire. May it ever be so.

REFERENCE: *The Life of William Wilberforce* (1838)

'A precious interval'

'Return unto thy rest, O my soul; for the LORD *hath dealt bountifully with thee.' Psalm 116:7*
SUGGESTED FURTHER READING: Hebrews 4:1–16

O blessed day which allows us a precious interval wherein to pause, to come out from the thickets of worldly concerns, and to give ourselves up to heavenly and spiritual objects. And oh what language can do justice to the emotions of gratitude which ought to fill my heart, and when I consider how few of my fellows know and feel its value and proper uses? Oh the infinite goodness and mercy of my God and Saviour!

FOR MEDITATION: The blessings of the Sabbath or Lord's Day were a recurring theme in Wilberforce's life. His was a life of great industry and demands, both in terms of his parliamentary duties and the private philanthropic pursuits he undertook. It was as he wrote in his book *A Practical View of Christianity*: 'we must be kept wakeful and active.'

Now while all this was true, no one was more grateful than he for the weekly gift of a day of rest. A day wherein he and his family could pause from the concerns of a busy life, attend church services, spend time in prayer, and take what he called contemplative or musing walks. He understood this to be the gift of God, and he cherished the gift. May we and our families also do the same.

REFERENCE: *The Life of William Wilberforce* (1838)

'A mystery of iniquity'

'The heart is deceitful above all things, and desperately wicked: who can know it?' Jeremiah 17:9
SUGGESTED FURTHER READING: Jeremiah 17:7–10

What a mystery of iniquity is the human heart! How forcibly do thoughts of worldly pursuits intrude into the mind during the devotional exercises, and how obstinately do they maintain their place, and when excluded, how incessantly do they renew their attacks!—which yet the moment our devotional exercises are over, fly away of themselves.

FOR MEDITATION: The sixteenth-century poet and devotional writer Francis Quarles said this of the heart: 'The heart is a small thing, but desireth great matters. It is not sufficient for a kite's dinner, yet the whole world is not sufficient for it.'

There are things about the human heart that are inscrutable, and yet God knows our hearts intimately. He fashioned them, and knows everything about us. The Book of Proverbs tells us many things about our hearts, including this verse: 'Hear thou, my son, and be wise, and guide thine heart in the way' (Proverbs 23:19).

And what is the good way to which we should direct our hearts? Four verses later, the writer tells us: 'Buy the truth, and sell it not; also wisdom, and instruction, and understanding' (Proverbs 23:23). These things we may ask of the Lord. These things he delights to give us.

REFERENCE: *The Life of William Wilberforce* (1838)

'How constantly I need the grace of God'

'Ye have not chosen me, but I have chosen you, and ordained you, that ye should go and bring forth fruit, and that your fruit should remain: that whatsoever ye shall ask of the Father in my name, he may give it you.' John 15:16

SUGGESTED FURTHER READING: Ephesians 1:1–6

How few are there in Parliament on whom the mercy of God has been so bounteously vouchsafed! Praise the Lord, O my soul, and forget not all his benefits. Above all, let me adore God's unspeakable kindness and long-suffering, in not being prevented from calling me to his fold, by the foreknowledge which he had of my hardness of heart and ingratitude. ... Let the impression of these incidents ever remain with me, to humble me, to keep me mindful how weak I am in myself, how constantly I need the grace of God. Let me meditate awhile on the majesty and holiness of God. I will read in a meditating way Witherspoon's[5] excellent sermon *A View of the Glory of God humbling to the Soul*. O Lord, let thy Spirit accompany me, let it make me see and feel towards sin as thou dost, and to be delivered from every remainder of my corruptions, and to be holy as thou art holy. Let me desire this day particularly to be full of love, meekness, and self-denial.

FOR MEDITATION: In the pages of *A Practical View of Christianity* Wilberforce stated his belief, based upon his reading of Scripture, that 'the offers to penitent sinners of pardon, and grace, and strength, are universal and unlimited.' Pardon, grace and strength. Can we find three words anywhere in the lexicon of the Christian that are a greater source of solace? We are forgiven. We have found favour with our Sovereign Lord. He will give us the strength each day and according to our need. We are blessed beyond measure.

REFERENCE: *The Life of William Wilberforce* (1838)

'A sort of birthday review'

'This I recall to my mind, therefore have I hope.' Lamentations 3:21
SUGGESTED FURTHER READING: Romans 8:1–11

Let me go now to confession and humiliation in direct prayer. Let me deplore my past sins—many years in which I lived without God in the world—then my sins since my having become acquainted with him in 1785–6. My actual state—my not having daily improved my talents—my chief besetting sins. This day therefore is to be a sort of birthday review. I am come here into the arbour by the river side.

How greatly are my sins aggravated by the extreme goodness to me of my God and Saviour! I am encumbered with blessings, my cup is so full of them as to overflow. During my life all has gone well with me, so far as God has ordered matters, and all the evil has been the result of my own follies. All that I enjoy has been from God—all I suffer from myself. Hitherto I have suffered nothing from the storms which have raged around me. To these blessings have been added most affectionate friends, and near relatives. My being honoured with the Abolition cause is a great blessing

FOR MEDITATION: These selections from a private devotional diary were written on 24 August 1803 (when Wilberforce turned forty-four). These thoughts reveal the great importance he placed on the Scriptural admonition to 'keep thy heart with all diligence' (Proverbs 4:23). As he also knew, the remainder of this verse underscores the value of this practice: 'for out of it are the issues of life.' Both the Old and New Testaments commend the practice of self-examination. We are, on the one hand, to ask for God's help in doing so, as Psalm 26:2 states: 'Examine me, O LORD, and prove me; try my reins and my heart.' On the other, 2 Corinthians 13:5 urges believers to 'Examine yourselves, whether ye be in the faith; prove your own selves.'

REFERENCE: *The Life of William Wilberforce* (1838)

'A most confined notion of benevolence'

*'And that, knowing the time, that now it is high time to awake out of sleep:
for now is our salvation nearer than when we believed.'* Romans 13:11
SUGGESTED FURTHER READING: 2 Corinthians 6:1–10

It is the true duty of every man to promote the happiness of his fellow-
creatures to the utmost of his power; and he who thinks he sees many
around him, whom he esteems and loves, labouring under a fatal error,
must have a cold heart, or a most confined notion of benevolence, if he
withhold his endeavours to set them right. Often has it filled me with
deep concern, to observe in orthodox Christians, scarcely any distinct
knowledge of the real nature and principles of the religion which they
profess. The subject is of infinite importance; let it not be driven out of
our minds by the bustle or dissipations of life. This present scene, and all
its cares and all its gaieties, will soon be rolled away, and 'we must stand
before the judgment-seat of Christ.'

FOR MEDITATION: James 4:17 tells us: 'Therefore to him that knoweth to
do good, and doeth it not, to him it is sin.' We are, or ought to be,
faithful stewards of the gifts, talents, opportunities and experiences God
has given us. Of these things, we are to give—as those to whom much has
been given (Luke 12:48). But how can we do this aright? And where can
we find the strength, wisdom and encouragement to do good to others?
The answer lies in a total reliance upon God, and in the integrity of a
right relationship with him. 'Draw nigh to God, and he will draw nigh to
you,' we read in James 4:8. When we draw near to God, he will help us to
come alongside others and make the best use of our opportunities to do
good.

REFERENCE: *A Practical View of Christianity* (1797)

'Barren generalities'

'Study to shew thyself approved unto God, a workman that needeth not to be ashamed, rightly dividing the word of truth.' 2 Timothy 2:15
SUGGESTED FURTHER READING: 1 Peter 3:15

Before proceeding to the consideration of any particular defects in the religious system of the bulk of professed Christians, it may be proper to point out the very inadequate conception which they entertain of the importance of Christianity in general, of its peculiar nature, and superior excellence. If we listen to their conversation, virtue is praised, and vice is censured; piety is, perhaps, applauded, and profaneness condemned. So far all is well: but let any one, who would not be deceived by these 'barren generalities,'[6] examine a little more closely, and he will find, that not to Christianity in particular, but at best to religion in general, perhaps to mere Morality, their homage is intended to be paid. With Christianity, as distinct from these, they are little acquainted; ... There are some few facts, and perhaps some leading doctrines and principles, of which they cannot be wholly ignorant; but of the consequences, and relations, and practical uses of these, they have few ideas, or none at all.

FOR MEDITATION: 'Christianity,' Wilberforce wrote in *A Practical View of Christianity*, is 'a revelation from God, and not the invention of man, discovering to us new relations, with their correspondent duties; containing also doctrines, and motives, and practical principles, and rules, peculiar to itself, and almost as new in their nature as supreme in their excellence. We cannot reasonably expect to become proficients in it by the accidental intercourses of life, as one might learn insensibly the maxims of worldly policy, or a scheme of mere morals.

'The diligent perusal of the Holy Scriptures would discover to us our past ignorance. We should cease to be deceived by superficial appearances, and to confound the Gospel of Christ with the systems of philosophers; we should become impressed with that weighty truth, so much forgotten, that Christianity calls on us, as we value our immortal souls, not merely in general, to be religious and moral, but specially to believe the doctrines, and imbibe the principles, and practise the precepts of Christ.'

REFERENCE: *A Practical View of Christianity* (1797)

'Hereditary religion'

'Lead me in thy truth, and teach me: for thou art the God of my salvation.' Psalm 25:5
SUGGESTED FURTHER READING: Psalm 90:10–17

In an age wherein it is confessed and lamented that infidelity abounds, do we observe in professed Christians any remarkable care to instruct their children in the principles of the faith which they profess, and to furnish them with arguments for the defence of it? They would blush, on their child's coming out into the world, to think him defective in any branch of that knowledge, or of those accomplishments which belong to his station in life; and accordingly these are cultivated with becoming assiduity. But he is left to collect his religion as he may: the study of Christianity has formed no part of his education; and his attachment to it, where any attachment to it exists at all, is, too often, not the preference of sober reason and conviction, but merely the result of early and groundless prepossession. He was born in a Christian country; of course he is a Christian: his father was the member of the Church of England; so is he. When such is the hereditary religion handed down among us by hereditary succession, it cannot surprise us to observe young men of sense and spirit beginning to doubt altogether of the truth of the system in which they have been brought up, and ready to abandon a profession which they are unable to defend.

FOR MEDITATION: The study of Christianity is deeply important, particularly the training of children and young persons in the faith tradition it is hoped they will embrace or have embraced. This lends a holy urgency to the work of Sunday school teachers as well as college and seminary professors. It also underscores the value of personal Bible study and prayer. Conviction is born of careful study. Let us take care to cherish, rightly understand and perpetuate our faith.

REFERENCE: *A Practical View of Christianity* (1797)

'The humiliating language of Christianity'

'For all have sinned, and come short of the glory of God.' Romans 3:23
SUGGESTED FURTHER READING: Romans 6:12–23

The bulk of professed Christians are used to speak of man as of a being, who naturally pure, and inclined to all virtue, is sometimes, almost involuntarily, drawn out of the right course, or is overpowered by the violence of temptation. Vice with them is rather an accidental and temporary, than a constitutional and habitual distemper; a noxious plant, which, though found to live and even to thrive in the human mind, is not the natural growth and production of the soil.

Far different is the humiliating language of Christianity. From it we learn that man is an apostate creature, fallen from his high original, degraded in his nature, and depraved in his faculties; indisposed to good, and disposed to evil; prone to vice—it is natural and easy to him: disinclined to virtue—it is difficult and laborious; that he is tainted with sin, not slightly and superficially, but radically and to the very core.

FOR MEDITATION: Many a Christian has learned about the 'Romans road.' These are Scriptures in Romans that clearly set out who we are without God, and why we need to seek forgiveness of him—in short, to come to faith in God. Romans 3:23 tells us: 'For all have sinned, and come short of the glory of God.'

Romans 6:22–23 tells us what happens when we confess our sins, ask God's forgiveness of them and place our faith in him: 'But now being made free from sin, and become servants to God, ye have your fruit unto holiness, and the end everlasting life. For the wages of sin is death; but the gift of God is eternal life through Jesus Christ our Lord.'

REFERENCE: *A Practical View of Christianity* (1797)

'A renovation of our nature'

'The goodness of God leadeth thee to repentance.' Romans 2:4
SUGGESTED FURTHER READING: Psalm 86:11–17

The Holy Scriptures speak of us as fallen creatures; in almost every page we shall find something that is calculated to abate the loftiness and silence the pretensions of man. 'The imagination of man's heart is evil, from his youth.' 'Who can say, I have made my heart clean, I am pure from my sin?' 'The *heart* is deceitful above all things, and desperately wicked, who can know it?' 'Behold, I was shapen in iniquity, and in sin did my mother conceive me.' 'We were by nature the children of wrath, even as others, fulfilling the desire, of the flesh and of the mind.' 'O wretched man that I am, who shall deliver me from the body of this death!'—Passages might be multiplied upon passages, which speak the same language, and these again might be illustrated and confirmed at large by various other considerations, drawn from the same sacred source; such as those which represent a thorough change, a renovation of our nature, as being necessary to our becoming true Christians.

FOR MEDITATION: In Romans 2:4 the apostle Paul cautions those who have not as yet placed their faith in God as the Lord and Saviour of their lives: 'Or despisest thou the riches of his goodness and forbearance and longsuffering; not knowing that the goodness of God leadeth thee to repentance?'

God, through his great goodness and mercy, calls to us—saying now is the day of your salvation (2 Corinthians 6:2). And what he intends for those who have not yet come to faith is described more fully by Paul in Ephesians 2:2–3. Paul continues: 'we…were by nature the children of wrath.'

But it was then, when we were seemingly furthest from God, that he was closest to us, calling us by name. Paul states: 'But God, who is rich in mercy, for his great love wherewith he loved us, even when we were dead in sins, hath quickened us together with Christ, (by grace ye are saved)' (Ephesians 2:4–5). May God grant us the grace to seek that renovation of our nature, if we have not yet done so.

REFERENCE: *A Practical View of Christianity* (1797)

'Our most secret cogitations'

'Shall not God search this out? for he knoweth the secrets of the heart.'
Psalm 44:21
SUGGESTED FURTHER READING: Psalm 139:1–16

As all nature bears witness to God's irresistible power, so we read in Scripture that nothing can escape his observation, or elude his discovery; not only our actions, but our most secret cogitations are open to his view. 'He is about our path and about our bed, and spieth out all our ways,' 'The Lord searcheth all hearts, and understandeth all the imaginations of the thoughts' (1 Chronicles 28:9). 'The Lord...will bring to light the hidden things of darkness, and will make manifest the counsels of the hearts' (1 Corinthians 4:5).

FOR MEDITATION: When we trust in God, as the one who knows us better than we know ourselves, Psalm 33:21 says: 'our heart shall rejoice in him.' The things that matter to us most deeply are known to God. Our hopes and desires, better disappointments and sources of pain—every aspect of our lives—all these things about us have been within his view since the day we were born.

God cares profoundly about us and every aspect of our lives. Psalm 139 tells many beautiful things about the ways in which God knows us and cares for us. Take time to read it carefully and prayerfully.

REFERENCE: *A Practical View of Christianity* (1797)

'Our hearts would have danced'

'Blessed are they which do hunger and thirst after righteousness: for they shall be filled.' Matthew 5:6
SUGGESTED FURTHER READING: Isaiah 55:1–13

Had we duly felt the burthen of our sins, accompanied with a deep conviction that the weight of them must finally sink us into perdition, our hearts would have danced at the sound of the gracious invitation, 'Come unto me, all ye that labour and are heavy laden, and I will give you rest.'

Are our hearts really filled with these things, and warmed by the love which they are adapted to inspire? Our minds are apt to stray to them almost unseasonably; or at least to hasten back to them when escaped from the estrangement imposed by the necessary cares and business of life. He was a masterly describer of human nature, who thus portrayed the characters of an undissembled affection:

Unstaid and fickle in all other things,
Save in the constant image of the object,
That is beloved.   Shakespeare, *Twelfth Night*

FOR MEDITATION: Psalm 149 presents us with one of the stirring images of dancing in the Scriptures. 'Let them praise his name in the dance: let them sing praises unto him with the timbrel and harp. For the Lord taketh pleasure in his people: he will beautify the meek with salvation' (Psalm 149:3–4).

Wilberforce's words above are most fitting. 'Are our hearts really filled with these things, and warmed by the love which they are adapted to inspire?'

REFERENCE: *A Practical View of Christianity* (1797)

'Holiness of heart and life'

'*Whereunto ye do well that ye take heed, as unto a light that shineth in a dark place, until the day dawn.*' 2 Peter 1:19
SUGGESTED FURTHER READING: John 6:47

If the love of Christ is languid in the bulk of nominal Christians, their joy and trust in him cannot be expected to be very vigorous. There is nothing which implies a mind acquainted with the nature of the Christian's privileges, and familiarized with their use. Habitually solace ourselves with the hopes held out by the gospel. We ought to be animated by the sense of its high relations.

The doctrine of the sanctifying operations of the Holy Spirit appears to have met with still worse treatment. It would be to convey a very inadequate idea of the scantiness of the conceptions on this head of the bulk of the Christian world to affirm merely, that they are too little conscious of the inefficacy of their own unassisted endeavours after holiness of heart and life; and that they are not daily employed in humbly and diligently using the appointed means for the reception and cultivation of the divine assistance.

FOR MEDITATION: Romans 8:26 tells us: 'Likewise the Spirit also helpeth our infirmities: for we know not what we should pray for as we ought: but the Spirit itself maketh intercession for us.'

Here the apostle Paul states that the Holy Spirit intercedes for us in the place of prayer. When we pursue holiness of heart and life, we should have a healthy sense of our own inabilities and infirmities. As with prayer, so it is with so many aspects of the pursuit of holiness of heart and life—we need the Holy Spirit's help. We should prayerfully seek it, and take comfort in the fact that the Holy Spirit is, in the language of Scripture, the Paraclete—the One who comes alongside us—and is our Helper (John 14:16, *Today's English Version*).

REFERENCE: *A Practical View of Christianity* (1797)

'A vigorous and active principle'

'I press toward the mark for the prize of the high calling of God in Christ Jesus.' Philippians 3:14
SUGGESTED FURTHER READING: 2 Timothy 2:1–15

The Christian religion implants a vigorous and active principle; it is seated in the heart, where its authority is recognized as supreme, whence by degrees it expels whatever is opposed to it, and where it gradually brings all the affections and desires under its complete control and regulation.

But though the heart be its special residence, it may be said to possess in a degree the ubiquity of its divine Author. Every endeavour and pursuit must acknowledge its presence; and whatever receives not its sacred stamp, is to be condemned as inherently defective, and is to be at once relinquished. It is like the principle of vitality, which, animating every part, lives throughout the whole of the human body, and communicates its kindly influence to the smallest and remotest fibres of the frame.

FOR MEDITATION: 1 Corinthians 9:24 speaks of how our pursuits as Christians must be undertaken in a spirit honouring to our profession of faith. 'Know ye not,' writes the apostle Paul, 'that they which run in a race run all, but one receiveth the prize? So run, that ye may obtain.'

How do we so run? In John's gospel, the Lord Jesus makes use of a word, 'abide,' that is the direct opposite of running. And yet, as he explains, unless we learn to abide in him, we cannot be all we should be for God: 'Abide in me, and I in you. As the branch cannot bear fruit of itself, except it abide in the vine; no more can ye, except ye abide in me. I am the vine, ye are the branches: he that abideth in me, and I in him, the same bringeth forth much fruit: for *without me ye can do nothing*' (emphasis added, John 15:4–5).

REFERENCE: *A Practical View of Christianity* (1797)

'We are become our own masters'

'If a man therefore purge himself from these, he shall be a vessel unto honour, sanctified, and meet for the master's use, and prepared unto every good work.' 2 Timothy 2:21
SUGGESTED FURTHER READING: 1 Corinthians 3:9–17

The promotion of the glory of God, and the possession of his favour, are no longer recognized as the objects of our highest regard, and most strenuous endeavours; as furnishing to us a vigorous, habitual, and universal principle of action. We set up for ourselves: we are become our own masters. The sense of constant homage and continual service is irksome and galling to us; and we rejoice in being emancipated from it, as from a state of base and servile villeinage [feudal tenancy]. Thus the very tenure and condition, by which life and all its possessions are held, undergo a total change: our faculties and powers are now our own: whatever we have is regarded rather as a property, than as a trust.

So little sense of responsibility seems attached to the possession of high rank, splendid abilities, affluent fortunes, or other means or instruments of usefulness. The instructive admonitions, 'give an account of thy stewardship' and 'Occupy till I come,' are forgotten.

FOR MEDITATION: 'I am the master of my fate,' wrote the nineteenth-century poet William Ernest Henley, 'I am the captain of my soul.' These lines come from a poem entitled *Invictus*—which is Latin for unconquered. And while there is certainly a level on which this poem can be read as a call to courage, and valued as such; a more literal reading that implies we are the masters of our destiny runs counter to the mindset that ought to characterize the Christian. 'Ye are not your own,' the apostle Paul writes in 1 Corinthians 6:19–20, 'for ye are bought with a price: therefore glorify God in your body, and in your spirit, which are God's.'

REFERENCE: *A Practical View of Christianity* (1797)

'Shall the benevolence of Christians want employment?'

'For we are his workmanship, created in Christ Jesus unto good works,
which God hath before ordained that we should walk in them.'
Ephesians 2:10
SUGGESTED FURTHER READING: 1 Corinthians 15:58

No man has a right to be idle—not to speak of that great work which we all have to accomplish, (and surely the *whole* attention of a short and precarious life is not more than an eternal interest may well require;) where is it that, in such a world as this, health, and leisure, and affluence may not find some ignorance to instruct, some wrong to redress, some want to supply, some misery to alleviate? Shall ambition and avarice never sleep? Shall they never want objects on which to fasten? Shall they be so observant to discover, so acute to discern, so eager, so patient to pursue, and shall the benevolence of Christians want employment? Yet thus life rolls away with too many of us in a course of 'shapeless idleness.'

FOR MEDITATION: Shakespeare wrote of 'shapeless idleness' in his celebrated play, Two Gentlemen of Verona (Act 1). In Scene 1, Valentine cautions Proteus not to 'wear out thy youth with shapeless idleness.'
   'True love,' Wilberforce wrote in the pages of his book *A Practical View of Christianity*, 'is an ardent and active principle.' *A Practical View* was a *cri de coeur*, or 'cry of heart'—for Christians to live out 'the real nature and principles of the religion which they profess.' Descriptions of active love or Christian benevolence are woven throughout the book.
   Elsewhere, in 1821, Wilberforce wrote of a transformation God had wrought through Christians in Britain during his own day: 'it pleased God to diffuse a spirit which began to display its love of God and love of man by the formation of societies of a religious and moral nature ... The diffusion of the sacred Scriptures, the establishment of societies for spreading throughout the world the blessings of religious light and of moral improvement, the growing attention to the education of our people, with societies and institutions for relieving every species of suffering which vice and misery can ever produce among the human race.' As Christians today, we ought similarly to commend our faith.

REFERENCE: *A Practical View of Christianity* (1797)

'To cultivate our hearts'

'Herein is my Father glorified, that ye bear much fruit; so shall ye be my disciples.' John 15:8
SUGGESTED FURTHER READING: Matthew 7:15–20

It is indeed true, and a truth never to be forgotten, that all pretensions to internal principles of holiness are vain when they are contradicted by [our] conduct; but it is no less true, that the only effectual way of improving the latter, is by a vigilant attention to the former. It was therefore our blessed Saviour's injunction, 'Make the tree good' as the necessary means of obtaining good fruit; and the Holy Scriptures abound in admonitions, to make it our chief business to cultivate our hearts with all diligence, to examine into their state with impartiality, and watch over them with continual care. Indeed it is the *Heart* which constitutes the *Man*.

FOR MEDITATION: Images of gardens and those who cultivate them are many in Scripture. Diligence, watchfulness and care are traits that all good gardeners possess. Gardeners take care that weeds do not overtake and choke healthy plants. Weeding, watering and pruning are often arduous tasks, but they are a testament to a gardener's diligence, watchfulness and care. Those who invest time and care in their gardens know what it is to harvest crops and fruit or to see the beauty of flowers. For those who rightly watch over their hearts it is much the same: the love of God flowers within them and bears good fruit. 'Blessed is the man,' we read in Psalm 1, '[whose] delight is in the law of the Lord; and in his law doth he meditate day and night. And he shall be like a tree planted by the rivers of water, that bringeth forth his fruit in his season; his leaf also shall not wither; and whatsoever he doeth shall prosper' (Psalm 1:1–3).

REFERENCE: *A Practical View of Christianity* (1797)

'The graces of the Christian temper'

'According to the grace of God which is given unto me, as a wise master builder, I have laid the foundation, and another buildeth thereon. But let every man take heed how he buildeth thereupon.' 1 Corinthians 3:10
SUGGESTED FURTHER READING: Romans 12:1–10

The vicious affections, like noxious weeds, sprout up and increase of themselves but too naturally; while the graces of the Christian temper, (exotics in the soil of the human heart), like the more tender productions of the vegetable world, [need] not only the light and breath of Heaven to quicken them, but constant superintendence and assiduous care on our part also, in order to their being preserved in health and vigour. But so far from these graces being earnestly sought for, or watchfully reared, with unremitted prayers to God for his blessing (without which all our labours must be ineffectual); no endeavours are used for their attainment, or they are suffered to droop and die, almost without an effort to preserve them.

FOR MEDITATION: There is a lovely image in Jeremiah 17:8—'For he shall be as a tree planted by the waters, and that spreadeth out her roots by the river.'

This recalls a passage from *The Life of William Wilberforce* in which Wilberforce's sons write of their father as he was in October 1803: 'He was a constant observer of the advice of Bishop Berkeley, "that modern scholars would like the ancients, meditate and converse in walks and gardens and open air." His favourite haunt at this time was a retired meadow which bordered on the Avon. A steep bank, shaded by some fine trees (one of which by its projection formed a promontory in a deep part of the stream) was his common seat.'

In its own way, this story shows how Wilberforce took time and care to cultivate the Christian graces in his life through prayer and the reading of God's word. That he did so among trees along the Avon only serves to show how we too might do this, and in so doing be like 'a tree planted by the waters, and that spreadeth out her roots by the river.' May we so grow in grace and in the knowledge of our Lord Jesus Christ.

REFERENCE: *A Practical View of Christianity* (1797)

'The illusions of vision'

'*While we look not at the things which are seen, but at the things which are not seen: for the things which are seen are temporal; but the things which are not seen are eternal.*' 2 Corinthians 4:18
SUGGESTED FURTHER READING: 1 Corinthians 2:9

It is the comprehensive compendium of the character of true Christians, that 'they are walking by faith, and not by sight.' By this description is meant, not merely that they so firmly believe in the doctrine of future rewards and punishments, as to be influenced by that persuasion to adhere in the main to the path of duty, but farther, that the great truths revealed in Scripture concerning the unseen world, are the thoughts for the most part uppermost in their minds... This state of mind contributes, if the expression may be allowed, to rectify the illusions of vision, to bring forward into nearer view those eternal things which from their remoteness are apt to be either wholly overlooked, or to appear but faintly in the utmost bounds of the horizon.

The true Christian knows from experience, however, that the former are apt to fade from the sight, and the latter again to swell on it. He makes it therefore his continual care to preserve those just and enlightened views, which through Divine mercy he has obtained. Not that he will retire from that station in the world which Providence seems to have appointed him to fill: he will be active in the business of life, and enjoy its comforts with moderation and thankfulness; but he will not be totally absorbed in those matters, he will not give up his whole soul to them, they will be habitually subordinate in his estimation to objects of more importance. This awful truth has sunk deep into his mind, that 'the things which are seen are temporal, but the things which are not seen are eternal;' and he is sobered by the still small voice which whispers to him, 'the fashion of this world passes away.'

FOR MEDITATION: To bring forward into nearer view those eternal things. In Colossians 3, the apostle Paul writes of our need to do this, saying: 'If ye then be risen with Christ, seek those things which are above, where Christ sitteth on the right hand of God. Set your affection on things above, not on things on the earth' (Colossians 3:1–2).

REFERENCE: *A Practical View of Christianity* (1797)

'The knowledge and love of heavenly things'

'Her ways are ways of pleasantness, and all her paths are peace.'
Proverbs 3:17
SUGGESTED FURTHER READING: Colossians 3:1–15

The true Christian walks in the ways of religion, not by constraint, but willingly; they are to him not only safe, but comfortable 'ways of pleasantness as well as of peace.' With earnest prayers, therefore, for the Divine help, with jealous circumspection, and resolute self-denial, he guards against, and abstains from, whatever might be likely again to darken his *enlightened judgment* or to vitiate his reformed taste; thus making it his unwearied endeavour to grow in the knowledge and love of heavenly things, and to obtain a warmer admiration and a more cordial relish of their excellence. That this is a just representation of the habitual judgment and of the leading disposition of true Christians, will be abundantly evident, if, endeavouring to form ourselves after our proper model, we consult the sacred Scripture.

FOR MEDITATION: In Hebrews 3, there are verses that focus on thoughts on 'the knowledge and love of heavenly things.' Here the writer of Hebrews states: 'Wherefore, holy brethren, partakers of the heavenly calling, consider the Apostle and High Priest of our profession, Christ Jesus' (Hebrews 3:1). We are to fix our eyes upon Jesus. In so doing, we are told that 'we are made partakers of Christ, if we hold the beginning of our confidence stedfast unto the end' (Hebrews 3:14). This complements what Wilberforce writes—that we are to make it our 'unwearied endeavour to grow in the knowledge and love of heavenly things, and to obtain a warmer admiration and a more cordial relish of their excellence.'

REFERENCE: *A Practical View of Christianity* (1797)

'A just sense of our weakness'

'For thus saith the high and lofty One that inhabiteth eternity, whose name is Holy; I dwell in the high and holy place, with him also that is of a contrite and humble spirit, to revive the spirit of the humble, and to revive the heart of the contrite ones.' Isaiah 57:15
SUGGESTED FURTHER READING: Psalm 25:4–9

It might perhaps be said to be the great end and purpose of all revelation, and especially to be the design of the gospel, to reclaim us from our natural pride and selfishness, and their fatal consequences; to bring us to a just sense of our weakness and *depravity*; and to dispose us, with unfeigned humiliation, to abase ourselves, and give glory to God. 'No flesh may glory in his presence;' 'he that glorieth, let him glory in the Lord.'—'The lofty looks of man shall be humbled, and the haughtiness of men shall be bowed down, and the Lord alone shall be exalted.'

FOR MEDITATION: In 2 Corinthians 12, we read the word of the Lord to the apostle Paul: 'And he said unto me: "My grace is sufficient for thee: for my strength is made perfect in weakness." Most gladly therefore will I rather glory in my infirmities, that the power of Christ may rest upon me.'

Wilberforce understood from his reading of Paul's Letters, most of which he had memorized, that we are to have a just sense of our weakness. It is as the hymn writer Annie S. Hawks wrote in 1872:

I need thee every hour, in joy or pain;
Come quickly and abide, or life is in vain.
I need thee, O I need thee;
Every hour I need thee;
O bless me now, my Saviour,
I come to thee.

REFERENCE: *A Practical View of Christianity* (1797)

'Highly dangerous possessions'

'But made himself of no reputation, and took upon him the form of a servant.' Philippians 2:7
SUGGESTED FURTHER READING: Philippians 2:3–10

Credit and reputation, in the judgment of the true Christian, stand on ground not very different from riches; which he is not to prize highly, or to desire and pursue with solicitude; but which, when they are allotted to him by the hand of Providence, he is to accept with thankfulness, and to use with moderation; relinquishing them, when it becomes necessary, without a murmur; guarding most circumspectly for so long as they remain with him, against that sensual and selfish temper, and no less against that pride and wantonness of heart, which they are too apt to produce and cherish; thus considering them as in themselves acceptable, but, from the infirmity of his nature, highly dangerous possessions; and valuing them not as instruments of luxury or splendour, but as affording the means of honouring his heavenly Benefactor, and lessening the miseries of mankind.

FOR MEDITATION: Another of Wilberforce's succinct and memorable passages, this paragraph is a potent reminder of how we need to keep many things in perspective as Christians. Honour and worldly estimation (fame in present language): 'Let this mind be in you, which was also in Christ Jesus; who, being in the form of God, thought it not robbery to be equal with God; but *made himself of no reputation*, and took upon him the form of a servant' (Philippians 2:5–7, emphasis added). Wilberforce had been willing to be thought a fool for his 'perennial resolution' during the 20–year fight to abolish the slave trade. He had been willing to sacrifice his 'sacred honour,' in as much as it referred to a choice between reputation and one's duty to his fellow man. Indeed, he showed most powerfully that he did not consider his reputation as something his work created. His reputation was a byproduct of his faithfulness to the path he felt called to follow.

REFERENCE: *A Practical View of Christianity* (1797)

'That better state'

'Lay not up for yourselves treasures upon earth, where moth and rust doth corrupt, and where thieves break through and steal. But lay up for yourselves treasures in heaven, where neither moth nor rust doth corrupt, and where thieves do not break through nor steal. For where your treasure is, there will your heart be also.' Matthew 6:19–21
SUGGESTED FURTHER READING: Hebrews 10:32–39

Christianity, be it remembered, proposes not to extinguish our natural desires, but to bring them under just control, and direct them to their true objects. In the case of both riches and honour, she maintains the consistency of her character. While she commands us not to set our hearts on *earthly* treasures, she reminds us that we have in *Heaven* 'a better and more enduring substance' than this world can bestow; and while she represses our solicitude respecting earthly credit, and moderates our attachment to it, she holds forth to us, and bids us habitually to aspire after, the splendours of that better state, where is true glory, and honour, and immortality.

FOR MEDITATION: Charles Spurgeon said that Thomas Brooks was the most readable of the Puritan divines. Here is what Brooks had to say of those who know they have 'in heaven a better and more enduring substance': 'If you would do gloriously, look to faith; give faith scope, give it elbow-room to work. Faith is a noble grace, and will ennoble the soul to do gloriously for God.

'Faith is that that will carry a man over all difficulties; faith will untie all knots; it will carry a man through the valley of darkness and over mountains of difficulties. Faith will not plead "there is a lion in the way," and that such and such men will frown if I do this or that for God and the general good. Faith will carry a man bravely over all. You know that story in Hebrews 11; you have several instances of the saints doing gloriously. But what enabled them? It is all along attributed to faith. By the power of faith they did gloriously: they stopped the mouths of lions; they turned to flight the armies of the aliens; they waxed valiant in fight; they refused to be delivered,—and all by the power of faith. Oh! faith will enable men to do gloriously.'

REFERENCE: *A Practical View of Christianity* (1824 EDITION)

'To rectify the motives and purify the heart'

'My son, give me thine heart, and let thine eyes observe my ways.'
Proverbs 23:26
SUGGESTED FURTHER READING: Proverbs 3:1–12

It is the distinguishing glory of Christianity not to rest satisfied with superficial appearances, but to rectify the *motives,* and purify the *heart.* The true Christian, in obedience to the lessons of Scripture, nowhere keeps over himself a more resolute and jealous guard, than where the desire of human estimation and distinction is in question. Nowhere does he more deeply feel the insufficiency of his unassisted strength, or more diligently and earnestly pray for divine assistance.

FOR MEDITATION: The Puritan divine Thomas Brooks (1608–1680) clearly understood why it is we ought to rectify our motives, and purify our hearts. 'Remember,' he wrote, 'a Christ highly prized will be Christ gloriously obeyed. As men prize the Lord Jesus Christ, so they will obey him. The great reason why Jesus Christ is no more obeyed, it is because he is no more prized. Men look upon him as a person of no worth, no dignity, no glory; they make slight of him, and that is the reason they are so poor in their obedience to him. Oh, if the sons of men did but more divinely prize Christ, they would more purely, and more fully, and more constantly obey him. Let this bespeak all your hearts highly to prize the Lord Jesus, who is your life.'

And if we prize the Lord Jesus aright we will be careful to do all that he has instructed us to do, especially that which he called the greatest commandment: 'Thou shalt love the Lord thy God with all thy heart, and with all thy soul, and with all thy mind' (Matthew 22:37).

REFERENCE: *A Practical View of Christianity* (1797)

'The undeserved bounty of Heaven'

'For by grace are ye saved through faith; and that not of yourselves: it is the gift of God: Not of works, lest any man should boast.' Ephesians 2:8–9
SUGGESTED FURTHER READING: Romans 5:11–21

The true Christian is much occupied in searching out, and contemplating his own infirmities. He endeavours to acquire and maintain a just conviction of his great unworthiness; and to keep in continual remembrance, that whatever distinguishes himself from others, is not properly his own, but that he is altogether indebted for it to the undeserved bounty of Heaven.

FOR MEDITATION: Romans 5:17 tells us this of God's grace—that which Wilberforce describes as the undeserved bounty of heaven: 'For if by one man's offence death reigned by one; much more they which receive abundance of grace and of the gift of righteousness shall reign in life by one, Jesus Christ.'

Abundance of grace and the gift of righteousness. Is anything to be compared with this? As Psalm 86:8 states: 'there is none like unto thee, O LORD; neither are there any works like unto thy works.' Psalm 71:19 strikes a similar note of praise: 'Thy righteousness also, O God, is very high, who hast done great things: O God, who is like unto thee!'

God can, through his grace, make of us a true servant of God. This was put forcefully by the eighteenth-century divine Philip Doddridge, who wrote: 'For to his Almighty grace nothing is hard, not even to transform a rock of marble into a man or a saint.' So may we become ornaments of grace in the hands of the Master Artist.

REFERENCE: *A Practical View of Christianity* (1797)

'Benevolent and useful schemes'

'Charge them that are rich in this world, that they be not highminded, nor trust in uncertain riches, but in the living God, who giveth us richly all things to enjoy; that they do good, that they be rich in good works, ready to distribute, willing to communicate.' 1 Timothy 6:17–18
SUGGESTED FURTHER READING: Romans 13:8–14

The Christian will studiously and diligently use any degree of worldly credit he may enjoy, in removing or lessening prejudices; in conciliating good-will, and thereby making way for the less obstructed progress of truth. He will make it his business to set on foot and forward benevolent and useful schemes; and where they require united efforts, to obtain and preserve for them this co-operation. He will endeavour to discountenance vice, to bring modest merit into notice; to lend as it were his light to men of real worth, but of less creditable name, and perhaps of less conciliating qualities and manners; that they may thus shine with a reflected lustre, and be useful in their turn, when invested with their just estimation. By these and various other means he strives to render his reputation, so long as he possesses it, subservient to advancing the cause of religion and virtue.

FOR MEDITATION: In his classic treatise *The Rise and Progress of Religion in the Soul*, Philip Doddridge had this to say of the source of Christian benevolence: 'The blessed Jesus designed himself to be a model for all his followers; and he is certainly a model most fit for our imitation: an example in our own nature and in circumstances adapted to general use: an example recommended to us at once by its spotless perfection, and by the endearing relations in which he stands to us, as our Master, our Friend, and our Head; as the person by whom our everlasting state is to be fixed, and in resemblance to whom our final happiness is to consist, if ever we are happy at all. Look then, into the life and temper of Christ, as described and illustrated in the Gospel, and search whether you can find any thing like it in your own. Have you any thing of his devotion, love, and resignation to God? Any thing of his humility, meekness, and benevolence to men?'

REFERENCE: *A Practical View of Christianity* (1797)

'Labour to enter into that rest'

'And have put on the new man, which is renewed in knowledge after the image of him that created him.' Colossians 3:10
SUGGESTED FURTHER READING: Psalm 27:7–14

Work out then thy own salvation. Purify thy heart, thou double-minded—labour to enter into that rest. The way is narrow, but then we have God and Christ on our side: we have heavenly armour; the crown is everlasting life, and the struggle how short, compared with the eternity which follows it!

FOR MEDITATION: After reading the Puritan Richard Baxter's classic devotional work *Saint's Everlasting Rest* (a book Wilberforce called his 'prime favourite') the Rev. John Janeway wrote: 'There is a duty, which, if it were exercised, would dispel all cause of melancholy: I mean heavenly meditation and contemplation of the things to which the true Christian religion tends. If we did but walk closely with God one hour in a day in this duty, O what influence would it have upon the whole day besides, and, duly performed, upon the whole life!'

In his diary, Wilberforce himself wrote of his own ardent desire to walk more closely with God: 'I feel true humiliation of soul from a sense of my own extreme unworthiness; a humble hope in the favour of God in Christ; some emotion from the contemplation of him who at this very moment was hanging on the cross; some shame at the multiplied mercies I enjoy; some desire to devote myself to him who has so dearly bought me; some degree of that universal love and good-will, which the sight of Christ crucified is calculated to inspire. Oh if the contemplation here can produce these effects on my hard heart … What gratitude is justly due from me (the vilest of sinners, when compared with the mercies I have received) who have been brought from darkness into light, and I trust from the pursuit of earthly things to the prime love of things above! Oh purify my heart still more by thy grace. Quicken my dead soul, and purify me by thy Spirit, that I may be changed from glory to glory, and be made even here in some degree to resemble my heavenly Father.'

REFERENCE: *A Practical View of Christianity* (1797)

'Quicken me, O Lord.'

'Thou, which hast shewed me great and sore troubles, shalt quicken me again, and shalt bring me up again from the depths of the earth.'
Psalm 71:20
SUGGESTED FURTHER READING: Psalm 119:25

Oh how difficult it is to keep alive in the soul any spark of the true spirit of religion! 'Quicken me, O Lord.' Form in me daily that new creature which is made after thy likeness. May I be endeavouring in all things to walk in wisdom to them that are without, redeeming the time ... and living soberly, righteously, and godly in this present world.

FOR MEDITATION: The following diary entry, though fragmentary, shows how deeply the desire to be quickened ran in Wilberforce, and also how this desire found voice in prayerful petitions:

I would now in prayer look back on the mercies of God through life. Oh how numerous and how freely bestowed! Pray for pardon, acceptance, holiness, peace— for courage, humility, and all that I chiefly want for love and heavenly mindedness. Pray for my country, both in temporal and spiritual things. Pray for the success of missions. Think over my enemies with forgiveness and love—over my friends and acquaintances, and pray for both. In the evening think how I may do good to my acquaintances and friends, and pray for wisdom here. I humbly bless God that my heart has been tender. What a solid satisfaction is it to reflect that our ascended Lord views us with a pitying and sympathetic eye; that he knows what it is to have a feeling of our infirmities, that he promises, and he is truth as well as love, that they who wait on him shall renew their strength!

May the Lord give us all those same desires after him.

REFERENCE: *The Life of William Wilberforce* (1838)

'How little has been our progress in virtue'

'For I delight in the law of God after the inward man. But I see another law in my members, warring against the law of my mind ...' Romans 7:22–23
SUGGESTED FURTHER READING: Romans 7:7–25

In spite of all our knowledge, how little has been our progress in virtue. It is now no less acknowledged than heretofore, that prosperity hardens the heart: that unlimited power is ever abused, instead of being rendered the instrument of diffusing happiness: that habits of vice grow up of themselves, whilst those of virtue, if to be obtained at all, are of slow and difficult formation: that they who draw the finest pictures of virtue, and seem most enamoured of her charms, are often the least under her influence, and by the merest trifles are drawn aside from that line of conduct, which they most strongly and seriously recommend to others.

FOR MEDITATION: A prayer of Philip Doddridge, composed in the language of Scripture, is fitting here. 'May thy grace, O Lord, which hath appeared unto all men, and appeared to me with such glorious evidence and lustre, effectually teach me to deny ungodliness and worldly lusts, and to live soberly, righteously, and godly. Work in my heart that godliness which is profitable unto all things; and teach me by the influence of thy blessed Spirit, to love thee, the Lord my God, with all my heart, and with all my soul, and with all my mind, and with all my strength. May I entertain the most faithful and affectionate regard to the blessed Jesus, thine incarnate Son, the brightness of thy glory, and the express image of thy person. Though I have not seen him, may I love him; and in him, though now I see him not, yet believing, may I rejoice with joy unspeakable and full of glory, and may the life which I live in the flesh be daily by the faith of the Son of God. May I be filled with the Spirit, and may I be led by it; and so may it be evident to others, and especially to my own soul, that I am a child of God, and an heir of glory. May I not receive the spirit of bondage unto fear, but the spirit of adoption, whereby I may be enabled to cry, Abba, Father. May he work in me, as the spirit of love, and of power, and of a sound mind, that so I may add to my faith virtue.'

REFERENCE: *A Practical View of Christianity* (1797)

'Trifling with everlasting interests'

'We pray you in Christ's stead, be ye reconciled to God.' 2 Corinthians 5:20
SUGGESTED FURTHER READING: Psalm 139:17–24

To any one who is seriously impressed with a sense of the critical state in which we are here placed [while on earth], a short and uncertain space in which to make our peace with God, and then the last judgment, and an eternity of unspeakable happiness or misery, it is indeed an awful and an affecting spectacle, to see men thus busying themselves in these speculations of arrogant curiosity, and trifling with their dearest, their everlasting interests. It is but a feeble illustration of this exquisite folly, to compare it to the conduct of some convicted rebel, who, brought into the presence of his Sovereign, instead of seizing the occasion to sue for mercy, should even neglect and trifle with the pardon which should be offered to him, and insolently employ himself in prying into his Sovereign's designs and criticizing his counsels.

FOR MEDITATION: At the close of his classic commendation of the gospel, *The Rise and Progress of Religion in the Soul* (1745), Philip Doddridge wrote: 'I have ventured my own everlasting interests on that foundation on which I have directed you to adventure yours. What I have recommended as the grand business of your life, I desire to make the business of my own; and the most considerable enjoyments which I expect or desire in the remaining days of my pilgrimage on earth, are such as I have directed you to seek and endeavoured to assist you in attaining. Such love to God, such constant activity in his service, such pleasurable views of what lies beyond the grave, appear to me (God is my witness) a felicity incomparably beyond anything else which can offer itself to our affection and pursuit; and I would not for ten thousand worlds resign my share in them, or consent even to the suspension of the delights which they afford, during the remainder of my abode here.'

REFERENCE: *A Practical View of Christianity* (1797)

'The unmerited goodness of God'

'For by grace are ye saved through faith; and that not of yourselves: it is the gift of God.' Ephesians 2:8
SUGGESTED FURTHER READING: Ephesians 2:1–10

In the sacred volume we are throughout reminded that we are originally the creatures of God's formation, and continual dependents on his bounty. There too we learn the painful lesson of man's degradation and unworthiness. We learn that humiliation and contrition are the tempers of mind best suited to our fallen condition, and most acceptable in the sight of our Creator. We learn that these it should be our habitual care to cherish and cultivate; studiously maintaining a continual sense that we are altogether indebted to the unmerited goodness of God.

FOR MEDITATION: We are continual dependents on God's bounty. This was well understood by the writer Philip Doddridge, whose writings greatly influenced Wilberforce. Speaking of our dependence upon God's bounty, Doddridge wrote: 'Reflect on the light and heat which the sun everywhere dispenses; on the air which surrounds all our globe; on the right temperature on which the life of the whole human race depends, and that of all the inferior creatures which dwell on the earth. Think on the suitable and plentiful provisions made for man and beast; the grass, the grain, the variety of fruits, and herbs, and flowers; everything that nourishes us, every thing that delights us, and say whether it does not speak plainly and loudly that our Almighty Maker is near, and that he is careful for us, and kind to us. God is present, present with you at this moment; even God your creator and preserver, God the creator and preserver of the whole visible and invisible world.'

REFERENCE: *A Practical View of Christianity* (1797)

'Means and instruments of influence'

'Let your light so shine before men, that they may see your good works, and glorify your Father which is in heaven.' Matthew 5:16
SUGGESTED FURTHER READING: Proverbs 8:13–21,32–36

We ought to have a due respect and regard to the approbation and favour of men. These however we should not value chiefly as they administer to our own gratification, but as furnishing means and instruments of influence, which we may turn to good account, by making them subservient to the improvement and happiness of our fellow-creatures, and thus conducive to the *glory of God*. On occasions like these we must also watch our hearts with the most jealous care, lest pride and self-love insensibly infuse themselves.

FOR MEDITATION: One of Wilberforce's favourite writers, Philip Doddridge had this to say of stewardship: 'On surveying the peculiar circumstances of your life and being, discover what opportunities of usefulness they now afford, and how those opportunities and capacities may be improved. Enter therefore into such a survey, not that you may pride yourself in the distinctions of divine Providence or grace towards you, or, "having received, may glory as if you had not received" (1 Corinthians 4:7) but that you may deal faithfully with the great Proprietor, whose steward you are, and by whom you are entrusted with every talent, which, with respect to any claim from your fellow-creatures, you may call your own. And here, "having gifts differing according to the grace that is given to us" (Romans 12:6), let us hold the balance with an impartial hand, that so we may determine what it is that God requires of us; which is nothing less than doing the most we can invent, contrive, and effect, for the general good. But, oh! how seldom is this estimate faithfully made! And how much does the world around us, and how much do our own souls suffer for want of that fidelity! Hath God given you genius and learning? It was not that you might amuse or deck yourself with it, and kindle a blaze which should only serve to attract and dazzle the eyes of men. It was intended to be the means of heading both yourself and them to the Father of lights.'

REFERENCE: *A Practical View of Christianity* (1797)

'By Christianity all these roughnesses are filed down'

'*And that ye put on the new man, which after God is created in righteousness and true holiness.*' Ephesians 4:24
SUGGESTED FURTHER READING: Ephesians 4:23–32

The virtues most strongly and repeatedly enjoined in Scripture, and by our progress in which, we may best measure our advancement in holiness, are the fear and love of God and of Christ; love, kindness, and meekness towards our fellow-creatures; indifference to the possessions and events of this life, in comparison with our concern about eternal things; self-denial, and humility.

In the case of these two last descriptions of Christian graces, the more attentively we consider them the more we shall be convinced that they afford mutual aid towards the acquisition of each other, and that when acquired, they all harmonize with each other in perfect and essential union. Take then the instances of loving-kindness and meekness towards others, and observe the solid foundation which is laid for them in self-denial, in moderation as to the good things of this life, and in humility. The chief cause of enmity among men is pride, and the consequent deference which they exact from others; the over-valuation of worldly possessions and of worldly honours, and in consequence, a too eager competition for them. The rough edges of one man rub against those of another, and the friction is often such as to injure the works, and disturb the motions of the social machine. But by Christianity all these roughnesses are filed down.

FOR MEDITATION: Those who are intent upon growing in grace will increasingly manifest elements of the Christian character. Meekness is one such character trait. Of this Philip Doddridge wrote: 'The Gospel will also teach you 'to put on meekness' (Colossians 3:12). Its gentle instructions will form you to calmness of temper under provocations. It will engage you to guard your words, lest you provoke and exasperate those you should rather study by love to gain, and by tenderness to heal. Meekness will render you slow in using any rough and violent methods, if they can by any means be lawfully avoided; and ready to admit, and even to propose a reconciliation, after they have been entered into, if there may yet be hope of succeeding. So far as this branch of the Christian temper prevails in your heart, you will take care to avoid every thing which might give unnecessary offence to others.'

REFERENCE: *A Practical View of Christianity* (1797)

'As if present things were to last'

'And they that use this world, as not abusing it: for the fashion of this world passeth away.' 1 Corinthians 7:31
SUGGESTED FURTHER READING: John 17:1–12

How can we go on as if present things were to last for ever, when so often reminded 'that the fashion of this world passes away'? Every day I live I see greater reason in considering this life but as a passage to another. And when summoned to the tribunal of God, to give an account of all things we have done in the body, how shall we be confounded by the recollection of those many instances, in which we have relinquished a certain eternal for an uncertain transitory good! You are not insensible to these things, but you think of them rather like a follower of Socrates than a disciple of Jesus. You see how frankly I deal with you, in truth I can no otherwise so well show the interest I take in your happiness.

FOR MEDITATION: The seventeenth-century preacher and writer Richard Baxter once wrote: 'I preached … as a dying man to dying men.' Present things will not last forever; and so we must give care to matters of eternity. In 1745 Philip Doddridge, a man much like Baxter, crafted a prayer that puts the things of eternity in perspective. It is the prayer of one who has come to see that this life is but as a passage to another: 'Gracious Father! I would not quit this earth of thine, without my grateful acknowledgments to thee for all that abundant goodness which thou hast caused to pass before me here. I thank thee, O my God! that this guilty, forfeited, unprofitable life, was so long spared; that it hath still been maintained by such a rich variety of thy bounty.

'I bless thee, O Lord! that I am not dying in an unregenerate and impenitent state; but that thou didst graciously awaken and convince me, that thou didst renew and sanctify my heart, and didst, by thy good Spirit, work in it an unfeigned faith, a real repentance, and the beginning of a divine life. Permit me to consign "this departing spirit to thine hand; for thou hast redeemed it O Lord God of truth!"'

REFERENCE: *The Life of William Wilberforce* (1838)

'I may be called to sharp trials'

'Wait on the Lord: be of good courage, and he shall strengthen thine heart: wait, I say, on the Lord.' Psalm 27:14
SUGGESTED FURTHER READING: Colossians 1:9–11

I would grow in love and tender solicitude for my fellow creatures' happiness, and in preparedness for any events which may befall me in this uncertain state. I may be called to sharp trials, but Christ is able to strengthen me for the event, be it what it may.

FOR MEDITATION: Psalm 145:15–18 speaks compellingly of walking closely with God. It is when we do so that we are given 'strength according to the day'—whether that day brings sharp trials or times when we are profoundly aware of God's blessing in our lives. When we wait upon the Lord, we begin to understand what it is to receive things from him in due season. When we draw near to him, he will draw near to us. He will show us the way wherein we should walk, and he will be beside us all along the way. As the psalmist has written:

The eyes of all wait upon thee;
and thou givest them their meat in due season.
Thou openest thine hand,
and satisfiest the desire of every living thing.
The Lord is righteous in all his ways,
and holy in all his works.
The Lord is nigh unto all them that call upon him,
to all that call upon him in truth.

REFERENCE: *The Life of William Wilberforce* (1838)

'The way of calumny'

'Blessed are ye, when men shall revile you, and persecute you, and shall say all manner of evil against you falsely, for my sake. Rejoice, and be exceeding glad: for great is your reward in heaven: for so persecuted they the prophets which were before you.' Matthew 5:11–12
SUGGESTED FURTHER READING: 1 Peter 2:21–23

After being charged with a falsehood Wilberforce wrote: 'Yet I endeavour I hope to fight against the bad tempers of revenge and pride which it is generating, by thinking of all our Saviour suffered in the way of calumny. St Stephen also and St Paul were falsely accused. Let me humbly watch myself, so far as this false charge may suggest matter of amendment; and also I ought to be very thankful that with the many faults of which I am conscious, it has pleased God that I have never been charged justly, or where I could not vindicate myself. How good is God!

FOR MEDITATION: Of what worth is a teachable heart? That Wilberforce had one is attested by this passage from his diary, and it was a key to the appeal of his Christian witness in public life. People see through pretence and sham. When they encounter someone who freely acknowledges faults, manifests a genuine humility, and willingness to learn from mistakes, they take notice. Wilberforce's contemporaries did, and the consistency of his character in this regard was winsome.

One of Wilberforce's spiritual mentors, Philip Doddridge, wrote of the traits that distinguish a teachable heart: 'If you are a Christian indeed, the mercies of God, and those of the blessed Redeemer, will work on your heart, to mould it to sentiments of compassion and generosity, so that you will feel the wants and sorrows of others. You will desire to relieve their necessities; and as you have an opportunity, you will do good, both to their bodies and their souls; expressing your kind affections in suitable actions, which may both evidence their sincerity and render them effectual. As a Christian, you will also maintain truth inviolable, not only in your solemn testimonies, when confirmed by an oath, but likewise in common conversation. You will be careful to keep a strict correspondence between your words and your actions, in such a manner as becomes a servant of the God of truth.'

REFERENCE: *The Life of William Wilberforce* (1838)

'Your faithful friend'

'But speaking the truth in love, may grow up into him in all things, which is the head, even Christ.' Ephesians 4:15
SUGGESTED FURTHER READING: Ephesians 4:11–16

It is my sincere prayer, my dear Pitt (British Prime Minister), that you may here be the honoured instrument of Providence for your country's good, and for the well-being of the civilized world; and much more that you may at length partake of a more solid and durable happiness and honour than this world can bestow. I am, and I trust I ever shall be, your affectionate and faithful friend.

FOR MEDITATION: Philip Doddridge, the writer so admired by Wilberforce, understood the importance of earnestly commending the faith. 'I hope,' he wrote, '[I may have] so far awakened the convictions of my reader, as to bring him to this purpose, "that some time or other he would attend to religious considerations." But give me leave to ask, earnestly and pointedly, "When shall that be?" "Go thy way for this time, when I have a convenient season I will call for thee" (Acts 24:25), was the language and ruin of unhappy Felix, when he trembled under the reasonings and expostulations of the apostle.

'Will you, dismiss me thus? For your own sake, and out of tender compassion to your perishing, immortal soul, I would not willingly take up with such a dismission and excuse—no, not though you shall fix a time. I would turn upon you, with all the eagerness and tenderness of friendly importunity, and entreat you to bring the matter to an issue even now.

'When I invite you to the care and practice of religion, it may seem strange that it should be necessary for me affectionately to plead the cause with you, in order to your immediate regard and compliance. What I am inviting you to is so noble and excellent in itself, so well worthy of the dignity of our rational nature, so suitable to it, so manly and so wise, that one would imagine you should take fire, as it were, at the first hearing of it; yea, that so delightful a view should presently possess your whole soul with a kind of indignation against yourself that you pursued it no sooner. "May I lift up my eyes and my soul to God!"'

REFERENCE: *The Life of William Wilberforce* (1838)

'This one true point of rest'

'Let not your heart be troubled: ye believe in God, believe also in me. In my Father's house are many mansions: if it were not so, I would have told you. I go to prepare a place for you. And if I go and prepare a place for you, I will come again, and receive you unto myself; that where I am, there ye may be also.' John 14:1–3
SUGGESTED FURTHER READING: Psalm 144:1–15

There is a perfect home, of love, and peace, and happiness, and we are invited to the enjoyment of it. Let every fresh proof therefore of the unsatisfactoriness of human things have the effect of urging us forward towards this one true point of rest.

FOR MEDITATION: Wilberforce wrote these words in a letter to his friend Lord Muncaster on 7 January 1800. They recall the words of *The Westminster Catechism*, which asks: 'What is the chief and highest end of man?' The answer: 'Man's chief and highest end is to glorify God, and fully to enjoy him forever.'

Several passages of Scripture attest this highest end. We read in 1 Corinthians 10:31—'Whether therefore ye eat, or drink, or whatsoever ye do, do all to the glory of God.' Romans 11:36 declares: 'For of him, and through him, and to him, are all things: to whom be glory for ever. Amen.' The psalmist writes: 'Thou shalt guide me with thy counsel, and afterward receive me to glory. Whom have I in heaven but thee? and there is none upon earth that I desire beside thee. My flesh and my heart faileth: but God is the strength of my heart, and my portion for ever' (Psalm 73:24–26). The gospel of John presents the words of our Lord: 'And the glory which thou gavest me I have given them; that they may be one, even as we are one … Father, I will that they also, whom thou hast given me, be with me where I am; that they may behold my glory, which thou hast given me: for thou lovedst me before the foundation of the world' (John 17:22, 24).

REFERENCE: *The Life of William Wilberforce* (1838)

'Miracles of mercy'

'Blessed be the God and Father of our Lord Jesus Christ, which according to his abundant mercy hath begotten us again unto a lively hope by the resurrection of Jesus Christ from the dead.' 1 Peter 1:3
SUGGESTED FURTHER READING: 1 Peter 1:1–9

Oh may I hear his voice, and open the door and let him in. May I be really a thriving Christian, bringing forth abundantly the fruits of the Spirit to the glory of God. O Lord, I am lost in astonishment at thy mercy and love. That thou shouldst not only quit the glory and happiness of heaven to be made man, and bear the most excruciating torments and bitter degradation for our deliverance and salvation; but that thou still bearest with us, though we, knowing all thy goodness, are still cold and insensible to it. That thou strivest with our perverseness, conquerest our opposition, and still waitest to be gracious; and that it was in the fore-knowledge of this our base ingratitude and stupid perverseness, that thou didst perform these miracles of mercy. Thou knewest me, and my hardness, and coldness, and unworthy return for all thy goodness. Thou calledst me from the giddy throng, and shone into my heart with the light of the glory of God, in the face of Jesus Christ.

FOR MEDITATION: Doddridge wrote this of the mercy and nearness of God: 'Look upward and look forward, and you will feel your heart animated by the view. Your General is near; he is near to aid you, he is near to reward you. When you feel the temptation press the hardest, think of him who endured even the cross itself for your rescue. View the fortitude of your Divine Leader, and endeavour to march on in his steps. Hearken to his voice, for he proclaims it aloud, "Behold, I come quickly, and my reward is with me" (Revelation 22:12). "Be thou faithful unto death, and I will give thee a crown of life" (Revelation 2:10).

'I make it my hearty prayer for you, my reader, that you may be "kept by the mighty power of God," kept, as in a garrison on all sides fortified in the securest manner, "through faith, unto salvation."'

REFERENCE: *The Life of William Wilberforce* (1838)

'We are to be pilgrims and strangers'

'For our conversation is in heaven; from whence also we look for the Saviour, the Lord Jesus Christ.' Philippians 3:20
SUGGESTED FURTHER READING: James 3:13–18

I have far too little thought of the dangers of great wealth, or rather of such affluence and rank in life as mine. O my soul, bethink thee of it; and at the same time bless God who has given thee some little knowledge of the way of salvation. How little also have I borne in mind that we are to be pilgrims and strangers on the earth! This impression can be kept up in those who are in such a state of prosperity and comfort as myself, by much prayer and meditation, and by striving habitually to walk by faith and to have my conversation in heaven. O Lord, direct me to some new line of usefulness, for thy glory, and the good of my fellow-creatures.

FOR MEDITATION: Philip Doddridge has written: 'Christ has told us, "that a man must deny himself, and take up his cross daily" (Luke 9:23), if he desires to become his disciple. Christ, the Son of God, the former and the heir of all things, "pleased not himself" (Romans 15:3) but submitted to want, to difficulties, and hardships, in the way of duty, and some of them of the extremest kind and degree, for the glory of God and the salvation of men. In this way we are to follow him. Attachment to this world, and an unwillingness to leave it, ill becomes those who are strangers and pilgrims on earth, and who expect so soon to be called away to that better country which they "profess to seek" (Hebrews 11:13,16).'

REFERENCE: *The Life of William Wilberforce* (1838)

'What can I say more?'

'*For he looked for a city which hath foundations, whose builder and maker is God.*' *Hebrews 11:10*
SUGGESTED FURTHER READING: Psalm 103:8–18

In truth, my dear friend, we are all too apt to forget that the time is short, and the fashion of this world passeth away; that here we are but strangers and pilgrims. Farewell, my dear Muncaster. I will not apologize for the serious strain into which I have just given. I know you wish me to say what is uppermost, to pour forth the effusions of the heart. Farewell once more, and may God bless you. When that is said seriously, as I say it, well may it be added in the phrase of the Orientals, 'What can I say more?'

FOR MEDITATION: Though words often seem inadequate Philip Doddridge, the author of the celebrated treatise *The Rise and Progress of Religion in the Soul* (1745), sought to convey some sense of the blessedness of the Christian faith: 'May I lift up my eyes and my soul to God! May I devote myself to him! May I even now commence a friendship with him—a friendship which shall last for ever, the security, the delight, the glory of this immortal nature of mine!'

Sometimes words fail us in trying to express our deep gratitude to a cherished friend or to God himself. But God knows what is in our hearts. So too, often, do friends who know us well.

And we do not always need words. Nor need we feel downcast if words fail us when our hearts are full. The humblest saint who seeks to live a life in service to the Lord understands and expresses something profoundly beautiful—something beautiful for God.

REFERENCE: *The Life of William Wilberforce* (1838)

'After our departure from the scene of our earthly pilgrimage'

'Wherefore seeing we also are compassed about with so great a cloud of witnesses …' Hebrews 12:1
SUGGESTED FURTHER READING: Matthew 25:31–40; Psalm 16:1–11

We are not told that Moses was to experience after death any thing different from mankind in general; and we know that he took part in the events of this lower world, and on the mount of transfiguration talked with Christ concerning his death which he was to undergo at Jerusalem. And I love to dwell on this idea, that after our departure from the scene of our earthly pilgrimage, we witness the development of the plans we may have formed for the benefit of our fellow-creatures; the growth and fruitage of the good principles we have implanted and cultivated in our children; and above all, the fulfilment of the prayers we have poured forth for them, in the large effusions on them of that heavenly grace, which above all things we have implored as their portion.

FOR MEDITATION: 'But as it is written,' we read in 1 Corinthians 2:9—'Eye hath not seen, nor ear heard, neither have entered into the heart of man, the things which God hath prepared for them that love him.'

We cannot conceive of the glories of heaven, but we shall be in the presence of the Lord, and of departed saints who have gone before us. Who can begin to tell how wonderful that will be!

And we have this blessed assurance from the apostle John: 'Beloved… we know that, when he shall appear, we shall be like him; for we shall see him as he is' (1 John 3:2). A century ago Charles Gabriel wrote verses that are lovely in their simplicity:

Friends will be there I have loved long ago;
Joy like a river around me will flow;
Yet just a smile from my Saviour, I know,
Will through the ages be glory for me.
O that will be glory for me,
Glory for me, glory for me,
When by his grace I shall look on his face,
That will be glory, be glory for me.

REFERENCE: *The Life of William Wilberforce* (1838)

'This is that simple faith'

'*Verily I say unto you, Except ye be converted, and become as little children, ye shall not enter into the kingdom of heaven.*' Matthew 18:3
SUGGESTED FURTHER READING: Psalm 4:1–5

How hard do I find it to trust Christ for all! Yet this is that simple faith, that humble, child-like principle, which produces love, and peace, and joy. Oh let me seek it diligently whilst it is called to-day! I should be filled also with the love of God and Christ, and of all mankind for his sake, with a fixed desire to please him and do all for his glory.

FOR MEDITATION: A fixed desire to please him and do all for his glory. May this be the continuing desire of our hearts.

It was the continuing desire of Philip Doddridge, the Christian teacher whom Wilberforce so admired. 'Lord God!' he wrote, 'thou searchest all hearts. and triest the reins of the children of men! (Jeremiah 17:10), Search me, O Lord, and know my heart; try me, and know my thoughts; and see if there be any wicked way in me, and lead me in the way everlasting (Psalm 139:23–24). May I know what it is to have my whole heart subdued by love; so subdued as to be crucified with him (Romans 6:6); to be dead to sin and dead to the world, but alive unto God, through Jesus Christ (Romans 6:11). In his power and love may I confide! To him may I without any reserve commit my spirit! His image may I bear! His laws may I observe! His service may I pursue! And may I remain, through time and eternity, a monument of the efficacy of his gospel, and a trophy of his victorious grace! O blessed God! if there be any thing wanting towards constituting me a sincere Christian, discover it to me, and work it in me!'

REFERENCE: *The Life of William Wilberforce* (1838)

'Let me seize proper occasions'

'Now the God of hope fill you with all joy and peace in believing, that ye may abound in hope, through the power of the Holy Ghost.' Romans 15:13
SUGGESTED FURTHER READING: 2 Corinthians 9:6–15

I have been praying with seriousness, and considering that the promises of grace, and repentance, and a new heart, and strength, and peace, and joy in believing, are made to all that wait on God through Christ, and will be performed in spite of Satan's hindrances. Oh may I be the temple of the Holy Ghost. I have found this morning the advantages of a little religious solitude. I have prayed three quarters of an hour—for myself, my country, and friends. Let me seize proper occasions for it, and not make my Sundays days of hurry.

FOR MEDITATION: Philip Doddridge understood what it meant to set aside time daily for communing with God. So too did he understand how such time might best be employed. 'For the government of our thoughts in solitude,' he wrote, 'let us accustom ourselves, on all occasions, to exercise a due command over our thoughts. Let us take care of those entanglements of passion, or those attachments to any present interest in view, which would deprive us of our power over them. Let us set before us some profitable subject of thought; such as the perfection of the blessed God, the love of Christ, the value of time, the certainty and importance of death and judgment, and the eternity of happiness or misery which is to follow. Let us also, at such intervals, reflect on what we have observed as to the state of our own souls, with regard to the advance or decline of religion; or on the last sermon we have heard or the last portion of Scripture we have read.'

Habits of the heart, time devoted to the Lord and spiritual reflection. These are keys to a vibrant walk with God.

REFERENCE: *The Life of William Wilberforce* (1838)

'In all my various relations'

'Now the just shall live by faith.' Hebrews 10:38
SUGGESTED FURTHER READING: Philippians 3:7–14

It is the more necessary for me to live by the faith of the Son of God. Do thou then, thou blessed Saviour and Friend of sinners, hear and have mercy on me. Let thy strength be magnified in my weakness. I will now form and note in my pocket-book such resolutions for this week's regulation, as are best adapted to my present circumstances; and do thou, O God, enable me to keep them. Let me constantly view myself in all my various relations

- as one who professes to be a Christian,
- as a Member of Parliament,
- as gifted by nature and fortune, as a son, brother, paterfamilias, friend, with influence and powerful connections.

FOR MEDITATION: After his self-described 'great change', or embrace of Christianity in 1786, Wilberforce kept lists of goals he wished to attain, traits he wished to cultivate or prayer requests. In this, he was not unlike many of his contemporaries who placed a high value on what was then called self-examination, the practice of trying to track one's progress in spiritual things.

There is much we can learn from such a practice. Do we wish to become more Christ-like? to honour our Christian profession? Wilberforce was deeply influenced regarding habits of self-examination by Philip Doddridge. Doddridge himself wrote: '[As concerns] the great and important work of self-examination. Let your own conscience answer, how far you have already attained it, and how far you desire it; and let the principal topics here touched upon be fixed in your memory and in your heart, that you may be mentioning them before God in your daily addresses to the throne of grace, in order to receive from him all necessary assistance for bringing them into practice.'

REFERENCE: *The Life of William Wilberforce* (1838)

'A cold, hard, unfeeling heart'

'Make a joyful noise unto God, all ye lands.' Psalm 66:1
SUGGESTED FURTHER READING: Psalm 100:1–5

We can scarcely indeed look into any part of the sacred volume without meeting abundant proofs, that it is the religion of the affections which God particularly requires … Joy [is] enjoined on us as our bounden duty, and commended to us as our acceptable worship … A cold, hard, unfeeling heart, is represented as highly criminal.

FOR MEDITATION: No better testimony to the joy that was the constantly manifested in Wilberforce's Christian walk can be found than that offered by his nephew Sir James Stephen (the grandfather of novelist Virginia Woolf): 'His presence was as fatal to dullness as to immorality. His mirth was irresistible as the first laughter of childhood.'

Faith fostered much that was childlike in Wilberforce. When staying with the Wordsworths (Dorothy and William) in the summer of 1818, Wilberforce took a two hour walk by Rydal and Grasmere, arriving home 'a good deal tired.' Weary though he was, his delight in retracing all the haunts he had so loved in his youth was undiminished. He pointed out to his children every well-remembered beauty. At the close of one day, he wrote, 'It doubles my own enjoyment to see my dear children enjoy these scenes with me.'

When taking sheltered walks among the trees with his children, he shared recollections, anecdotes, and reflections with them—many stemming from his long service in political life. He described what he had observed of the lives of others, passages of Scripture, and favourite or well-remembered poems. The times he spent with them in this way underscored, as they saw it, the two main pillars of his faith—'the first, that God is love; the second, that God is truth.'

REFERENCE: *A Practical View of Christianity* (1797)

'More and more out of sight'

'I will delight myself in thy statutes: I will not forget thy word.'
Psalm 119:16
SUGGESTED FURTHER READING: Psalm 119:65–72

The fatal habit of considering Christian morals as distinct from Christian doctrines insensibly gained strength. Thus the peculiar doctrines of Christianity went more and more out of sight, and as might naturally have been expected, the moral system itself also began to wither and decay, being robbed of that which should have supplied it with life and nutriment.

FOR MEDITATION: First principles, for the Christian, flow from faith. Many systems of ethics exist; and Wilberforce was familiar with the ethical systems set forth by many philosophers. But his reading of Scripture taught him that without God, and faith in God, no true basis for ethics exists. All moral principles have their source in him who is the source of all righteousness.

The Scriptures abound in such declarations. Psalm 48:10 tells us: 'According to thy name, O God, so is thy praise unto the ends of the earth: thy right hand is full of righteousness.' Psalm 119:42 states: 'Thy righteousness is an everlasting righteousness, and thy law is the truth.' In 1 Corinthians 1:30 the apostle Paul writes: 'But of him are ye in Christ Jesus, who of God is made unto us wisdom, and righteousness.'

Romans 10:3 cautions us not to seek a righteousness of our own devising—that is, not to separate our system of ethics from God. Here Paul writes: 'For they being ignorant of God's righteousness, and going about to establish their own righteousness, have not submitted themselves unto the righteousness of God.'

REFERENCE: *A Practical View of Christianity* (1797)

'That humble, peaceful, confiding hope'

'If ye keep my commandments, ye shall abide in my love; even as I have kept my Father's commandments, and abide in his love.' John 15:10
SUGGESTED FURTHER READING: 1 John 2:24–29

I bless God that I feel more than of late I have done, that humble, peaceful, confiding hope in the mercy of God, reconciled in Christ Jesus, which tranquillizes the mind, and creates a desire after that blessed state, where we shall be completely delivered from the bondage of our corruptions, as well as from all our bodily pains and sicknesses, and all our mental anxieties and griefs; where the injustice, oppression, and cruelty, the wickedness, the falsehood, the selfishness, the malignity, of this bad world shall be no more; but peace, and truth, and love, and holiness, shall prevail for ever. O Lord, purify my heart, and make me meet for that blessed society.

FOR MEDITATION: Wilberforce's words above recall those of the apostle Paul in Philippians 4:

Be careful for nothing; but in every thing by prayer and supplication with thanksgiving let your requests be made known unto God. And the peace of God, which passeth all understanding, shall keep your hearts and minds through Christ Jesus. Finally, brethren, whatsoever things are true, whatsoever things are honest, whatsoever things are just, whatsoever things are pure, whatsoever things are lovely, whatsoever things are of good report; if there be any virtue, and if there be any praise, think on these things. Those things, which ye have both learned, and received, and heard, and seen in me, do: and the God of peace shall be with you (Philippians 4:6–9).

REFERENCE: *The Life of William Wilberforce* (1838)

'Privilege and hopes'

'These things have I spoken unto you, that my joy might remain in you, and that your joy might be full.' John 15:11
SUGGESTED FURTHER READING: Ephesians 2:7–18

My grand objection to the religious system still held by many who declare themselves to be orthodox Churchmen is that it tends to render Christianity so much a system of prohibitions rather than of privilege and hopes, and thus the injunction to rejoice, so strongly enforced in the New Testament, is practically neglected, and religion is made to wear a forbidding and gloomy air and not one of peace and hope and joy.

FOR MEDITATION: Wilberforce wrote that if our love for Christ is as a lamp burning brightly, we will have 'a mind acquainted with the nature and familiarized with the use of the Christian's privileges, habitually solacing itself with the hopes held out by the gospel, animated by the sense of its high relations and its glorious reversion.'

He felt that the Sabbath, or Lord's Day, was a time particularly suited to reflection upon the privileges accorded us through our Christian faith. 'It might,' he wrote, 'be deemed a privilege thus to spend the Sabbath in the more immediate presence of our Heavenly Father, in the exercises of humble admiration and grateful homage; of the benevolent and domestic, and social feelings, and of all the best affections of our nature, prompted by their true motives, conversant about their proper objects, and directed to their noblest end; all sorrows mitigated, all cares suspended, all fears repressed, every angry emotion softened, every envious or revengeful, or malignant passion expelled; and the bosom, thus quieted, purified, enlarged, ennobled, partaking almost of a measure of the heavenly happiness, and become for a while the seat of love, and joy, and confidence, and harmony.'

REFERENCE: QUOTED IN JOHN POLLOCK, *Wilberforce*, P. 46

'At chosen seasons'

'I will bless the Lord, who hath given me counsel.' Psalm 16:7
SUGGESTED FURTHER READING: Psalm 16

Thus, at chosen seasons, the Christian exercises himself; and when, from this elevated region, he descends into the plain below, and mixes in the bustle of life, he still retains the impressions of his retired hours. By these he realizes to himself the unseen world: he accustoms himself to speak and act as in the presence of 'an innumerable company of angels, and of the spirits of just men made perfect, and of God the Judge of all;' the consciousness of their approbation cheers and gladdens his soul under the scoffs and reproaches of a misjudging world, and to his delighted ear their united praises form a *harmony* which a few discordant earthly voices cannot interrupt.

FOR MEDITATION: In late August 1817, Wilberforce wrote a tender letter to his family that breathes the same spirit as his words above: 'For myself, I can truly say, that scarcely any thing has at times given me more pleasure than the consciousness of living as it were in an atmosphere of love; and heaven itself has appeared delightful in that very character of being a place, in which not only every one would love his brethren, but in which every one would be assured that his brother loved *him*, and thus that all was mutual kindness and harmony, without one discordant jarring; all sweetness without the slightest acescency [sourness].'

Many were the seasons throughout Wilberforce's life when such a consciousness of the blessings of love, peace and harmony was present to him. More often than not these seasons sprang from the devotional time he spent daily with God. Increasingly, he came to realize just how important these daily interludes of prayer and Scripture reading were. And so we find him writing in his diary: 'let me therefore endeavour to secure to myself frequent seasons of uninterrupted converse with God.'

REFERENCE: *A Practical View of Christianity* (1797)

'The day of rest'

'Remember the Sabbath day, to keep it holy.' Exodus 20:8
SUGGESTED FURTHER READING: Exodus 20:3–17

Blessed be God, who hath appointed these solemn returns of the day of rest to remind us of those most important realities, of which we grow forgetful amidst the hurry of business and the vanities of the world.

FOR MEDITATION: We are surrounded by that which is fleeting—by things that clamour for our attention, yet are not truly the first things of our life as Christians. Verses from the Old Testament Book of Isaiah put this starkly: 'I, even I, am he that comforteth you: who art thou, that thou shouldest be afraid of a man that shall die, and of the son of man which shall be made as grass; and forgettest the LORD thy maker, that hath stretched forth the heavens, and laid the foundations of the earth' (Isaiah 51:12–13).

There are times when we need to be still and know that the Lord is God (Psalm 46:10). Sundays are such days. But we also need to take time each day, whether in the morning or evening, to set the business of the day aside and enter the presence of him who has given us the day.

All that we seek to do in life is best informed or best guided by him who is the Author of life. In a world of dizzy change and great busyness, may we be careful to seek out our daily and weekly Sabbaths. They are gifts to us from a loving God.

REFERENCE: *The Life of William Wilberforce* (1838)

'Write thy law in my heart'

'Bless the LORD, *O my soul, and forget not all his benefits.' Psalm 103:2*
SUGGESTED FURTHER READING: Psalm 116:7–14

Oh blessed be God who hath appointed the Sabbath, and interposes these seasons of serious recollection. May they be effectual to their purpose; may my errors be corrected, my desires sanctified, and my whole soul quickened and animated in the Christian course. I trust God will enable me to turn to him in righteousness. Write, I beseech thee, thy law in my heart, that I may not sin against thee.

FOR MEDITATION: Wilberforce cherished Psalm 119. He committed it to memory, and used to recite it to himself while walking home from the House of Commons through Hyde Park to his home, Gore House—or, as it was sometimes called, Kensington Gore. Early on in this great psalm we read:

With my whole heart have I sought thee
O let me not wander from thy commandments.
Thy word have I hid in mine heart,
that I might not sin against thee.
Blessed art thou, O Lord:
teach me thy statutes.

The Sabbath affords seasons of recollection, seasons of renewal, seasons of rest. We have great need of them. And God, knowing our need, has given them to us. May we seek them and him aright.

REFERENCE: *The Life of William Wilberforce* (1838)

'To live a life of faith'

'But without faith it is impossible to please him: for he that cometh to God must believe that he is, and that he is a rewarder of them that diligently seek him.' Hebrews 11:6

SUGGESTED FURTHER READING: 1 Peter 1:13–21

Let me therefore make a spirited effort, not trusting in myself, but in the strength of the Lord God. Let me labour to live a life of faith, and prayer, and humility, and self-denial, and heavenly-mindedness, and sobriety, and diligence. Oh that the blessed day may come, when in the words of St Paul, I may assert of myself that my conversation is in heaven; that the life I now lead in the flesh, I live by faith in the Son of God, who loved me and gave himself for me!

FOR MEDITATION: In 1868, the hymn writer Thomas Pollock penned verses that reveal a great desire, like Wilberforce's above, to live a life of faith:

Faithful Shepherd, feed me	Hold me fast, and guide me
In the pastures green;	In the narrow way;
Faithful Shepherd, lead me	So, with thee beside me,
Where thy steps are seen.	I shall never stray.
Daily bring me nearer	Hallow every pleasure,
To the heav'nly shore;	Every gift and pain;
Make my faith grow clearer,	Be thyself my treasure,
May I love thee more.	Though none else I gain.

REFERENCE: *The Life of William Wilberforce* (1838)

'I went home with it ringing in my ears'

'Of whom the world was not worthy: they wandered in deserts, and in mountains, and in dens and caves of the earth.' Hebrews 11:38
SUGGESTED FURTHER READING: Psalm 68:1–11

In 1819, Wilberforce spoke of the blessings that he derived from attending 'Christian assemblies, in hearing of the general diffusion of the word of God, and of the labours, and sufferings, and blessed be God the triumphs also, of those zealous missionaries who are devoting their lives in distant lands to the service of their Divine Master.'

'I shall never forget,' said a friend who thus heard him, 'the effect of a short speech of his upon my own mind. He was alluding to some natural difficulties which had impeded the success of missions, which ought not to discourage us; for nature seemed often, as well as man, to fight against St Paul. He was not merely "scourged with rods," but "thrice he suffered shipwreck." The tone, the manner, the voice in which he brought out this simple thought was so overpowering, that I went home with it ringing in my ears for days.'

FOR MEDITATION: The life, ministry and writings of the apostle Paul were a source of great inspiration for Wilberforce. He memorized the Pauline epistles, and remarked time and again of how Paul's writings spoke powerfully to him and guided him in the course of his Christian life.

Missionaries follow in the steps of Paul. And so they ought to be the subject of our continuing prayers, and people for whom we provide support from the resources God has given us. Not everyone can be a missionary, but we can all be missions-minded.

REFERENCE: *The Life of William Wilberforce* (1838)

'The poor publican's plea'

'And the publican, standing afar off, would not lift up so much as his eyes unto heaven, but smote upon his breast, saying, God be merciful to me a sinner.' Luke 18:13
SUGGESTED FURTHER READING: Psalm 119:89–96

The Quaker reformer Joseph John Gurney, a friend of many years, recalled the last conversation he had with Wilberforce—just a few weeks before his death. 'How admirable are the harmony and variety of St Paul's smaller Epistles!' he told Gurney. 'You might well have given an argument upon it in your little work on evidence [*Essays on the Evidences, Doctrines and Practical Operations of Christianity*]. The Epistle to the Galatians contains a noble exhibition of doctrine. That to the Colossians is a union of doctrine and precept, showing their mutual connection and dependence; that to the Ephesians, is seraphic; that to the Philippians, is all love.'

Gurney long remembered Wilberforce's closing words. '"With regard to myself," he added, "I have nothing whatsoever to urge, but the poor publican's plea, 'God be merciful to me a sinner.'"' These words were expressed with peculiar feeling and emphasis, and have since called to my remembrance his own definition of the word mercy—"kindness to those that deserve punishment."'

FOR MEDITATION: Until we surrender to Christ, we all have prodigal hearts. And so for all of us the parable of the Prodigal Son (Luke 15:11–32) is true. Our wayward hearts are as of the son who left his father for a far-off country. Our heavenly Father is as the father in the story—longing for our lost hearts to be found. 'And when [the son] came to himself, he said...I will arise and go to my father...and will say unto him, Father, I have sinned...' May those of us who have submitted to Christ always remember what we once were.

REFERENCE: *The Life of William Wilberforce* (1838)

'Some breach of truth or of Christian charity'

'But the wisdom that is from above is first pure, then peaceable, gentle, and easy to be intreated, full of mercy and good fruits, without partiality, and without hypocrisy.' James 3:17
SUGGESTED FURTHER READING: Psalm 119:33–48

When the Christian's character is mistaken or his conduct misconstrued, he will not wrap himself up in a mysterious sullenness, but will be ready, where he thinks any one will be ready to listen to him with patience and candour, to clear up what has been dubious, to explain what has been imperfectly known, and 'speaking the truth in love,' to correct, if it may be, the erroneous impressions that have been conceived of him. He may sometimes feel it his duty publicly to vindicate his character from unjust reproach, and to repel false charges of his enemies; but he will carefully watch against being led away by pride, or being betrayed into some breach of truth or of Christian charity.

FOR MEDITATION: 'I remember, owing to some occurrence,' wrote the nineteenth-century preacher William Jay, 'Mr Wilberforce gave me an admonition never to notice *any* thing concerning one's-self in the public prints. "If you do," said he, "you must notice *every* thing; or what passes unnoticed will pass for truth which cannot be refuted," adding, "our character and conduct must be both our defenders and advocates."

'He then mentioned the following imputation concerning himself: "Some time ago, in Benjamin Flower's *Cambridge Journal,* it was said, 'Behold an instance of the Pharisaism of St Wilberforce! He was lately seen walking up and down in the Bath Pump Room, reading his prayers, like his predecessors of old, who prayed in the corners of the streets, to be seen of men.'"

'Wilberforce went on to say: "As there is generally some slight circumstance which perverseness turns into a charge or reproach, I began to reflect; and I soon found the occasion of the calumny; and it was this:—I was walking in the Pump Room in conversation with General ——; a passage was quoted from Horace, the accuracy of which was questioned; and, as I had a [volume of] Horace in my pocket, I sought and found, and read the words. This was the plain *bit of wire* which factious malignity sharpened into a pin to pierce my reputation."'

REFERENCE: *A Practical View of Christianity* (1797)

'The best things this world has to offer'

'Let not mercy and truth forsake thee: bind them about thy neck; write them upon the table of thine heart. So shalt thou find favour and good understanding in the sight of God and man.' Proverbs 3:3–4
SUGGESTED FURTHER READING: Proverbs 3:1–6

Worldly favour and distinction are amongst the best things this world has to offer; but the Christian knows it is the very condition of his calling, *not* to have his portion here; and as in the case of any other earthly enjoyments, so in that also of worldly honour, he dreads, lest his supreme affections being thereby gratified, it should be hereafter said to him (as of the rich man of the parable), 'Remember that thou in thy lifetime receivedst thy good things and likewise Lazarus evil things: but now he is comforted, and thou art tormented' (Luke 16:25).

FOR MEDITATION: Psalm 16 reminds of where and in whom we have our portion:

The Lord is the portion of mine inheritance and of my cup: thou maintainest my lot. The lines are fallen unto me in pleasant places; yea, I have a goodly heritage. I will bless the Lord, who hath given me counsel: my reins also instruct me in the night seasons. I have set the Lord always before me: because he is at my right hand, I shall not be moved. Therefore my heart is glad, and my glory rejoiceth: my flesh also shall rest in hope. Thou wilt shew me the path of life: in thy presence is fullness of joy; at thy right hand there are pleasures for evermore (Psalm 16:5–9, 11).

REFERENCE: *A Practical View of Christianity* (1797)

'Proud piety and ostentatious charity'

'Be clothed with humility: for God resisteth the proud, and giveth grace to the humble.' 1 Peter 5:5
SUGGESTED FURTHER READING: Proverbs 15:23–33

The Christian too is well aware that the excessive desire of human approbation is a passion of so subtle a nature, that there is nothing into which it cannot penetrate; and from much experience, learning to discover it where it would lurk unseen, and to detect it under its most specious disguises, he finds, that elsewhere disallowed and excluded, it is apt to insinuate itself into his very religion, where it especially delights to dwell, and obstinately maintains its residence. Proud piety and ostentatious charity, and all the more open effects it there produces, have been often condemned, and we may discover the tendencies to them in ourselves, without difficulty.

FOR MEDITATION: Pride is one of the most severely censured things in all of Scripture. 'Pride goeth before destruction,' we read in Proverbs 16:18, 'and an haughty spirit before a fall.' Pride is indeed subtle, subtle as the serpent who beguiled Eve into sin and hence Adam. Pride is at the root of so many hurtful things, cutting remarks, hatred and derision. 1 Peter 5:5 puts the matter starkly: 'God resisteth the proud.'

But for those who are clothed with humility or who seek to be, we have this blest assurance: God 'giveth grace to the humble.' May we be as those who are grace-filled, because we are those who earnestly seek after humility.

REFERENCE: *A Practical View of Christianity* (1797)

'Small as well as great occasions'

'In whom we have boldness and access with confidence by the faith of him.' Ephesians 3:12
SUGGESTED FURTHER READING: Psalm 20:1–9

The Christian watches himself also on small as well as on great occasions: the latter indeed, in the case of many persons, can hardly ever be expected to occur, whereas the former are continually presenting themselves. Thus, whilst on the one hand they may be rendered highly useful in forming and strengthening a just habit of mind in the particular in question, so, on the other, they are the means most at hand for enabling us to discover our own real character.

Let not this be lightly passed over. If anyone finds himself shrinking from disrepute or disesteem in little instances, but apt to solace himself with the persuasion that his spirits being fully called forth to the encounter, he could boldly stand the brunt of sharper trials; let him be slow to give entertainment to so beguiling a suggestion; and let him not forget that these little instances, where no credit is to be got, and the vainest can find small room for self-complacency, furnish perhaps the truest test whether we are ashamed of the Gospel of Christ, and are willing, on principles really pure, to bear reproach for the name of Jesus.

FOR MEDITATION: In the parable of the talents in Luke 19, the servant receives praise and reward from his lord because he had 'been faithful in a very little'. We are no different. God's blessing rests upon those who are faithful in the small things. Such faithfulness attests the growth of Christian character within us.

REFERENCE: *A Practical View of Christianity* (1797)

'Cause for continual watchfulness'

'Thy word have I hid in mine heart, that I might not sin against thee.'
Psalm 119:11
SUGGESTED FURTHER READING: Psalm 119:65–72

Eloquence in its right sense is of great effect in every free community; and as it has pleased God to endow me with a certain natural turn for public speaking, and by his providence to place me in a situation in which there is room for the use of that talent, it seems to be my duty to improve that natural faculty, and cultivate that true eloquence which alone is suitable to the character of a follower of the Saviour, who was full of love, truth, and lowliness.

Besides, the very basis of eloquence, in the sense in which I use it, is wisdom and knowledge, a thorough acquaintance with one's subject, the sure possession of it, and power of promptly calling up and using it. But let me ever remember here what cause there is for continual watchfulness and godly jealousy, lest the pursuit should lead to an inordinate love of worldly estimation to vanity and pride; and if to them in its consequence to the malignant passions.

FOR MEDITATION: It has been said that those who are most eloquent are so when they have something to speak of which has captured their heart. Christians are custodians or stewards of the greatest story ever told. Ours is the high privilege of sharing what we have come to know of that story with others. For some of us, eloquence may well be through public speaking. Others have the kind of eloquence that springs from a life lived well and faithfully in service to God and their fellow-citizens. But whatever capacity for eloquence we possess, may we strive to cultivate it as we ought to do—as good stewards of our Lord.

REFERENCE: *The Life of William Wilberforce* (1838)

'Activity and fidelity'

'A faithful man shall abound with blessings.' Proverbs 28:20
SUGGESTED FURTHER READING: Titus 2:6–15

Whatever dreams of ambition I may have indulged, it now seems clear that my part is to give the example of an independent Member of Parliament, and a man of religion, discharging with activity and fidelity the duties of his trust, and not seeking to render his parliamentary station a ladder by which to rise to a higher eminence. What has passed of late years (the number of country gentlemen made peers, etc.), renders it particularly necessary to give this lesson; and from whom can it be required, if not from him who professes to have set his affections on things above, and to consider himself as a stranger and a pilgrim on the earth? If it should ever please God to call me to any situation of power, or to any higher eminence, which I do not expect, he would furnish me with the talents necessary for the discharge of its duties. But as this is highly improbable, I should do wrong to sacrifice an opportunity of usefulness which is within my reach, in order to qualify myself for a station I am not likely ever to fill.

FOR MEDITATION: In the summer of 1802, Wilberforce had reason to think he might be appointed to high political office under Prime Minister Henry Addington (1801–04). He was not ultimately appointed, but that he prayerfully besought the Lord on this occasion attested his heart's desire to be a good steward.

That, in the end, is what we should always strive to be—faithful wherever the Lord has called us. The circumstances of our lives are subject to change, but if we have learned faithfulness we will do well whatever changes are in store.

REFERENCE: *The Life of William Wilberforce* (1838)

'A sense of my great sinfulness'

'A broken and a contrite heart, O God, thou wilt not despise.' Psalm 51:17
SUGGESTED FURTHER READING: Psalm 51:1–19

'I had received into my understanding the great truths of the gospel, and believed that its offers were free and universal; and that God had promised to give his Holy Spirit to them that asked for it. At length such thoughts as these completely occupied my mind, and I began to pray earnestly.' Thus Mr Wilberforce returned home from the continent—another man in his inner being.

Upon the 10th November 1785 he reached Wimbledon, and as Parliament did not meet until the following February, he was much alone and had leisure to commune with himself. The more he reflected, the deeper became his new impressions. 'It was not so much,' he said, 'the fear of punishment by which I was affected, as a sense of my great sinfulness in having so long neglected the unspeakable mercies of my God and Saviour; and such was the effect which this thought produced, that for months I was in a state of the deepest depression from strong convictions of my guilt. Indeed nothing which I have ever read in the accounts of others, exceeded what I then felt.'

Whilst this struggle was at its height, he commenced a private journal, with the view of making himself 'humble, and watchful.' The sky was now brightening over him into clearer sunshine. 'By degrees,' he said in the calm retrospect of a peaceful age, 'the promises and offers of the gospel produced in me something of a settled peace of conscience. I devoted myself for whatever might be the term of my future life, to the service of my God and Saviour, and with many infirmities and deficiencies, through his help, I continue until this day.'

FOR MEDITATION: Humility and watchfulness ought to be twin pillars of our Christian life. They are kindred traits of the Christian character. May they attend us on our journey of faith.

REFERENCE: *The Life of William Wilberforce* (1838)

'The book which he studied most carefully'

'And he answering said, Thou shalt love the Lord thy God with all thy heart, and with all thy soul, and with all thy strength, and with all thy mind.' Luke 10:27
SUGGESTED FURTHER READING: Psalm 119:17–24

The following week Mr Wilberforce arrived at Wilford, the seat of his cousin Samuel Smith; he remained almost two months, diligently employing the quiet time afforded him by its retirement. A keen remembrance of wasted time and a sense of his deficiency in the power of steady application, led him to set about educating himself. Various and accurate were now his studies, but the book which he studied most carefully, and by which perhaps above all others his mental faculties were perfected, was the Holy Scripture. This was his chief occupation at Wilford. It was now his daily care to instruct his understanding and discipline his heart.

His diary entries reflect this resolve. 'O God! do thou enable me to live more to thee, to look to Jesus with a single eye, and by degrees to have the renewed nature implanted in me, and the heart of stone removed.'

'On this day,' he wrote on 24th August, 'I complete my twenty-seventh year. What reason have I for humiliation and gratitude! May God, for Christ's sake, increase my desire to acquire the Christian temper and live the Christian life, and enable me to carry this desire into execution.'

A few days later, on September 3rd, he added, 'I am just returned from receiving the sacrament. I was enabled to be earnest in prayer, and to be contrite and humble under a sense of my unworthiness, and of the infinite mercy of God in Christ. I hope that I desire from my heart to lead henceforth a life more worthy of the Christian profession. May it be my meat and drink to do the will of God, my Father. May he daily renew me by his Holy Spirit, and may I walk before him in a frame made up of fear, and gratitude, and humble trust, and assurance of his fatherly kindness and constant concern for me.'

FOR MEDITATION: 2 Timothy 2:15 tells us of the diligence we ought to bring to bear on our study of the Scriptures: 'Study to shew thyself approved unto God, a workman that needeth not to be ashamed, rightly dividing the word of truth.'

REFERENCE: *The Life of William Wilberforce* (1838)

'He has called me from darkness to light'

'Giving thanks unto the Father, which hath made us meet to be partakers of the inheritance of the saints in light: who hath delivered us from the power of darkness, and hath translated us into the kingdom of his dear Son.' Colossians 1:12–13
SUGGESTED FURTHER READING: Ephesians 1:3–12

I do not think I have a sufficiently strong conviction of sin; yet I see plainly that I am an ungrateful, stupid, guilty creature. I believe that Christ died that all such, who would throw themselves on him, renouncing every claim of their own and relying on his assurance of free pardon, might be reconciled to God, and receive the free gift of his Holy Spirit to renew them after the image of God in righteousness and true holiness; and I hope in time to find such a change wrought by degrees in myself, as may evidence to me that he has called me from darkness to light, and from the power of Satan unto God.

FOR MEDITATION: The apostle Paul writes in Ephesians 4: 'If so be that ye have heard him, and have been taught by him, as the truth is in Jesus: that ye put off concerning the former conversation the old man, which is corrupt according to the deceitful lusts; and be renewed in the spirit of your mind; and that ye put on the new man, which after God is created in righteousness and true holiness' (Ephesians 4:21–24).

As Wilberforce writes above, God is the One who will help us to put on the new person which after God is created in righteousness and true holiness. Earlier in Ephesians, we are given the assurance that God 'is able to do exceeding abundantly above all that we ask or think, according to the power that worketh in us' (Ephesians 3:20).

REFERENCE: *The Life of William Wilberforce* (1838)

'Renew my heart'

'But the hour cometh, and now is, when the true worshippers shall worship the Father in spirit and in truth: for the Father seeketh such to worship him.' John 4:23
SUGGESTED FURTHER READING: Joshua 24:14–25

Do thou, O God, renew my heart—fill me with that love of thee which extinguishes all other affections, and enable me to give thee my heart, and to serve thee in spirit and in truth.

FOR MEDITATION: Such a brief prayer, and yet it says so much. In God we live and move and have our being. All that we are and ever hope to be rests in him. Sometimes it seems as though there is so very little that we can give him, yet the one thing he truly desires is precisely the one thing we can give him. Long ago, the poet Christina Rossetti wrote of this in her timeless Christmas hymn *In the Bleak Midwinter*:

What can I give him, poor as I am?
If I were a shepherd, I would bring a lamb;
If I were a Wise Man, I would do my part;
Yet what I can I give him: give my heart.

In response to the giving of our hearts to the Lord, Psalm 51:17 tells us: 'a contrite heart, O God, thou wilt not despise.' May Wilberforce's prayer be ours: 'fill me with that love of thee which extinguishes all other affections, and enable me to give thee my heart.'

REFERENCE: *The Life of William Wilberforce* (1838)

'When we desire to love God with all our hearts'

'I can do all things through Christ which strengtheneth me.' Philippians 4:13
SUGGESTED FURTHER READING: Psalm 27:1–14

I pray God to enable me to serve him in newness of life. It is when we desire to love God with all our hearts, and in all things to devote ourselves to his service, that we find our continual need of his help, and such incessant proofs of our own weakness, that we are kept watchful and sober, and may hope by degrees to be renewed in the spirit of our minds. Oh may I be thus changed from darkness to light! Solitude and quiet are favourable to reflection and to sober-mindedness; let me therefore endeavour to secure to myself frequent seasons of uninterrupted converse with God.

FOR MEDITATION: If it is our continual prayer that God will fill us with his love, that he will fill us with himself, we will be able to do that which the Lord has called us to do. Those who are filled with love—or charity, as the King James Bible has it—are marked by beautiful traits. In 1 Corinthians 13 we read:

Charity suffereth long, and is kind; charity envieth not; charity vaunteth not itself, is not puffed up, doth not behave itself unseemly, seeketh not her own, is not easily provoked, thinketh no evil; rejoiceth not in iniquity, but rejoiceth in the truth; beareth all things, believeth all things, hopeth all things, endureth all things (1 Corinthians 13:4–7).

May we desire to love God with all our hearts, and may our hearts be filled with his love.

REFERENCE: *The Life of William Wilberforce* (1838)

'Take now and then a solitary walk'

'We took sweet counsel together, and walked unto the house of God in company.' Psalm 55:14
SUGGESTED FURTHER READING: Psalm 86:1–17

Look up to God with feelings of filial confidence and love, and to Christ as to an advocate and a friend. The more you do this the better. Use yourself, my dearest Samuel, to take now and then a solitary walk, and in it to indulge in these spiritual meditations. The disposition to do this will gradually become a habit, and a habit of unspeakable value. I have long considered it as a great misfortune, or rather, I should say, as having been very injurious to your brother William, that he never courted solitude in his walks, or indeed at any time. Some people are too much inclined to it, I grant; they often thereby lose the inestimable benefit which results from having a friend to whom we open our hearts, one of the most valuable of all possessions both for this world and the next. When I was led into speaking of occasional intervals of solitude—

when Isaac, like the solitary saint,
Walks forth to meditate at eventide,[7]

—you remember the passage, I doubt not, I was mentioning that holy, peaceful, childlike trust in the fatherly love of our God and Saviour which gradually diffuses itself through the soul and takes possession of it, when we are habitually striving to walk by faith under the influence of the Holy Spirit.

FOR MEDITATION: The words of John Sammis capture so much of what Wilberforce was writing of above:

When we walk with the Lord in the light of his Word,
What a glory he sheds on our way!
While we do his good will, he abides with us still,
And with all who will trust and obey.

REFERENCE: *Private Papers of William Wilberforce* (1897)

'Those who love and serve God'

'When the people are gathered together, and the kingdoms, to serve the LORD.' *Psalm 102:22*
SUGGESTED FURTHER READING: Psalm 145:1–21

No man has perhaps more cause for gratitude to God than myself. But of all the various instances of his goodness, the greatest of all, excepting only his Heavenly Grace, is the many kind friends with whom a gracious Providence has blessed me. Oh remember, my dearest boy, to form friendships with those only who love and serve God, and when once you have formed them, then preserve them as the most valuable of all possessions.

FOR MEDITATION: Friends are those who come alongside us when we take walks. They are those from whom letters are most welcome. They delight to show kindnesses, small and great, to those for whom they have regard.

Friends have that capacity to listen when we most need it, and the capacity for sharing a word in season when we most require it. They stay the course with us when the storms of life break over us. They take almost as much joy as we do in the high moments of life, when something long desired is achieved, such as a marriage or birth of a child. They share in countless common moments of life, which are no less valued for being commonplace—one thinks of meals that add season and savour to life.

When we are old, friends are those with whom we look back upon the passage of years, and find that at so many important times they were they with us. It is then that they, and we, have cause to offer thanks to God for the gift of friends and friendship.

REFERENCE: *Private Papers of William Wilberforce* (1897)

'To be a truly religious man'

'That ye might walk worthy of the Lord unto all pleasing, being fruitful in every good work, and increasing in the knowledge of God.' Colossians 1:10
SUGGESTED FURTHER READING: Hebrews 13:10–17

My dear Samuel, the best preparation for being a good politician, as well as a superior man in every other line, is to be a truly religious man. For this includes in it all those qualities which fit men to pass through life with benefit to others and with reputation to ourselves. Whatever is to be the effect produced by the subordinate machinery, the mainspring must be the desire to please God, which, in a Christian, implies faith in Christ and a grateful sense of the mercies of God through a Redeemer, and an aspiration after increasing holiness of heart and life.

FOR MEDITATION: In Psalm 5:12 we read: 'For thou, LORD, wilt bless the righteous; with favour wilt thou compass him as with a shield.' The Book of Proverbs tells us: 'Righteousness exalteth a nation: but sin is a reproach to any people' (Proverbs 14:34).

The eighteenth-century bishop, George Berkeley penned a phrase in keeping with these Scriptures. 'To be a good patriot,' he wrote, 'a man must consider his countrymen as God's creatures, and himself as accountable for his acting towards them.' Wilberforce himself summed up the importance of individual righteousness and integrity to a nation when he quoted a well-known phrase in his book *A Practical View of Christianity.* 'The best man,' he wrote, 'is the truest patriot.'

REFERENCE: *Private Papers of William Wilberforce* (1897)

'The one thing needful'

'The fear of the LORD *is the beginning of wisdom: and the knowledge of the holy is understanding.' Proverbs 9:10*
'But one thing is needful: and Mary hath chosen that good part, which shall not be taken away from her.' Luke 10:42
SUGGESTED FURTHER READING: Proverbs 15:20–24

Above all remember *the one thing needful*. I had far rather that you should be a true Christian than a learned man, but I wish you to become the latter through the influence of the former.

FOR MEDITATION: Wilberforce's words above recall the story of Solomon in 1 Kings 3. It is there that we read of how God came to Solomon in a dream, saying: 'Ask what I shall give thee. And Solomon said, Thou hast shewed unto thy servant David my father great mercy, according as he walked before thee in truth, and in righteousness, and in uprightness of heart with thee; and thou hast kept for him this great kindness, that thou hast given him a son to sit on his throne, as it is this day. And now, O LORD my God, thou hast made thy servant king instead of David my father: and I am but a little child: I know not how to go out or come in. And thy servant is in the midst of thy people which thou hast chosen, a great people, that cannot be numbered nor counted for multitude. Give therefore thy servant an understanding heart to judge thy people, that I may discern between good and bad: for who is able to judge this thy so great a people?

'And the speech pleased the Lord, that Solomon had asked this thing. And God said unto him, Because thou hast asked this thing, and hast not asked for thyself long life; neither hast asked riches for thyself, nor hast asked the life of thine enemies; but hast asked for thyself understanding to discern judgment; behold, I have done according to thy words: lo, I have given thee a wise and an understanding heart' (1 Kings 3:5–12).

Now not one of us will be asked to rule a kingdom, as Solomon was. But we can, like him, ask of the Lord the one thing needful.

REFERENCE: *Private Papers of William Wilberforce* (1897)

'Almighty prayer'

'And if we know that he hear us, whatsoever we ask, we know that we have the petitions that we desired of him.' 1 John 5:15
SUGGESTED FURTHER READING: Psalm 20:1–9

All may be done through prayer—almighty prayer, I am ready to say; and why not? for that it is almighty is only through the gracious ordination of the God of love and truth. Oh then, pray, pray, pray, my dearest boy. But then remember to estimate your state on self-examination not by your prayers, but by what you find to be the effects of them on your character, tempers, and life.

FOR MEDITATION: Philip Doddridge, whose writings and Christian walk Wilberforce so admired, wrote this concerning prayer and ardently seeking after God:

I beseech you, reader, whoever you are, that you would now look seriously into your own heart, and ask it this one plain question; Am I truly religious? Is the love of God the governing principle of my life? Do I walk under the sense of his presence? *Do I converse with him from day to day, in the exercise of prayer and praise?* And am I, on the whole, making his service my business and my delight, regarding him as my master and my father?

Prayer was a subject close to the heart of Charles Spurgeon. He, like Wilberforce, understood how prayer should inform our character, tempers, and life. 'Sometimes a fog,' Spurgeon wrote, 'will settle over a vessel's deck and yet leave the topmast clear. Then a sailor goes up aloft and gets a lookout which the helmsman on deck cannot get. So prayer sends the soul aloft, lifts it above the clouds in which our selfishness and egotism befog us and gives us a chance to see which way to steer.'

REFERENCE: *Private Papers of William Wilberforce* (1897)

'The habit of living in Christ'

'Recompense to no man evil for evil. Provide things honest in the sight of all men.' Romans 12:17
SUGGESTED FURTHER READING: Romans 12:9–18

The second view is that which most belongs to our present inquiry—that, I mean, of the society in which it may appear necessary to take a share on grounds of conformity (where there is nothing wrong) to the ordinary customs of life, and even on the principle of 'providing things honest in the sight of all men' and not suffering your good to be evil spoken of.

Now in considering this question, I am persuaded I need not begin in my dear Samuel's instance with arguing for, but may assume the principle that there are no indifferent actions properly speaking, I should rather say none with which religion has nothing to do. This however is the commonly received doctrine of those who consider themselves as very good Christians. Just as in law it is an axiom,

De minimis non curat lex.
The law does not care about trivial things

A true Christian holds, in obedience to the injunction, 'Whatever you do in word or deed' that the desire to please his God and Saviour must be universal. It is thus that the habit of living in Christ, and to Christ is to be formed. And the difference between real and nominal Christians is more manifest on small occasions than on greater. In the latter all who do not disclaim the authority of Christ's commands must obey them, but in the former only they will apply them who do make religion their grand business, and pleasing their God and Saviour, and pleasing, instead of grieving the Spirit, their continual and habitual aim.

FOR MEDITATION: Ephesians 2:10 tells us: 'For we are his workmanship, created in Christ Jesus unto good works, which God hath before ordained that we should walk in them.'

REFERENCE: *Private Papers of William Wilberforce* (1897)

'The obligation under which they lie'

'But whoso hath this world's good, and seeth his brother have need, and shutteth up his bowels of compassion from him, how dwelleth the love of God in him?' 1 John 3:17

SUGGESTED FURTHER READING: Acts 2:41–47

When we read the *strong* passage in the 15th of Deuteronomy, and still more when we remember our Saviour's language in the 25th of St Matthew, we shall see reason to be astonished that the *generality* of those who do fear God, and mean in the main to please him, can give away so small a proportion of their fortunes, and so little appear sensible of the obligation under which they lie to economize as much as they can for the purpose of having the funds for giving away within their power.

What pleasure will a true Christian sometimes feel in sparing himself some article which he would be glad to possess, and putting the price instead into his charity purse, looking up to his Saviour and in heart offering it up to his use. And really, when I consider it merely in the view of the misery that may be alleviated, and the tears that may be wiped away by a very little money judiciously employed, I grow ashamed of myself for not practising more self-denial that I may apply my savings to such a purpose.

FOR MEDITATION: James 2:15–17 provides a bracing challenge for us to be continually thinking about how we can help those in need: 'If a brother or sister be naked, and destitute of daily food, and one of you say unto them, Depart in peace, be ye warmed and filled; notwithstanding ye give them not those things which are needful to the body; what doth it profit? Even so faith, if it hath not works, is dead.'

REFERENCE: *Private Papers of William Wilberforce* (1897)

'Cultivating spirituality of mind'

'Look thou upon me, and be merciful unto me, as thou usest to do unto those that love thy name.' Psalm 119:32
SUGGESTED FURTHER READING: Proverbs 18:10–15

Oh, my very dear Samuel, be not satisfied with the name of Christian. But strive to be a Christian 'in life and in power and in the Holy Ghost.' I think a solitary walk or ride now and then would afford an excellent opportunity for cultivating *spirituality of mind*, the grand characteristic of the thriving Christian.

FOR MEDITATION: 'And be not conformed to this world,' we read in Romans 12:2, 'but be ye transformed by the renewing of your mind, that ye may prove what is that good, and acceptable, and perfect, will of God.' 1 John 3:18 is a kindred verse: 'My little children, let us not love in word, neither in tongue; but in deed and in truth.'

This is where prayer and the reading of God's word are crucial, for in no other ways can we cultivate spirituality in our lives as believers. All of us must take time alone with God so that we may better walk with God.

Philip Doddridge had this to say of focusing our best energies upon our walk with God: 'Examine, then, I entreat you, the temper of your heart with regard to the blessed God. Do you find there a reverential fear, and a supreme love and veneration for his incomparable excellencies, a desire after him as the highest good, and a cordial gratitude towards him as your supreme benefactor? Can you trust his care? Can you credit his testimony? Do you desire to pay an unreserved obedience to all that he commands, and an humble submission to all the disposals of his providence? Do you design his glory as your noblest end, and make it the great business of your life to approve yourself to him? Is it your governing care to imitate him, and to "serve him in spirit and in truth?" (John 4:24).'

REFERENCE: *Private Papers of William Wilberforce* (1897)

'He delighteth in mercy'

'All the paths of the Lord are mercy and truth unto such as keep his covenant and his testimonies.' Psalm 25:10
SUGGESTED FURTHER READING: Psalm 25:1–22

What a comfort it is to know that our Heavenly Father is ever ready to receive all who call upon him. He delighteth in mercy, and ever remember that as you have heard me say, mercy is kindness to the guilty, to those who deserve punishment. What a delightful consideration it is that our Saviour loves his people better than we love each other, than an earthly parent loves his child.

FOR MEDITATION: In 1875, the hymn writer Samuel Francis wrote of the love of Jesus:

O the deep, deep love of Jesus, vast, unmeasured, boundless, free!
Rolling as a mighty ocean in its fullness over me!
Underneath me, all around me, is the current of thy love
Leading onward, leading homeward to thy glorious rest above!

O the deep, deep love of Jesus, spread his praise from shore to shore!
How he loveth, ever loveth, changeth never, nevermore!
How he watches o'er his loved ones, died to call them all his own;
How for them he intercedeth, watcheth o'er them from the throne!

O the deep, deep love of Jesus, love of every love the best!
'Tis an ocean full of blessing, 'tis a haven giving rest!
O the deep, deep love of Jesus, 'tis a heaven of heavens to me;
And it lifts me up to glory, for it lifts me up to thee!

REFERENCE: *Private Papers of William Wilberforce* (1897)

'Associating with such good young men'

'Also Jonathan, David's uncle was a counsellor, a wise man'
1 Chronicles 27:32
SUGGESTED FURTHER READING: Proverbs 1:1–9

I have been for some days thinking of writing to you, in consequence of my having heard that your friend Ryder and Sir George Prevost were reading classics with Mr Keble. Could you not have been allowed to make it a triumvirate? Much as I value classical scholarship, I prize still more highly the superior benefit to be derived from associating with such good young men as I trust the two gentlemen are whose names I have mentioned, and I have the satisfaction of knowing that you have the privilege of calling them your friends.

FOR MEDITATION: The 'Mr Keble' Wilberforce writes of above was John Keble, the author of many treasured hymns. Keble's hymn *New Every Morning is the Love* speaks of the cordials of Christian friendship:

New every morning is the love
Our wakening and uprising prove;
Through sleep and darkness safely brought,
Restored to life and power and thought.

New mercies, each returning day,
Hover around us while we pray;
New perils past, new sins forgiven,
New thoughts of God, new hopes of heaven.

Old friends, old scenes, will lovelier be,
As more of heaven in each we see;
Some softening gleam of love and prayer
Shall dawn on every cross and care.

REFERENCE: *Private Papers of William Wilberforce* (1897)

'A peculiar people'

'And whatsoever ye do in word or deed, do all in the name of the Lord Jesus, giving thanks to God and the Father by him.' Colossians 3:17
SUGGESTED FURTHER READING: 1 Peter 2:6–10

I will remind you of an idea which I threw out on the day preceding your departure—that I feared I had scarcely enough endeavoured to impress on my children the idea that they must as Christians be a peculiar people. I am persuaded that you cannot misunderstand me to mean that I wish you to affect singularity in indifferent matters. The very contrary is our duty. But from that very circumstance of its being right that we should be like the rest of the world in exterior, manners, etc., results an augmentation of the danger of our not maintaining that diversity, nay, that contrast, which the eye of God ought to see in us to the worldly way of thinking and feeling on all the various occasions of life, and in relation to its various interests.

The man of the world considers religion as having nothing to do with 99–100ths of the affairs of life, considering it as a medicine and not as his food, least of all as his refreshment and cordial. He naturally takes no more of it than his health requires. How opposite this to the apostle's admonition, 'Whatever ye do in word or deed, do all in the name of the Lord Jesus, giving thanks to God the Father through him.' This is being spiritually-minded, and being so is truly declared to be life and peace.

FOR MEDITATION: 'To be spiritually minded is life and peace.' Here, Wilberforce is quoting Romans 8:6. The precepts of Scripture were ever-present to his mind, because he took time and care to memorize portions of the word of God. If we would be a people of the book, as the phrase has it, we should take care to ensure that its precepts have found an abiding place in our hearts.

REFERENCE: *Private Papers of William Wilberforce* (1897)

'I love your considering and treating me as a friend'

'A wise man will hear, and will increase learning; and a man of understanding shall attain unto wise counsels.' Proverbs 1:5

SUGGESTED FURTHER READING: Proverbs 27:5–11

Let me assure you that you give me great pleasure by telling me unreservedly any doubts you may entertain of the propriety of my principles or conduct. I love your considering and treating me as a friend, and I trust you will never have reason to regret your having so done, either in relation to your benefit or your comfort. In stating my suspicions that I had not sufficiently endeavoured to impress on my children, and that you were scarcely enough aware of the force of the dictum that Christians were to be a peculiar people, I scarcely need assure you that I think the commands, 'Provide things honest in the sight of all men, whatever things are lovely, whatsoever of good report,' etc., clearly prove that so far from being needlessly singular, we never ought to be so, but for some special and good reason.

Again, I am aware of what you suggest that, in our days, in which the number of those who profess a stricter kind of religion than the world of *soi-disant*[8] Christians in general, there is danger lest a party spirit should creep in with its usual effects and evils. Against this, therefore, we should be on the watch. And yet, though not enlisting ourselves in a party, we ought, as I think you will admit, to assign considerable weight to any opinions or practices which have been sanctioned by the authority of good men in general.

FOR MEDITATION: It was Philip Doddridge who wrote: 'If a criminal, condemned by human laws, has but the least shadow of hope that he may escape, he is all attention to it. If there be a friend who he thinks can help him, with what strong importunity does he entreat the interposition of that friend?' This casts into sharp relief the idea that we are to cherish a friend who cares deeply about our welfare. In the Christian life, God raises up companions for us who can dispense the cordials of friendship.

REFERENCE: *Private Papers of William Wilberforce* (1897)

'Let your religion consist much in prayer'

'Epaphras, who is one of you, a servant of Christ, saluteth you, always labouring fervently for you in prayers, that ye may stand perfect and complete in all the will of God.' Colossians 4:12
SUGGESTED FURTHER READING: James 5:10–20

I finish this letter after hearing an excellent sermon from Robert Hall. It was not merely an exhibition of powerful intellect, but of fervent and feeling piety, especially impressing on his hearers to live by the faith of the love of Christ daily, habitually looking to him in all his characters. Prayer, prayer, my dear Samuel; let your religion consist much in prayer. May you be enabled more and more to walk by faith and not by sight, to feel habitually as well as to recognize in all your more deliberate calculations and plans, that the things that are seen are temporal, but the things that are not seen are eternal. Then you will live above the world, as one who is waiting for the coming of the Lord Jesus Christ.

FOR MEDITATION: 'Religion,' it has been said, ' is such a sense of God in the soul, and such a conviction of our obligations to him, and of our dependence upon him, as shall engage us to make it our great care to conduct ourselves in a manner which we have reason to believe will be pleasing to him.'

Prayer, we know from Scripture, pleases the Lord. Proverbs 15:8 tells us: 'the prayer of the upright is his delight.' There are so many things we need of God, and prayer is means by which they are sought. Wisdom is one. Of this we read in James 1:5—'If any of you lack wisdom, let him ask of God, that giveth to all men liberally, and upbraideth not; and it shall be given him.' Are we in need of strength? Psalm 27:14 states: 'Wait on the Lord: be of good courage, and he shall strengthen thine heart: wait, I say, on the Lord.'

REFERENCE: *Private Papers of William Wilberforce* (1897)

'A holy awe and reverence'

'My heart standeth in awe of thy word.' Psalm 119:161
SUGGESTED FURTHER READING: Hebrews 12:28—*'Wherefore we receiving a kingdom which cannot be moved, let us have grace, whereby we may serve God acceptably with reverence and godly fear.'*

There is, in Jonathan Edwards on the *Religious Affections*, a book from which you will, I think, gain much useful matter, a very striking passage, in which he condemns with great severity, but not at all too great, *me judice*,[9] that familiarity with the Supreme King which was affected by some of the religionists of his day. Edwards remarks very truly that Moses and Elijah, and Abraham the friend of God (and all of them honoured by such especial marks of the Divine condescension), always manifested a holy awe and reverence when in the Divine presence.

FOR MEDITATION: Awe, reverence, deep and abiding respect—these things are what Wilberforce and Edwards are writing with respect to God. In our Christian walk we must never lose sight of God's majesty. He is the One who spoke and the world was made. From nothing he created all that we see in nature and in the universe beyond. It is as the psalmist said: 'great is the LORD and greatly to be praised' (Psalm 48:1).

This psalm also speaks of 'the mountain of his holiness.' God is holy. And although Moses, Elijah and Abraham enjoyed a special relationship with God—they were in awe of him and reverential in the place of worship and prayer. So we ought to be.

REFERENCE: *Private Papers of William Wilberforce* (1897)

'Such deep views of Christianity'

'O LORD, *how great are thy works! and thy thoughts are very deep.*'
Psalm 92:5
SUGGESTED FURTHER READING: Proverbs 20:5–12

Pascal's *Thoughts on Religion* is a collection of fragments, but they are the fragments of a master like the study of Michelangelo. I know no book whatever which appears to me to contain such deep views of Christianity.

FOR MEDITATION: Wilberforce once wrote that 'Pascal's *Thoughts on Religion* is a book abounding in the deepest views of practical Christianity.' He also long remembered a conversation on another occasion about Pascal: 'I well remember Lady Liverpool telling me at the Royal Pavilion many years ago, that she and Lord Liverpool used to contend each for the favourite of each, Pascal or Fenelon; and that Pascal is an author who has many "pregnant propositions," as Lord Bacon calls them.'

Wilberforce read Pascal for hours at time when he was undergoing his self-described great change or embrace of Christianity. It was at this time of his life and after one session of reading Pascal that he wrote: 'Another body of proof [in favor of Christianity] is derived from the nature of Man, (see Pascal's *Thoughts*) and from Christianity's being the great remedy by which the diseases of his nature are to be cured. Man is to be made a pure and ennobled creature, fitted for a better world of more exalted beings.'

The writings of wise Christians like Pascal have much to teach us. They understand what it is to love God with their minds (Luke 10:27). For this reason, we ought to seek out and savour the great Christian classics.

REFERENCE: *Wilberforce, in a letter to Arthur Young* (1797)

'To embrace any little opportunity'

'As we have therefore opportunity, let us do good unto all men, especially unto them who are of the household of faith.' Galatians 6:10
SUGGESTED FURTHER READING: Psalm 34:11–22

I well remember that when first it pleased God to touch my heart, now rather above forty years ago, it had been reported of me that I was deranged, and various other rumours were propagated to my disadvantage. It was under the cloud of these prejudices that I presented myself to some old friends, and spent some time with them (after the close of the parliamentary session) at Scarborough. I was careful to embrace any little opportunity of pleasing them (little presents often have no small effects), and I endeavoured to impress them with a persuasion that I was not less happy than before.

The consequence was all I could desire, and I well recollect that the late Mrs Henry Thornton's mother, a woman of very superior powers and of great influence in our social circle, one day broke out to my mother—she afterwards said to me something of the same kind, not without tears—'Well, I can only say if *he* is deranged I hope we all shall become so.'

To your young friend again I need not suggest the duty of constant prayer for his nearest relatives. By degrees they will become softened, and he will probably enjoy the delight of finding them come over to the blessed path he is himself pursuing. He will also find that self-denial, and a disposition to subject himself to any trouble or annoyance in order to promote his friends' comfort, or exemption from some grievance, will have a very powerful effect in conciliating his friends.

FOR MEDITATION: Written on 28 July 1826, this letter reveals much about what we can do to commend our faith to family members and friends who are sceptical of Christianity. 2 Corinthians 5:20 states: 'Now then we are ambassadors for Christ, as though God did beseech you by us: we pray you in Christ's stead, be ye reconciled to God.' Let us be prayerful that God will help us to best perform our embassy.

REFERENCE: *Private Papers of William Wilberforce* (1897)

'In all that concerns my children'

'Casting all your care upon him; for he careth for you.' 1 Peter 5:7
SUGGESTED FURTHER READING: Psalm 37:1–9

The Almighty has been so signally kind to me even in my worldly affairs, and so much more gracious than I deserved in my domestic concerns, that it would indicate a heart never to be satisfied were I not disposed in all that concerns my children, to cast all my care on him.

FOR MEDITATION: Psalm 55:22 tells us: 'Cast thy burden upon the Lord, and he shall sustain thee: he shall never suffer the righteous to be moved.'

Nothing is dearer to a parent than those things which concern their children. Parents think back to the times when they watched over their infants in the night, even checking to make sure their little ones—so frail and new—were breathing. Parents realize that they never thought they could care so deeply about anything as they do their children.

Added to all this is the knowledge that God loves us, and our children, more deeply and profoundly than we could ever understand. 1 John 4:16 beautifully describes this: 'And we have known and believed the love that God hath to us. God is love; and he that dwelleth in love dwelleth in God, and God in him.'

And so we may fully and completely entrust our children to God's care. He will watch over them and us. Together, we and our children may dwell in God's love. Praise his name.

REFERENCE: *Private Papers of William Wilberforce* (1897)

'That our joy may be full'

'Now the God of hope fill you with all joy and peace in believing, that ye may abound in hope, through the power of the Holy Ghost.' Romans 15:13
SUGGESTED FURTHER READING: Romans 14:13–19

We ought to be always making it our endeavour to be experiencing peace and joy in believing, and that we do not enjoy more of this sunshine of the breast is, I fear, almost always our own fault. We ought not to acquiesce quietly in the want of them, whereas we are too apt to be satisfied if our consciences do not reproach us with anything wrong, if we can on good grounds entertain the persuasion that we are safe; and we do not sufficiently consider that we serve a gracious and kind master who is willing that we should taste that he is gracious. Both in St John's first general Epistle, and in our Lord's declaration in John 15, we are assured that our Lord's object and the apostles' in telling us of our having spiritual supplies and communion, is that our joy may be full. To be spiritually-minded is both life and peace.

FOR MEDITATION: The writer Philip Doddridge once said: 'I will joyfully proclaim the glad tidings of pardon and salvation by Christ Jesus our Lord, which is all the support and confidence of my own soul.'

When one thinks of joy in the Lord, one often thinks of this Christmas carol, written by Isaac Watts in 1719:

Joy to the world, the Lord is come!
Let earth receive her King;
Let every heart prepare him room,
And Heaven and nature sing.

Joy to the earth, the Saviour reigns!
Let men their songs employ;
While fields and floods, rocks, hills and plains
Repeat the sounding joy.

REFERENCE: *Private Papers of William Wilberforce* (1897)

'I say ditto'

'For the children ought not to lay up for the parents, but the parents for the children.' 2 Corinthians 12:14
SUGGESTED FURTHER READING: Proverbs 6:20–23

An admirable expedient has this moment suggested itself to me, which will supersede the necessity for my giving expression to sentiments and feelings, for which you will give me full credit, though unexpressed. It is that of following the precedent set by a candidate for the City of Bristol in conjunction with Edmund Burke. The latter had addressed his electors in a fuller effusion of eloquence than was used to flow even from his lips, when his colleague, conscious that he should appear to great disadvantage were he to attempt a speech, very wisely confined himself to, 'Gentlemen, you have heard Mr Burke's excellent speech. I say ditto to the whole of it.' Sure I am that no language of mine could give you warmer or more sincere assurances of parental affection than you will have received in the letter of your dear mother, which she has just put into my hands to be inserted into my letter. To all she has said, therefore, I say ditto.

FOR MEDITATION: It is the joy of parents to second the love a spouse has shown for their children. How many a parent has heard a spouse say something particularly special to a child, only to find they themselves have no words or that no words are necessary—just a smile of agreement and acknowledgment. We often marvel too at the love God has for his children—a love that leaves us at a loss for words. As we read in 1 John 3:1—'Behold, what manner of love the Father hath bestowed upon us, that we should be called the sons of God.'

REFERENCE: *Private Papers of William Wilberforce* (1897)

'The rest shall be prayer'

'That our sons may be as plants grown up in their youth; that our daughters may be as corner stones, polished after the similitude of a palace.' Psalm 144:12

SUGGESTED FURTHER READING: Psalm 90:11–17

I hope I am deeply thankful to the bountiful Giver of all good for having granted me in you a son to whose future course I can look with so much humble hope, and even joyful confidence. It is also with no little thankfulness that I reflect on your domestic prospects, from the excellent qualities of your, let me say *our,* dear Emily. I must stop, the rest shall be prayer, prayer for both of you, that your course in this life may be useful and honourable, and that you may at length, accompanied by a large assemblage of the sheep of Christ, whom you have been the honoured instrument of bringing to the fold of Christ, have an abundant entrance into the everlasting kingdom of God.

FOR MEDITATION: Wilberforce wrote this letter to his third son Samuel, and was speaking of the joy he had experienced in coming to know and cherish Emily, Samuel's newlywed wife. In the Gospel of Mark we read of marriage as described by the Lord Jesus: 'from the beginning of the creation God made them male and female. For this cause shall a man leave his father and mother, and cleave to his wife; and they twain shall be one flesh: so then they are no more twain, but one flesh. What therefore God hath joined together, let not man put asunder' (Mark 10:6–9).

REFERENCE: *Private Papers of William Wilberforce* (1897)

'He who rolls the spheres along'

'When I consider thy heavens, the work of thy fingers, the moon and the stars, which thou hast ordained.' Psalm 8:3
SUGGESTED FURTHER READING: Luke 12:6–7, 27–31

How much do they lose of comfort, as well as, I believe, in incentives to gratitude and love, and if it be not their own fault thereby in the means of practical improvement, who do not accustom themselves to watch the operations of the Divine Hand.

I have often thought that, had it not been for the positive declarations of the Holy Scriptures concerning the attention of the Almighty Governor of the universe to our minutest comforts and interests ... we should not dare to be so presumptuous as to believe, that he who rolls the spheres along, would condescend thus to sympathize with our feelings, and attend to our minutest interests. Here also Dr Chalmers' suggestions, derived from the discoveries made to us through the microscope, come in to confirm the same delightful persuasion. I am persuaded that many true Christians lose much pleasure they might otherwise enjoy from not sufficiently watching the various events of their lives, more especially in those little incidents, as we rather unfitly term them; for, considering them as links in the chain, they maintain the continuity, as much as those which we are apt to regard as of greater size and consequence.

FOR MEDITATION: The psalmist marvelled at the works of God, and worshipped him as the Creator of the universe: 'The heavens declare the glory of God; and the firmament sheweth his handywork' (Psalm 19:1). The psalmist has also written: 'O LORD our Lord, how excellent is thy name in all the earth! who hast set thy glory above the heavens.'

REFERENCE: *Private Papers of William Wilberforce* (1897)

'There is no great and little to God'

'He will bless them that fear the Lord, both small and great.' Psalm 115:13
SUGGESTED FURTHER READING: Proverbs 29:23–27

On 26 August 1827 Wilberforce recorded the events of a dinner and the conversation that followed in his diary: 'Dined at Samuel Hoare's at Hampstead, with Dr and Mrs Lushington, and William Allen, who still goes on doing good. Miss Joanna Baillie came in the evening—so like her father the Doctor, as quite to affect me. Dr Lushington acting a most important part in changing the condition of the coloured class through the whole West Indies. He and Miss Baillie were asked if they believed in a particular providence.

'"Yes," they replied, "on great occasions."'

Wilberforce reflected: 'As unphilosophical as unscriptural—must not the smallest links be as necessary for maintaining the continuity, as the greatest? Great and little belong to our littleness, but there is no great and little to God.'

FOR MEDITATION: Scripture tells us the very hairs on our head are numbered. God, we also learn, takes note of one tiny sparrow that falls. We read of these things in the gospel of Matthew, Chapter Ten: 'Are not two sparrows sold for a farthing? and one of them shall not fall on the ground without your Father. But the very hairs of your head are all numbered. Fear ye not therefore, ye are of more value than many sparrows' (Matthew 10:29–31).

Truly there is no great and little to God. And it is just as true that he who cares about the minutest parts of his creation cares deeply and profoundly about each one of us.

REFERENCE: *The Life of William Wilberforce* (1838)

'The Christian's hope and peace and joy'

'My flesh and my heart faileth: but God is the strength of my heart, and my portion for ever.' Psalm 73:26
SUGGESTED FURTHER READING: Psalm 5:1–11

We ought not to expect this life to flow on smoothly without rubs or mortification. Indeed, it is a sentiment which I often inculcate on myself that, to use a familiar phrase, we here have more than our bargain, as Christians, in the days in which we live; for I apprehend the promise of the life that now is, combined with that which is to come, was meant to refer rather to mental peace and comfort, than to temporal prosperity. My thoughts have been of late often led into reflections on the degree in which we are wanting to ourselves, in relation to the rich and bright prospects set before us as attainable in the Word of God. More especially I refer to that of the Christian's hope and peace and joy.

Again and again we are assured that joy is ordinarily and generally to be the portion of the Christian. Yet how prone are but too commonly those, whom we really believe to be entitled to the name of Christians, disposed to remain contented without the possession of this delightful state of heart; and to regard it as the privilege of some rarely gifted, and eminently favoured Christians, rather than as the general character of all. It is to be obtained through the Holy Spirit, and therefore when St Paul prays for the Roman Christians that they may be filled with all *peace* and *joy* in believing, and may abound in hope, it is added, through the power of the Holy Ghost.

FOR MEDITATION: In a life so often filled with uncertainties, it is most comforting and reassuring to read over and over again of how much God longs for us to know and experience joy. It is marvellous too that so often in the Scriptures joy is spoken in tandem with peace. They are two sides of the same precious coin. May God grant us both in good measure.

REFERENCE: *Private Papers of William Wilberforce* (1897)

'In what pleasant places my lines were fallen'

'The lines are fallen unto me in pleasant places; yea, I have a goodly heritage.' Psalm 16:6
SUGGESTED FURTHER READING: Psalm 61:1–8

The 1st of January, I consider, except perhaps my birthday, as the most important of the whole year. For a long period (as long as I lived in the neighbourhood of the Lock Chapel, or rather not far from it) I used to receive the sacrament, which was always administered there on New Year's Day. And the heart must be hard and cold, which that sacred ordinance in such a relations would not soften and warm into religious sensibility and tenderness. I was naturally led into looking backwards to the past days of my life, and forward to the future; led to consider in what pleasant places my lines were fallen, how goodly was my heritage, that the bounds of my life should be fixed in that little spot, in which, of the whole earth, there has been the greatest measure of temporal comforts, and of spiritual privileges.

That it should be also in the eighteenth century, for where should I have been, a small, weakly man, had I been born either among our painted or skin-clothed ancestors, or in almost any other before or after it? As they would have begun by exposing me, there need be no more inquiry as to the sequel of the piece. Next take my station in life, neither so high as naturally to intoxicate me, nor so low as to excite to envy or degradation. Take then the other particulars of my condition, both personal and circumstantial. But I need go no farther, but leave it to you to supply the rest. And you will likewise, I doubt not, pursue the same mental process in your own instance also, and find, as may well be the case, that the retrospect and prospect afford abundant matter for gratitude and humiliation (I am sure I find the latter most powerfully called forth in my heart by my own survey).

FOR MEDITATION: The Book of Psalms is the book of the Bible where the word 'remember' most often occurs (in the King James translation). This is most fitting, for remembrance of what God has done for us should be a prominent part of our praise to him. Bless his name for the things he has done.

REFERENCE: *Private Papers of William Wilberforce* (1897)

'A good name which is better than great riches'

'A good name is rather to be chosen than great riches, and loving favour rather than silver and gold.' Proverbs 22:1
SUGGESTED FURTHER READING: Psalm 35:10–28

Passing our lives in this vagarious mode calls forth emotions of gratitude to the Giver of all good, who has raised up for me so many and so kind friends. I ought not to forget, while a gracious Providence has granted me a good name which is better than great riches, that many public men as upright as myself have been the victims of calumny. I myself indeed have had its envenomed shafts at times directed against me. But on the whole few men have suffered from them so little as myself.

FOR MEDITATION: The psalmist knew what it was to be downcast because of calumnies and reproaches, and yet there was an abiding source of hope that he knew and could resort to in time of trouble. He writes of this in Psalm 119:

Princes also did sit and speak against me: but thy servant did meditate in thy statutes.
Thy testimonies also are my delight and my counsellors.
My soul cleaveth unto the dust: quicken thou me according to thy word.
I have declared my ways, and thou heardest me: teach me thy statutes.
Make me to understand the way of thy precepts: so shall I talk of thy wondrous works.
My soul melteth for heaviness: strengthen thou me according unto thy word (Psalm 119:23–28).

REFERENCE: *Private Papers of William Wilberforce* (1897)

'Let us all be found in our several stations'

'Be sober, be vigilant.' 1 Peter 5:8
SUGGESTED FURTHER READING: Psalm 130:1–8

I own I am sadly alarmed for the Church. There is such a combination of noxious elements fermenting together, that I am ready to exclaim, 'There is death in the pot,' and there will be, I fear, no Elisha granted to us to render the mess harmless. But yet I am encouraged to hope that the same gracious and long-suffering Being who would have spared Sodom for ten, and Jerusalem even for one righteous man's sake, may spare us to the prayers of the many who do, I trust, sincerely sigh and cry in behalf of our proud, ungrateful land. Yet, again, when I consider what light we have enjoyed, what mercies we have received, and how self-sufficient and ungrateful we have been, I am again tempted to despond. I wish I could be a less unprofitable servant. Yet I must remember Milton's sonnet,

They also serve who only stand and wait

Let us all be found in our several stations doing therein the Lord's work diligently and zealously.

FOR MEDITATION: Words penned by Wilberforce's favourite poet William Cowper are fitting here:

Did ever mourner plead with thee,
And thou refuse that mourner's plea?
Does not the Word still fixed remain
That none shall seek thy face in vain?

That were a grief I could not bear,
Didst thou not hear and answer prayer;
But a prayer hearing, answering God
Supports me under every load.

REFERENCE: *Private Papers of William Wilberforce* (1897)

'Hymns and hymn tunes'

'The Lord is my strength and my shield; my heart trusted in him, and I am helped: therefore my heart greatly rejoiceth; and with my song will I praise him.' Psalm 28:7

SUGGESTED FURTHER READING: Psalm 40:3—*'And he hath put a new song in my mouth, even praise unto our God: many shall see it, and fear, and shall trust in the Lord.'*

I will put down in any letter I may write to you any hymns and hymn tunes which I like ('Happy the heart where graces reign,' Lock tune), and you may add together the *disjecta membra*[10] into one list. But I have no hymn-books here except G. Noel's. At Highwood I have a considerable number.

Happy the heart where graces reign,
When faith and hope shall cease,
'Tis this shall strike our joyful strings
In the sweet realms of bliss.
Before we quite forsake our clay,
Or leave this dark abode,
The wings of love bear us away
To see our smiling God.

This is the grace that lives and sings
Where love inspires the breast;
Love is the brightest of the train,
And strengthens all the rest.
Knowledge, alas! 'Tis all in vain,
And all in vain our fear,
Our stubborn sins will fight and reign
If love be absent there.

FOR MEDITATION: Joseph Brown eulogized Wilberforce in the *Christian Observer* for January 1834, saying: 'Mr Wilberforce was also a most cheerful Christian. His harp appeared to be always in tune; no "gloomy atmosphere of a melancholy moroseness" surrounded him; his sun appeared to be always shining: hence he was remarkably fond of singing hymns, both in family prayer and when alone. He would say, "A Christian should have joy and peace in believing: It is his duty to abound in praise."'

REFERENCE: *Private Papers of William Wilberforce* (1897)

'The heirs of glory'

'And if ye be Christ's, then are ye Abraham's seed, and heirs according to the promise.' Galatians 3:29
SUGGESTED FURTHER READING: Galatians 4:21–31

We went to prayers, and after about half an hour, surely well spent, we returned to the common room and renewed our reading, which I now stopped, finding how late it was, and being in the singularly favoured circumstances of an old fellow, who is allowed to say 'Come or go, do this or do that,' without the appearance of fretfulness.

We have been reading an article on Gibbon and Madame de Stael, and latterly also on Voltaire. You remember, I doubt not, the last sentence in Gibbon's *Autobiography*; I have engaged my young friend to write under it Watts's beautiful hymn, ending with the line—'Foretells a bright rising again.'

In old age the consolation of hope is reserved for the tenderness of parents, who commence a new life in their children.   *Edward Gibbon*

How fine has the day been! how bright was the sun!
How lovely and joyful the course that he run;
Though he rose in a mist when his race he begun,
And there followed some droppings of rain:
But now the fair traveller's come to the west,
His rays are all gold, and his beauties are best;
He paints the skies gay as he sinks to his rest,
And foretells a bright rising again.

This is one of Watts's *Hymns for Children*, but surely it is for the children of God, for the heirs of glory, [whether] you compare it either in point of good sense, or imagination, or sterling value, or sustaining hope, with the considerations and objects which feed the fancy, or exercise the understanding or affections.

FOR MEDITATION: The lines above should prompt this prayer: may God grant us a heart ever ready to sing his praise.

REFERENCE: *The Life of William Wilberforce* (1838)

'Oh may I hear his voice'

'The voice of joy, and the voice of gladness, the voice of the bridegroom, and the voice of the bride, the voice of them that shall say, Praise the LORD of hosts: for the LORD is good; for his mercy endureth for ever: and of them that shall bring the sacrifice of praise into the house of the Lord.' Jeremiah 33:11
SUGGESTED FURTHER READING: Jeremiah 42:1–6

'O Lord, I humbly hope that it is thou who knockest at the door of my heart, who callest forth these more than usually lively emotions of contrition, desire, faith, trust, and gratitude. Oh may I hear his voice, and open the door and let him in. May I be really a thriving Christian, bringing forth abundantly the fruits of the Spirit to the glory of God. O Lord, I am lost in astonishment at thy mercy and love. That thou shouldst not only quit the glory and happiness of heaven to be made man, and bear the most excruciating torments and bitter degradation for our deliverance and salvation; but that thou still bearest with us, though we, knowing all thy goodness, are still cold and insensible to it. That thou strivest with our perverseness, conquerest our opposition, and still waitest to be gracious.'

FOR MEDITATION: Wilberforce knew John Wesley, and it was from Wesley that Wilberforce received the last letter Wesley ever wrote. Verses that Wesley wrote have a place in this entry:

Thou waitest to be gracious still;	Faithful, O Lord, thy mercies are,
Thou dost with sinners bear,	A rock that cannot move!
That, saved, we may thy goodness feel,	A thousand promises declare
And all thy grace declare.	Thy constancy of love.

Throughout the universe it reigns,
Unalterably sure;
And while the truth of God remains,
The goodness must endure

REFERENCE: *The Life of William Wilberforce* (1838)

'Majestic though in ruin'

'*What fruit had ye then in those things whereof ye are now ashamed? for the end of those things is death. But now being made free from sin, and become servants to God, ye have your fruit unto holiness, and the end everlasting life.*' Romans 6:21–22
SUGGESTED FURTHER READING: Romans 6:12–23

Far different is the humiliating language of Christianity. From it we learn that man is an apostate creature, fallen from his high original, degraded in his nature, and depraved in his faculties; indisposed to good, and disposed to evil; prone to vice, it is natural and easy to him; disinclined to virtue, it is difficult and laborious; that he is tainted with sin, not slightly and superficially, but radically and to the very core. These are truths which, however mortifying to our pride, one would think none would be hardy enough to attempt to controvert. I know not any thing which brings them home so forcibly to my own feelings, as the consideration of what still remains to us of our primitive dignity, when contrasted with our present state of moral degradation.

Into what depth thou seest,
From what height fallen!'[11]

Examine first with attention the natural powers and faculties of man; invention, reason, judgment, memory; a mind 'of large discourse,' 'looking before and after,'[12] reviewing the past, and thence determining for the present, and anticipating the future; discerning, collecting, combining, comparing: capable not merely of apprehending but of admiring the beauty of moral excellence: with fear and hope to warn and animate; with joy and sorrow to solace and soften; with love to attach, with sympathy to harmonize, with courage to attempt, with patience to endure, and with the power of conscience, that faithful monitor within the breast, to enforce the conclusions of reason, and direct and regulate the passions of the soul. Truly we must pronounce him 'majestic though in ruin'.[13]

FOR MEDITATION: That we have been created in the image of God is cause for our highest praise. That we bear the marks of the fall reveals our deepest need for God, his forgiveness and our redemption.

REFERENCE: *A Practical View of Christianity* (1797)

'A complete renewal into thine image'

'I have called thee by thy name; thou art mine.' Isaiah 43:1
SUGGESTED FURTHER READING: Isaiah 45:2–12

Thou knewest me, and my hardness, and coldness, and unworthy return for all thy goodness, when thou calledst me from the giddy throng, and shone into my heart with the light of the glory of God, in the face of Jesus Christ. O well may we exclaim, 'Thy ways are not as our ways, nor thy thoughts as our thoughts; but as the heavens are higher than the earth, so are thy ways higher than our ways, and thy thoughts than our thoughts.'

O Lord, I cast myself before thee, O spurn me not from thee; unworthy though I am of all thy wonderful goodness. O grant me more and more of humility, and love, and faith, and hope, and longing for a complete renewal into thine image. Lord, help me and hear me. I come to thee as my only Saviour. O be thou my help, my strength, my peace, and joy, and consolation; my Alpha and Omega; my all in all. Amen.

FOR MEDITATION: Wilberforce's prayers so often breathe a spirit of deep longing for God, and a renewal into God's image. This desire is also expressed in verses written by William Cowper:

I sometimes think myself inclined	Oh make this heart rejoice, or ache;
To love thee if I could;	Decide this doubt for me;
But often feel another mind,	And if it be not broken, break,
Averse to all that's good.	And heal it, if it be.

My best desires are faint and few,
I fain would strive for more;
But when I cry, 'My strength renew!'
Seem weaker than before.

REFERENCE: *The Life of William Wilberforce* (1838)

'Looking for a better country'

'These all died in faith, not having received the promises, but having seen them afar off, and were persuaded of them, and embraced them, and confessed that they were strangers and pilgrims on the earth.'
Hebrews 11:13
SUGGESTED FURTHER READING: Hebrews 11:1–16

O Lord, cause me to live in a more practical sense of the shortness and uncertainty of all human things; and oh bring my soul, more effectually than ever hitherto, to God in Christ, and give me a large measure of thy Spirit. May I be enabled to live by faith above the world, looking for a better country, with my heart supremely set on it. O Lord, I know too well my own weakness, but thou canst strengthen the weakest, and hast promised that thou wilt, if we earnestly pray to thee. Lord, be with me, and strengthen me. Enable me to maintain a closer walk with thee; and while I live a life of faith and hope, having my affections set on things above, may I discharge the duties of my station, so to let my light shine before men, and adorn the doctrine of God my Saviour in all things. Amen, and Amen.

FOR MEDITATION: 'To maintain a closer walk with thee.' These were words close to the heart of William Cowper as well:

O for a closer walk with God,
A calm and heavenly frame,
A light to shine upon the road
That leads me to the Lamb!

So shall my walk be close with God,
Calm and serene my frame;
So purer light shall mark the road
That leads me to the Lamb.

REFERENCE: *The Life of William Wilberforce* (1838)

'The main-spring of the machine'

'So will not we go back from thee: quicken us, and we will call upon thy name.' Psalm 80:18
SUGGESTED FURTHER READING: Psalm 119:25–40

I pray above all for the love of God and my Redeemer, that this blessed principle may be like the main-spring of the machine, prompting all the movements, and diffusing its practical influence through every disposition, action, plan, and design. May the God of hope fill me with all joy and peace in believing. O Lord, do thou break, soften, quicken, warm my cold heart; and teach me to feel an overflowing love and gratitude, or rather a deep and grateful sense of obligation, not as a transient effusion, but as the settled temper and disposition, the practical habit of my soul: that so I may here begin the song of praise, to be sung with more purified and warm affections in heaven, Worthy is the Lamb; and blessing, honour, glory, and power, etc.

FOR MEDITATION: 'May the God of hope fill me with all joy and peace in believing.' It is in the Scriptures that we find words of hope, joy and peace. May they be our continual meditation and strengthen our belief and trust in God.

O How I love thy holy Word,
Thy gracious covenant, O Lord!
It guides me in the peaceful way,
I think upon it all the day.

What are the mines of shining wealth,
The strength of youth, the bloom of health!
What are all joys compared with those
Thine everlasting Word bestows! William Cowper

REFERENCE: *The Life of William Wilberforce* (1838)

'Casting all my care on thee'

'Cast thy burden upon the Lord, and he shall sustain thee: he shall never suffer the righteous to be moved.' Psalm 55:22
SUGGESTED FURTHER READING: Psalm 55

Buonaparte now busy in Italy—it is supposed planning partition of Turkey. This man is manifestly an instrument in the hands of Providence; when God has done with him, he will probably show how easily he can get rid of him. Meanwhile may we be of the number of those who trust in him, and all will be well. Lord, prepare and fit me for discharging the duties of my station, in a manner honourable to my Christian profession, and useful to my fellow-creatures. O Lord, teach me to see thy hand in all things, and to refer all to thee, bearing in mind continually thy overruling providence, and casting all my care on thee.

FOR MEDITATION: The princes of this world, Wilberforce knew from his reading of Scripture, come and go. God is the Author of history. When we refer all to God, we are reminded anew of his overruling Providence. Despite the storms that darken the horizon of the world and its kingdoms, we may always and safely cast our care on God.

Many writers have penned telling thoughts about God's Providence. The early nineteenth-century poet Thomas Haynes Bayly, like Wilberforce, lived in the time when Napoleon wrought such havoc throughout the world. He wrote: 'fear not, but trust in Providence,/wherever thou may'st be.' The eighteenth-century essayist and poet Joseph Addison was another writer Wilberforce knew well. Addison wrote: 'and pleas'd th' Almighty's orders to perform,/rides in the whirlwind and directs the storm.'

REFERENCE: *The Life of William Wilberforce* (1838)

'But an instrument in the hand of the Almighty'

'And it shall come to pass at that day, saith the LORD, that the heart of the king shall perish, and the heart of the princes.' Jeremiah 4:9
SUGGESTED FURTHER READING: Isaiah 10:5–25

What an extraordinary spectacle is now exhibiting in Spain! Surely Bonaparte would not have proceeded as he has done, if he had not been absolutely intoxicated by his prosperity. To publish to the world that [his brother] Joseph Bonaparte was to be king, and his children in hereditary succession to succeed to the crown after his death; and failing his issue, Louis and his heirs; and failing Louis, Jerome and his heirs; and failing all these, to revert to us, Napoleon! Surely this is so heaping insult on injury, that he might have foreseen that human nature would scarcely bear it. I have often thought that it might perhaps please God to pull down this giant when raised to his highest elevation, and apparently glorying the most reasonably, as well as most proudly, in his strength. Do you recollect the chapter in Isaiah, in which the prophet introduces the King of Assyria as at first boasting of his victories, and after having been reminded that he was but an instrument in the hand of the Almighty, he is represented as brought down to the pit amid contempt and derision. Lowth,[14] I remember, justly states it to be, for its length, the finest poem almost in existence.

FOR MEDITATION: Wilberforce wrote these words on 19 July 1808, at time when it seemed the world would never be free of the scourge that was Napoleon. And while the Old Testament Book of Isaiah contains many passages that speak of kings who devastated the ancient near east, there are so many assurances that God will bring peace at the last. In fact, the word 'peace' occurs more often in the Book of Isaiah (in the King James translation) than in any other book of the Bible. Isaiah 52:7 declares: 'How beautiful upon the mountains are the feet of him that bringeth good tidings, that publisheth peace; that bringeth good tidings of good, that publisheth salvation; that saith unto Zion, Thy God reigneth!' In Isaiah 39:8 we read: 'Then said Hezekiah to Isaiah, Good is the word of the LORD which thou hast spoken. He said moreover, For there shall be peace and truth in my days.'

REFERENCE: *The Life of William Wilberforce* (1838)

'Those who come to him'

'Why art thou cast down, O my soul? and why art thou disquieted within me? hope thou in God: for I shall yet praise him, who is the health of my countenance, and my God.' Psalm 42:11
SUGGESTED FURTHER READING: Psalm 37:23–31

What a resource does Christianity offer to disappointed men, and yet offer it in vain! How merciful and condescending is our God! willing to take the world's leavings, and to accept those who come to him (if they will but come) only when they have nowhere else to go.

FOR MEDITATION: The words above were written in a letter to Hannah More from Eastbourne on 2 August 1808. These reflections from Wilberforce remind one of some of the most comforting words to be found in Scripture—Psalm 73:23–26. 'Thou hast holden me by my right hand,' the passage begins,

Thou shalt guide me with thy counsel, and afterward receive me to glory.
Whom have I in heaven but thee? and there is none upon earth that I desire beside thee.
My flesh and my heart faileth: but God is the strength of my heart, and my portion for ever.

In the Book of Isaiah, we also have an assurance that is a balm to the troubled soul: 'When the poor and needy seek water, and there is none, and their tongue faileth for thirst, I the LORD will hear them, I the God of Israel will not forsake them.' (Isaiah 41:17)

REFERENCE: *The Life of William Wilberforce* (1838)

'In the calmness of the morning'

'*My voice shalt thou hear in the morning, O* LORD; *in the morning will I direct my prayer unto thee, and will look up.*' *Psalm 5:3*
SUGGESTED FURTHER READING: Psalm 59:5–17

In 1838, Wilberforce's biographer sons wrote of him: 'The first hours in the morning were all that he could strictly call his own, and these were spent in devotional exercises. "I always find," he said, "that I have most time for business, and it is best done, when I have most properly observed my private devotions." His common observation was: "In the calmness of the morning, before the mind is heated and wearied by the turmoil of the day, you have a season of unusual importance for communing with God and with yourself."'

FOR MEDITATION: The great reformer Martin Luther is reputed to have said: 'I pray an hour every day, except when I get very busy. Then I pray two hours a day.'

Luther, like Wilberforce, was a man who could spontaneously craft a brief and very memorable phrase. In a collection of his 'table talk,' Luther had this to say of prayer: 'Upright Christians pray without ceasing; though they pray not always with their mouths, yet their hearts pray continually, sleeping and waking; for the sigh of a true Christian is a prayer.'

Luther's words—and Wilberforce's, powerfully underscore the importance of prayer. Both accomplished great things for God. Both were incredibly busy. And both knew that they would not have been able to do anything of lasting value for God and his kingdom without prayer. May we, like them, heed the scriptural admonition to 'pray without ceasing.'

REFERENCE: *The Life of William Wilberforce* (1838)

'Our times and seasons'

'And he said unto them, It is not for you to know the times or the seasons, which the Father hath put in his own power.' Acts 1:7
SUGGESTED FURTHER READING: Psalm 16:1–11

Though I have not heard from you, I have heard of you, and that more especially from our friend the Dean;[15] and it gave me sincere pleasure to receive so favourable a report of the state of your health and strength. I am inclined to hope it will please God still to grant you a fine autumn of life; a season which, with better reason than the historian of nature, as Mr Gibbon terms him, you might find peculiarly grateful. However, our times and seasons are in the disposal of One who knows far better than we do what is most eligible for us, and who, if it be not our own fault, will cause all things to work together for our good.

FOR MEDITATION: Wilberforce's words above were written in a letter to his friend William Hey, an eminent physician and reformer in Leeds. They were close friends and maintained an important correspondence. Each had occasion to thank God for the other, and the ways in which they were able to encourage one another in matters of faith and philanthropy.

How often we need to be reminded of God's love for us and the ways in which he, in his sovereignty, causes all things to work together for our good. We read of this in the Scriptures, and yet we are like the person in a mirror who sees their reflection, steps away for a moment, and then returns—because it seems as though they have immediately forgotten what they look like. Our hearts seem to have short memories, these memories of the good things of God must be strengthened and renewed. How fine a thing to receive such a reminder from a close friend.

REFERENCE: *The Life of William Wilberforce* (1838)

'Guide me right in this great business'

'Commit thy works unto the LORD*, and thy thoughts shall be established.' Proverbs 16:3*
SUGGESTED FURTHER READING: Psalm 37:1–7

Lord, guide me right in this great business that is now going on. May I be enabled to judge, and speak, and act with a simple desire to please God, free entirely from vanity or love of popular favour on the one side, and from the fear of man on the other. O Lord, above all teach me to look to thee, and set my affections on things above.

FOR MEDITATION: In the midst of a great scandal in the early 1800s, involving the Duke of York and corruption in the military, Wilberforce penned these words above. The threat from Napoleon's army was greater than ever before, and yet there was widespread corruption in Britain's armed forces—and a royal duke was involved. Things were very dire indeed.

So often in our lives, things can become very dire. It is then that we, like Wilberforce, must learn to look to God. He sees all ends and knows all things. He is all-wise and all-powerful. In our days of trouble, he is our strong tower. He is our shield. He is our strength and deliverer. The last two verses of Psalm 27 are most fitting: 'I had fainted, unless I had believed to see the goodness of the Lord in the land of the living. Wait on the Lord: be of good courage, and he shall strengthen thine heart: wait, I say, on the Lord' (Psalm 27:13–14).

REFERENCE: *The Life of William Wilberforce* (1838)

'A work to wonder at'

'Many, O LORD my God, are thy wonderful works which thou hast done, and thy thoughts which are to us-ward: they cannot be reckoned up in order unto thee: if I would declare and speak of them, they are more than can be numbered.' Psalm 40:5
SUGGESTED FURTHER READING: Psalm 9:1–11

From a parsonage where he was staying in Newport Pagnell, Wilberforce wrote to Lord Muncaster in September 1809: 'I must own that from my earliest days, at least my earliest travelling days, I never passed a parsonage in at all a pretty village without my mouth watering to reside in it. And this longing has been still more powerful since the only objection, that of solitude, has been removed by my bringing my own society along with me. The best of this place is that though the immediate neighbourhood has no other beauties than those of peaceful rural scenery, yet we are near the scene of Cowper's rambles, and devoted as I am to Cowper, the idea of treading in his track is not a little delightful. It is quite classic ground to me and I shall read both his prose and his verse here with a double relish. I have once already carried some cold meat to a venerable old oak to which he was strongly attached.'

Mr John Bowdler's sketch of this time of peaceful harmony is so happily expressed that though it has appeared in print already it will be read again with pleasure.

'I arrived here last Saturday morning at breakfast time having been kept by Mr Wilberforce much longer than I intended but he is like the old man in Sinbad's Voyage—woe be to the traveller that falls into his grasp! It required a considerable effort to disengage myself and I have promised another short visit on my return which will be greatly to my inconvenience and delight. Mr Wilberforce I think enjoys his parsonage as much as possible: to say that he is happier than usual is being very bold but certainly he is as happy as I ever beheld a human being. He carried me one day to Weston and we wandered over many a spot which Cowper's feet had trod and gazed on the scenes which his pen has immortalized.'

FOR MEDITATION: Psalm 132:6–7 reads: 'we found it in the fields of the wood. We will go into his tabernacles: we will worship at his footstool.'

REFERENCE: *The Life of William Wilberforce* (1838)

'There is a Sun behind the clouds'

'But unto you that fear my name shall the Sun of righteousness arise with healing in his wings.' Malachi 4:2
SUGGESTED FURTHER READING: Psalm 78:14–24

My dear Muncaster ... I feel no comfort in beginning upon political subjects. Oh! it is a gloomy sky, but there is a Sun behind the clouds. In one particular I quite agree with you, in ascribing all the great events which are taking place to a higher hand. Indeed he is always the supreme Agent, but there are times, and this seems to be one of them, when his arm is lifted up, and his hand displayed with more than common plainness. This consideration administers the greatest comfort to my mind. For being persuaded that there are many among us who still love, and fear, and serve the great Governor of the universe, I cannot but hope that, though justly deserving the vengeance, we shall still experience the mercy of Heaven.

FOR MEDITATION: The writer Philip Doddridge also wrote of the sun and the clouds as they relate to the things of God: 'He strengthens my graces; thus he is wisely contriving to bring me nearer to himself and to ripen me for the honours of his heavenly kingdom. It is, if need be, that "I am in heaviness," (1 Peter 1:6) and he surely knows what that need is better than I can pretend to teach him, and knows what peculiar propriety there is in this affliction to answer my present necessity, and to do me that peculiar good which he is graciously intending me by it. This tribulation shall "work patience, and patience experience," and "experience a more assured hope," even a hope which "shall not make ashamed," while the love of God is shed abroad in my heart, (Romans 5:3,5) and shines through my affliction, like the sun through a gentle descending cloud, darting in light upon the shade, and mingling fruitfulness with weeping.'

REFERENCE: *The Life of William Wilberforce* (1838)

'To be living thus in peace'

'And my people shall dwell in a peaceable habitation, and in sure dwellings, and in quiet resting places' Isaiah 32:18
SUGGESTED FURTHER READING: Isaiah 26:11–21

Wilberforce's sons write of the Cowperizing summer their father spent in the parsonage at Newport Pagnell: 'Here he could walk undisturbed in the solitary fields communing with God, or as he did "two mornings, reading Pope and Horace, and getting his *Odes* by heart; had quite forgotten them, but found them easily regained." A little more exertion carried him to Cowper's Weston Woods. "I wish you were a horseman," writes a distant friend, "that I might go and see them by proxy, and hear from you what the place resembles; but your feats of equestrianism are confined to your septennial ride into the Castle Yard; so there are no hopes of your getting into Cowper's classic ground." He had far more activity and spring of body than his appearance seemed to indicate, and twice already had he made this excursion. In this unusual quiet, "reading much, correcting the *Practical View* for a new edition," and much with his family, the weeks passed happily away. "Oh what a blessing it is to be living thus in peace! Surely no one has so much reason to say, that goodness and mercy have followed me all the days of my life."'

FOR MEDITATION: There are Sabbaths that we observe from week to week, and then there are those Sabbaths in metaphor—Sabbaths when we are granted rest and renewal. They are the gift of God. And when we are among family or friends in treasured places, God helps us to find rest from our busy lives—to slow down or to stop—and to savour the moments he gives when we do.

REFERENCE: *The Life of William Wilberforce* (1838)

'Cultivating communion with God'

'The grace of the Lord Jesus Christ, and the love of God, and the communion of the Holy Ghost, be with you all. Amen.'
2 Corinthians 13:14
SUGGESTED FURTHER READING: Psalm 90:1–17

Whilst he thanked God for 'this wholesome retirement,' he was most anxious to turn it to the best account. 'O Lord,' he prayed, 'direct and guide me, so as to make my residence here a blessing to me.' Here therefore, as well as in the crowded life of London, he could exclaim upon his Sundays, 'blessed days these, which call us from the bustle of life, and warrant us in giving up our studies and our business, and cultivating communion with God.'

FOR MEDITATION: The celebrated hymn writer Fanny Crosby, who was blind, knew what it was to cultivate communion with God in ways most of us cannot begin to understand. In 1874, she wrote the following verses:

Thou my everlasting Portion, more than friend or life to me,
All along my pilgrim journey, Saviour, let me walk with thee.
Close to thee, close to thee, close to thee, close to thee,
All along my pilgrim journey, Saviour, let me walk with thee.

The dictionary defines communion as fellowship with God. This is a staggering thought. We may know and enjoy fellowship with the Creator of all that exists. This the psalmist knew, and this he treasured: 'But it is good for me to draw near to God,' he wrote in Psalm 73:28. And in James 4:8 we have this incredible promise: 'Draw nigh to God, and he will draw nigh to you.'

REFERENCE: *The Life of William Wilberforce* (1838)

'The promise is sure'

'Whereby are given unto us exceeding great and precious promises: that by these ye might be partakers of the divine nature.' 2 Peter 1:4
SUGGESTED FURTHER READING: 2 Corinthians 1:13–22

How should I be ashamed if others could see me just as I really am! I often think I am one grand imposture. My heart is heavy; oh, there is nothing that can speak peace to the wounded spirit but the gospel promises—and the promise is sure. God is love; and is able to save to the uttermost, and he will cast out none who come to him. He it is I trust who has excited in me a disposition to come, and I will therefore press forward, humbly indeed, but trusting to his mercy who has promised so many blessings to them that seek him. O Lord, yet strengthen me, and, if it please thee, fill me with all peace and joy in the Holy Ghost. Amen.

FOR MEDITATION: Philip Doddridge, whom Wilberforce so admired, had delved deeply into the word of God, and he knew well that the promises of God are sure. He had this to say of them: 'God has helped the very greatest sinners or all that have yet applied themselves to him; and he has made thee offers of grace and salvation in the most engaging and encouraging terms. "If any man thirst, let him come unto me and drink" (John 7:37); "let him that is a-thirst come; and whosoever will, let him take of the water of life freely" (Revelation 22:17). "Come unto me, all ye that labour and are heavy laden, and I will give you rest" (Matthew 11:28). And once more, "Him that cometh unto me, I will in no wise cast out" (John 4:37). Take his words as they stand, and drink in the consolation of them.'

REFERENCE: *The Life of William Wilberforce* (1838)

'Mercies of all sorts and sizes'

'But the God of all grace, who hath called us unto his eternal glory by Christ Jesus, after that ye have suffered a while, make you perfect, stablish, strengthen, settle you.' 1 Peter 5:10

SUGGESTED FURTHER READING: 1 Corinthians 1:3–9

I humbly hope that I have felt this day, and still feel, somewhat of the powers of the world to come. I feel indeed the deepest sense of my own sinfulness; but blessed be God for his gracious promises. To thee, O Lord, I humbly devote myself; O confirm me to the end. Make me perfect, stablish, strengthen, settle me.

O praeclarum illum diem.
O greatest of days,
when I shall hasten to that divine assembly
and gathering of souls, and when I shall
depart from this crowd and rabble of life! Cicero, *De Senectute*

'What cause have I for thankfulness! Which way soever I look I am heaped up with blessings, mercies of all sorts and sizes. Oh let me record the loving kindness of the Lord.'

FOR MEDITATION: Psalm 63:3–4 declares: 'Because thy lovingkindness is better than life, my lips shall praise thee. Thus will I bless thee while I live: I will lift up my hands in thy name.' May this be the song in our hearts, and may an abiding sense of the lovingkindness of the Lord be ever with us.

REFERENCE: *The Life of William Wilberforce* (1838)

'That I really may be of use in my generation'

'Now also when I am old and grayheaded, O God, forsake me not; until I have shewed thy strength unto this generation, and thy power to every one that is to come.' Psalm 71:18
SUGGESTED FURTHER READING: Psalm 24:1–10

I have a vast multiplicity of objects soliciting my attention and I seem to myself to be failing in the discharge of the duties of my several relations, as Member of Parliament, as father, and as a master [of household servants]. To thee, O God, I fly, through the Saviour; enable me to live more worthy of my holy calling; to be more useful and efficient, that my time may not be frittered away unprofitably to myself and others, but that I really may be of use in my generation, and adorn the doctrine of God my Saviour. I am a poor, helpless creature, Lord, strengthen me.

FOR MEDITATION: To be more useful and efficient. Wilberforce learned early in his career as a reformer from the writings of Philip Doddridge, who wrote: 'nothing conduces more to the advancement of grace than the lively exercise of love to God, and a holy joy in him. I would remind the real Christian of those mercies which tend to excite that love and joy; and in the view of them to animate him to those vigorous efforts of usefulness in life, which so well become his character.' Doddridge then concluded with the following prayer: 'Nor would I forget to acknowledge thy favour in rendering me capable of serving others, and giving me in any instance to know how much "more blessed it is to give than to receive" (Acts 20:35). I thank thee for a heart which feels the sorrows of the necessitous, and a mind which can make it my early care and refreshment to contrive, according to my little ability, for their relief; for "this also cometh forth from thee, O Lord!" (Isaiah 28:29) the great Author of every benevolent inclination, of every prudent scheme, of every successful attempt to spread happiness around us, or in any instance to lessen distress.'

REFERENCE: *The Life of William Wilberforce* (1838)

'My Laodicean heart'

'And God is able to make all grace abound toward you; that ye, always having all sufficiency in all things, may abound to every good work'
2 Corinthians 9:8
SUGGESTED FURTHER READING: Philippians 1:1–11

I have been hearing an excellent sermon from [Charles] Simeon, on Aaron's death, pressing towards the close on torpid believers; alas! alas! to me that name belongs; but blessed be God it need not belong always; thou hast declared that thou wilt be found of them that seek thee. To thee, O Lord, I fly; O forgive and receive thy unworthy wanderer! O come and dwell within me! O Lord fill me with love, with brotherly kindness, and grateful humility. How thankful I should be for my signal privileges, and how candid and tender in speaking, or judging, or thinking of those who have been destitute of the advantages I have enjoyed! If they had possessed my advantages they would most likely be far superior to me. How shocking is it to think that now for twenty-four years I have been seeking after God, and that my progress has been so little! Yet, O Lord, I would humbly hope that though I am weakly and feeble, yet that Christ is knocking at the door of my Laodicean heart, and that I shall open the door and admit my heavenly visitant. O Lord, rouse me effectually, and make me an active, zealous, fruitful Christian.

FOR MEDITATION: Wilberforce wrote these words in the late autumn/early winter of 1809. As an adult, he had begun to seek the Lord earnestly in 1785. Now, twenty-four years later, he still sought the Lord earnestly. His prayer is one that should be ours: 'O Lord, rouse me effectually, and make me an active, zealous, fruitful Christian.'

REFERENCE: *The Life of William Wilberforce* (1838)

'Let me beware'

'But shewing all good fidelity; that they may adorn the doctrine of God our Saviour in all things.' Titus 2:10
SUGGESTED FURTHER READING: Psalm 63:1–11

Let me beware of getting into the way so forcibly described by [John] Owen, as a trade of sinning and repenting. Oh most blessed promise, I will give to him that is athirst of the water of life freely! The main spring having thus been set flowing, may it water every distant branch, and may I fulfil the duties of all my various relations—as M.P., master, acquaintance, etc. now so ill performed. Oh how little have I adorned thy doctrine. Lord, do thou completely sanctify me. Amen.

FOR MEDITATION: How little have I adorned thy doctrine. Is this something about which we ourselves are concerned? Like Wilberforce, each of us play, many roles in our lives, being parents, pursuing professions and many other things besides. Does our faith, like flowing water, flow to each branch of our endeavours in life?

The noted nineteenth-century American hymn writer Fanny Crosby wrote these verses about the water of life:

Jesus the water of life will give,
Freely, freely, freely;
Jesus the water of life will give,
Freely to those who love him.
Come to that fountain, oh drink, and live!
Freely, freely, freely;
Come to that fountain, oh, drink and live!
Flowing for those that love him.

REFERENCE: *The Life of William Wilberforce* (1838)

'I have not played with him at cricket for I know not how long'

'Lo, children are an heritage of the Lord: and the fruit of the womb is his reward. As arrows are in the hand of a mighty man; so are children of the youth. Happy is the man that hath his quiver full of them.' Psalm 127:3–5
SUGGESTED FURTHER READING: Psalm 147:7–14

My dear Muncaster, The kindness which I have ever experienced at your hands assures me, that if you were to hear a loose report of my having been confined up-stairs for a week in a recumbent posture, you would become very uneasy till you should receive some authenticated report of my well-doing. You would, and you will nevertheless laugh heartily when you hear the whole story:—That playing at cricket with Mr Babington, a ball struck my foot with great violence, and that by the positive injunctions of my surgeon, I have been ever since sentenced to a sofa.

It will lessen the marvel, and render the tale less laughable, to hear that my son William was the personage in the *dramatis personae* of the cricket players, and I have not played with him at cricket before, for I know not how long. But here, as in so many other instances, I have abundant cause for thankfulness to the good providence of God; for Mr Pearson (and there is not a more able surgeon in London) declares that if the ball had struck me an inch or two higher, and it is very uncommon for a ball to come along shaving the ground as that did, it would almost certainly have broken my leg.

FOR MEDITATION: The nineteenth-century writer John Ruskin once said: 'Give a little to love a child, and you get a great deal back.' Wilberforce's love for and activities with his children showed how deeply he believed they were an heritage of the Lord. One senses that despite the pain of his injury, he felt it was all worth it to have spent the time he had with his children. May we all cherish our children, as he clearly did.

REFERENCE: *The Life of William Wilberforce* (1838)

'He never seemed to allude to any Scriptural facts or ideas'

'Thy word is a lamp unto my feet, and a light unto my path.' Psalm 119:105
SUGGESTED FURTHER READING: Psalm 119:124–133

It was said poor Windham's accident was a mere trifle at first, and perhaps if it had been attended to in its earliest stages, the bad effects might have been checked. Poor fellow! I really felt for him. He had some fine qualities, though I must own I did not rate him so highly as some persons did, except for conversation in which I really think he was *facile princeps*,[16] decidedly the most agreeable, scholar-like gentleman, or gentleman-like scholar, I ever remember to have seen.

It is certainly true that he wrote to Dr Fisher the day but one before the operation, to say that, the issue being doubtful, he wished to prepare for what might be the consequence in the most solemn manner, and therefore desired him to administer the sacrament to him. Sir W. Scott, who told me this at Lord Camden's, added, that he did receive it with the greatest fervour and emotion.

It is very remarkable, that with an imagination far more fertile and combining than any I ever knew, he never seemed to allude to any Scriptural facts or ideas. Burke did continually.

FOR MEDITATION: Wilberforce wrote the words above following the death of William Windham, of Felbrigg Hall (1750–1810). Windham was M.P. for Norwich from 1784, Secretary at War from 1794 to 1801, and War and Colonial Secretary from 1806–7. On 8 July 1809, he saw a fire in Conduit Street, which threatened to spread to the house of a friend named North, who possessed a valuable library. In his efforts to save the books, Windham fell and bruised his hip. A tumour formed, which was removed; but the operation greatly weakened him and he died on 4 June 1810. Wilberforce admired and respected Windham greatly, and mourned his loss.

REFERENCE: *The Life of William Wilberforce* (1838)

'Never was religion seen in a more engaging form'

'But godliness with contentment is great gain.' 1 *Timothy 6:6*
SUGGESTED FURTHER READING: Luke 12:22–31

Wilberforce's biographer sons described their childhood days in this way:
During the [parliamentary] session indeed he was so busy, and so much
from home, that he could see little of them through the week; but Sunday
was his own, and he spent it in the midst of his family. His children, after
meeting him at prayers, went with him to the house of God; repeating to
him in the carriage hymns or verses, or passages from his favourite
Cowper. Then they walked with him in the garden, and each had the
valued privilege of bringing him a Sunday nosegay, for which the flowers
of their little gardens had been hoarded all the week. Then all dined
together at an early hour.

'*Better,*' was one of his Sunday commonplaces, 'says the wise man, *is a
dinner of herbs where love is, than a stalled ox and hatred therewith*; but,
my children, how good is God to us! He gives us the stalled ox and love
too.'

Never was religion seen in a more engaging form. When the session
was over, and he had retired into the country, it was his delight to live
amongst his children. His meals were as far as possible taken with them;
he carried them out with him on little pleasurable excursions, and joined
often in their amusements. Every day too he read aloud with them,
setting apart some time in the afternoon for lighter and more
entertaining books [or] selecting one of them to read more serious works
to him while he dressed. The young performer who was chosen for the
office drew forth all a father's tenderness.

FOR MEDITATION: How we commend our faith to our children says
everything about the character of our faith.

REFERENCE: *The Life of William Wilberforce* (1838)

'God can effect whatever he will'

'In whom also we have obtained an inheritance, being predestinated according to the purpose of him who worketh all things after the counsel of his own will.' Ephesians 1:11

SUGGESTED FURTHER READING: Isaiah 44:24–45:4

God can effect whatever he will, by means the most circuitous, and the least looked for.

FOR MEDITATION: Wilberforce had a gift for crafting short phrases that stayed in the memory. The words above were of a piece with his ardent belief in an all-powerful, sovereign God. In *A Practical View of Christianity*, he described God as a being of 'exalted Majesty and infinite power.' Elsewhere in this same book he stated: 'the Christian's hope is founded, not on the speculations or the strength of man, but on the declaration of him who cannot lie, on the power of Omnipotence.'

Wilberforce was greatly moved by instances from nature that spoke to him of God's power. 'How wonderful an ordination of providence is it,' he declared, 'that the sand should be placed as the boundary to the roaring sea. "Who placed the *sand* for a bound to the sea by a perpetual decree etc." Here we see the power of omnipotence: had counsel been asked of man, he would have said: "place the granite rock, the adamant bar to restrain the swelling ocean." But no, God places the sand, that which would seem the weakest of barriers, that which is proverbial for instability, as the bound to the sea which it cannot pass over.'

REFERENCE: *The Life of William Wilberforce* (1838)

'Wakeful with continual gratitude'

'But unto every one of us is given grace according to the measure of the gift of Christ.' Ephesians 4:7
SUGGESTED FURTHER READING: Psalm 125

This is the Christian love of God! A love compounded of admiration, of preference, of hope, of trust, of joy; chastised by reverential awe, and wakeful with continual gratitude.

The elementary principles which have been above enumerated may exist in various degrees and proportions. A difference in natural disposition, in the circumstances of the past life, and in numberless other particulars, may occasion a great difference in the predominant tempers of different Christians. In one, the love, in another the fear of God may have the ascendancy; trust in one, and in another gratitude; but in greater or less degrees, a cordial complacency in the sovereignty, an exalted sense of the perfections, a grateful impression of the goodness, and a humble hope of the favour of the Divine Being, are common to them all— Common—the determination to devote themselves without exceptions, to the service and glory of God—Common—the desire of holiness and an abasing consciousness of their own unworthiness.

FOR MEDITATION: The Christian family, like any family, is one where differences may be noted. In an age where these differences, particularly between Anglicans and dissenters, were considerable, Wilberforce's faith fostered within him a charity that stood out. His writings are full of references which show a desire to find common ground wherever he could with fellow believers of other denominations. In this, he followed the dictum of the Christian writer he most revered, the seventeenth-century Puritan Richard Baxter: 'In necessary things, unity; in doubtful things, liberty; in all things, charity.'

REFERENCE: *A Practical View of Christianity* (1797)

'How easily can God confound the wisdom of the wise'

'All the ways of a man are clean in his own eyes; but the LORD *weigheth the spirits.' Proverbs 16:2*
SUGGESTED FURTHER READING: Proverbs 16:1–11

After Wilberforce heard of the death of a political acquaintance and the tragic circumstances that attended it, he wrote: 'Poor S.'s end was awful beyond measure, all circumstances considered. He was ill a fortnight, but his mind was so harassed with worldly affairs, that he would not pursue any medical advice till too late. I hear that dining lately with a small party of contemporaries, he boasted that, in his own words, "he should see them all out"—one was too fat, and another something else. His life appears to have been completely thrown away; yet he was one of the most sensible practical men I ever knew. Oh how easily can God confound the wisdom of the wise, and bring to nothing the understanding of the prudent! What a contrast is Miles Atkinson's death! meek, humble, and confident.'

FOR MEDITATION: 'My times are in thy hand', wrote the psalmist in Psalm 31:15. None of us knows when God will summon us to eternity. The cautionary story Wilberforce relates above reminds us of the story in Luke, Chapter 12:16–21, 31:

And he spake a parable unto them, saying, The ground of a certain rich man brought forth plentifully: and he thought within himself, saying, What shall I do, because I have no room where to bestow my fruits? And he said, This will I do: I will pull down my barns, and build greater; and there will I bestow all my fruits and my goods. And I will say to my soul, Soul, thou hast much goods laid up for many years; take thine ease, eat, drink, and be merry. But God said unto him, Thou fool, this night thy soul shall be required of thee: then whose shall those things be, which thou hast provided? So is he that layeth up treasure for himself, and is not rich toward God … But rather seek ye the kingdom of God; and all these things shall be added unto you.

REFERENCE: *The Life of William Wilberforce* (1838)

'That true honour which cometh from God'

'The fear of the LORD *is the instruction of wisdom; and before honour is humility.' Proverbs 15:33*
SUGGESTED FURTHER READING: Proverbs 15:28–33

But after all, it is of little real importance what judgment is formed of us by our fellow-creatures. To obtain the approbation of the man within the breast, as conscience has been well called, should be our object, and to seek for that true honour which cometh from God.

FOR MEDITATION: To seek for that true honour which cometh from God. In the pages of *A Practical View of Christianity,* Wilberforce added a complementary thought to the one just given: 'act from a pure principle and leave the event to God.'

There are times when we need to take a stand for principle's sake as Christians. It can be a lonely and sometimes hurtful step when others don't understand or agree. It is then that we should try to remember that ours is the privilege of serving an audience of One, the Lord Jesus Christ. In our day of trouble, he will provide strength, solace, discernment and encouragement. He will help us to remain firm in our constancy. He will help us to acquit ourselves as our consciences dictate. And to this we are given an assurance written in the Scriptures: 'I will never leave you, nor forsake you.'

REFERENCE: *The Life of William Wilberforce* (1838)

'Who I have been, and what God has done for me'

'Come and hear, all ye that fear God, and I will declare what he hath done for my soul.' Psalm 66:16
SUGGESTED FURTHER READING: Psalm 26:1–12

Wilberforce wrote on 24 August 1811: My birthday again—born in 1759, so fifty-two complete. Let me not omit the duty of praise and thanksgiving! Who was ever so loudly called on to perform it! Who has been so highly favoured!

Surely when I look over in detail for the last forty years (Deuteronomy 8:2) the course of my heart and life; when I call to mind who I have been, and what God has done for me, and by me; when I sum up all together, and recollect that consideration which should never be forgotten, that all the past, present, and to come, are under the view of God in lively colours, I am lost in astonishment, and can only exclaim 'Thy ways are not as our ways nor thy thoughts as our thoughts.' I will try to look back through my past life, and to affect my heart, as by the review it ought to be, with humiliation, gratitude, love, and confidence.

FOR MEDITATION: Wilberforce loved the liturgy of the Church of England. He felt it contained 'grand truths,' that fostered within him an increase in the religious affections and a transforming influence in the heart. 'What lively emotions,' he wrote in *A Practical View of Christianity,* 'are these grand truths calculated to excite in us of self-abasement, abhorrence of our sins, humble hope, firm faith, heavenly joy, ardent love and active, unceasing gratitude!'

It was much the same with his birthday, an anniversary which he always marked after his 'great change' with recollection and reflection. He found that such a review, like the liturgy he so loved, fostered within him a properly Christian sense of humiliation, gratitude, love, and confidence.

REFERENCE: *The Life of William Wilberforce* (1838)

'The true honour'

'For ye are bought with a price: therefore glorify God in your body, and in your spirit, which are God's.' 1 Corinthians 6:20
SUGGESTED FURTHER READING: 1 Corinthians 6:11–20

To serve God is the true honour of those who are not their own, but are bought with a price; and the point is, to learn what his will is.

FOR MEDITATION: Wilberforce wrote these words when he was deciding to resign his seat as MP for Yorkshire in 1812. He had represented the entire county of Yorkshire for 28 years, and it was then one of the most powerful elected seats in the national legislature. Historians are generally agreed that had he chosen not to resign, so secure was his hold on the affections of his constituents that he could have held the seat with little effort for the rest of his life.

So why resign? His health was one factor, for he had always been prone to dangerous bouts of stress-induced illness. Ulcerative colitis appears to have been the chief culprit.

But in the main, it was concern over his family that led him to take the step of resignation. His young children were growing up and he felt he was too seldom there for them. Wishing to take a more active role in rearing them, particularly in their education—this was Wilberforce's primary inducement to relinquish his seat as MP for Yorkshire. He would still continue in politics, as member for the less taxing constituency of Bramber, but he could now embark on what he felt to be a calling from God that was just as important—more actively parenting his six children.

REFERENCE: *The Life of William Wilberforce* (1838)

'The promised Sabbath'

'There remaineth therefore a rest to the people of God.' Hebrews 4:9
SUGGESTED FURTHER READING: 1 John 3:1–3

Elmdon, Sunday, Sept. 29 1811. Walked a little with [a volume of] Cowper—the beautiful end of the 6th book—'the promised Sabbath'. What a prospect! Oh the unspeakable mercies of God; what can I desire which he has not granted me?

The groans of nature in this nether world,
Which Heav'n has heard for ages, have an end.
Foretold by prophets, and by poets sung,
Whose fire was kindled at the prophets' lamp,
The time of rest, the promis'd Sabbath, comes.
Six thousand years of sorrow have well-nigh
Fulfill'd their tardy and disastrous course
Over a sinful world; and what remains
Of this tempestuous state of human things
Is merely as the working of a sea
Before a calm, that rocks itself to rest:
For he, whose care the winds are, and the clouds
The dust that waits upon his sultry march,
When sin hath mov'd him, and his wrath is hot,
Shall visit earth in mercy; shall descend,
Propitious, in his chariot pav'd with love;
And what his storms have blasted and defac'd
For man's revolt shall with a smile repair.[17]

And then when I compare my state with that of all the rest of the world, in other countries, and even in this little oasis of security, and prosperity, and peace! Oh that I were more grateful! Oh let me strive more to love God and Christ, to delight in them, and be grateful to them in some proportion to what I ought.

FOR MEDITATION: The promised Sabbath—what a glorious prospect.

REFERENCE: *The Life of William Wilberforce* (1838)

'His grateful voice sang its own joy'

'And he hath put a new song in my mouth, even praise unto our God.'
Psalm 40:3
SUGGESTED FURTHER READING: Psalm 9:1–11

During the summer recess of 1790 Wilberforce stayed at Yoxall Lodge, the home of his cherished friends, Thomas and Mary Gisborne. There he devoted ten or twelve hours every day to studying evidence against the slave trade and writing his book *A Practical View of Christianity*. This summer sojourn to a welcoming home and its beautiful surroundings also helped to lift Wilberforce's spirits, for the preceding session of Parliament had been gruelling. 'Mr. Wilberforce,' wrote his sons, 'sallied forth always for a walk a short time before dinner, amongst the holly groves of the then unenclosed Needwood forest, where:

His grateful voice
Sang its own joy, and made the woods rejoice.

'"Often," said his host, "have I heard its melodious tones at such times, amongst the trees from the distance of full half a mile."'

FOR MEDITATION: The great seventeenth-century divine Richard Baxter, in his classic book *The Saint's Everlasting Rest*, wrote of the joys and the songs that flow from religious contemplation, particularly that of heaven: 'The next affection to be excited in heavenly contemplation, is desire,' he wrote. 'O blessed souls who see a thousand times more clearly what I have seen at a distance, and through dark, interposing clouds. I am sighing, and they are singing. They have none of my cares and fears; they weep not in secret; they languish not in sorrows; these "tears are wiped away from their eyes." O happy, a thousand times happy souls! They are of one heart and voice, and daily sound forth the hallelujahs of heaven with perfect harmony.'

REFERENCE: *The Life of William Wilberforce* (1838)

'Friendly expostulation'

'But to them that rebuke him shall be delight, and a good blessing shall come upon them.' Proverbs 24:25
SUGGESTED FURTHER READING: Deuteronomy 5:1–12

To the house of Edward Eliot at Burton Pynsent, Mr Wilberforce made an excursion upon the 30th of June 1791. 'Set off early for [Edward] Eliot's. Dined with G. his friend. G. sadly taking God's name in vain.'

To any of his friends who had contracted this irreverent habit, he made a practice of addressing by letter his most serious admonitions; and he has often said that by this custom he never lost, and but once endangered the continuance of a friendship.

'I wrote to the late Sir ——, and mentioned to him this bad habit. He sent me in reply an angry letter, returning a book that I had given him; and asking for one he had given me. Instead of it I sent him a second letter of friendly expostulation, which so won him over, that he wrote to me in the kindest tone, and begged me to send him back again the book he had so hastily returned.'

FOR MEDITATION: It is a rare person who can rebuke in such a way as to win over the person to whom the rebuke is given. The dictionary states that expostulation is the act of reasoning earnestly with someone in an effort to dissuade or correct.

We risk much when we do this. Our motives may never be understood as we might wish them to be by the person with whom we are expostulating. We may lose a friend. Admonishing someone is never to be undertaken lightly, but it ought always to be done charitably. God is in no other wise honoured by our action.

REFERENCE: *The Life of William Wilberforce* (1838)

'The Author of my mercies'

'And being made perfect, he became the author of eternal salvation unto all them that obey him.' Hebrews 5:9
SUGGESTED FURTHER READING: Psalm 89:1–8

August 24, 1797. I have no time to write, but let me use the few minutes I have in praying to God in Christ, the Author of my mercies, beseeching him to hear me, to fill me with spiritual blessings, and enable me to live to his glory. My marriage and the publication of my book are the great events of the past year. In both I see much to humble me, and to fill my mouth with praises. Let me resign myself to God, who has hitherto led me by ways that I knew not, and implore him yet to bless me.

FOR MEDITATION: Wilberforce had a habit of observing the anniversaries of special, often providential events in his life. They reminded him powerfully that God is the one who holds our times in his hands (Psalm 31:15). His birthday was one such day, the day he escaped drowning in the Avon River another. In 1818 he wrote: 'Tomorrow, the 25th of October, is the anniversary of the day on which I experienced that notable escape from being drowned in the Avon, when we lodged at Bath Easton. Praise the Lord, O my soul.'

Wilberforce's near drowning occurred in 1803, at which time he had written: 'Walked with pencil and book and wrote. A charming day. I was sitting by the river-side, with my back to the water, on a portable seat, when suddenly it struck me that it was not quite safe. Writing, I might be absent, and suddenly slip off, etc. I moved therefore a few yards, and placed my stool on the grass, when in four or five minutes it suddenly broke, and I fell flat on my back, as if shot. Had it happened five minutes sooner, as I cannot swim, I must, a thousand to one, have been drowned, for I sat so that I must have fallen backwards into the river I had not the smallest fear or idea of the seat's breaking with me; and it is very remarkable, that I had rather moved about while by the river, which would have been more likely to break it, whereas I sat quite still when on the grass. A most providential escape. Let me praise God for it.'

REFERENCE: *The Life of William Wilberforce* (1838)

'The multiplied mercies of God'

'Thou preparest a table before me in the presence of mine enemies: thou anointest my head with oil; my cup runneth over.' Psalm 23:5
SUGGESTED FURTHER READING: Psalm 136:1–9

'I could not be quiet yesterday,' Wilberforce wrote the day after his birthday, 25 August 1799, 'though I got a contemplative walk and even today I have less time than I could wish for looking back through the year, and awakening pious gratitude for the multiplied mercies of God.

'How often have I been sick and restored! How few, if any, days of suffering, either bodily or mental! My wife and child going on well, and a daughter born (July 21st) and doing well. Instances repeatedly heard of my book [*Practical View*] doing good. How gracious is God through Christ, to fill my cup with blessings.'

FOR MEDITATION: A young woman was once asked to read a text for a class in oral interpretation, that is to say, public speaking. She selected Psalm 136, which begins: 'O give thanks unto the Lord; for he is good: for his mercy endureth for ever.' Each of the twenty-six verses in this psalm ends with the same refrain: 'for his mercy endureth for ever.'

As this young woman continued to read, a powerful sense of the meaning of that refrain overcame her. She quietly began to weep. Overcome, she took her seat amidst a silent classroom. It was then that her professor rose to speak. Normally he would have given an evaluation of her presentation on the spot, as he done with others who had gone before.

But he didn't. Instead this professor—who was not known for mincing words—showed himself to be one who understood what grace and mercy are. 'That was beautiful,' he said gently, 'thank you.'

REFERENCE: *The Life of William Wilberforce* (1838)

'The best of all medicines'

'Then are they glad because they be quiet; so he bringeth them unto their desired haven.' Psalm 107:30
SUGGESTED FURTHER READING: Psalm 107:1–7

Leaving Broomfield in the beginning of September [1804] Mr Wilberforce moved with his whole family[18] to Lyme in Dorsetshire, where he hoped 'to enjoy something of to me the greatest of all luxuries, as well as the best of all medicines, quiet.'

'The place,' he told [Thomas] Babington, 'suits me mightily: a bold coast; a fine sea view—the clouds often shrouding the tops of the cliffs; a very varied surface of ground; a mild climate and either fresh air or sheltered walks as you please. I allow myself two or three hours open air daily, and have enjoyed more than one solitary stroll with a Testament, a Cowper, or a Psalter for my companion. Excepto quod non simul esses, etc.[19] I wish you were here and all your house but if the presence of some friends would be a most valuable addition the absence of the multitude of callers is a most valuable loss. We have not had one call since we came. I never was at any place where I had so much the command of my own time and the power of living as I please.'

He could now too indulge in some degree his keen relish of natural beauties and the common air. He read 'much out of doors and wrote with a pencil,' and 'had many a delightful walk along the rough, resounding shore, meditating on better things than poor blind Homer knew or sung of.'

FOR MEDITATION: Psalm 107:23–24 tells us: 'They that go down to the sea in ships ... these see the works of the Lord, and his wonders in the deep.' The whole of Psalm 107 is worthy of careful study. The security of the Lord's people should be a constant theme for our praise.

REFERENCE: *The Life of William Wilberforce* (1838)

'When soured and fretted by the bustle and the business of life'

'From the rising of the sun unto the going down of the same the Lord's name is to be praised.' Psalm 113:3
SUGGESTED FURTHER READING: Psalm 141:1–10

'I am now writing at the parsonage of James Stephen's eldest son [William], in one of the most rural villages in Oxfordshire, secured almost to the point of being impregnable by the badness of the roads, but surrounded with beech woods, and truly dulcifying to the mind, as [Edmund] Burke would have said, when soured and fretted by the bustle and the business of life.'

'Yesterday,' he told Mrs Wilberforce from the same place, 'I was fully occupied until the evening, when it would have been almost sacrilege and ingratitude not to walk for half an hour at least enjoying one of the finest sun-settings and moon-risings which my eyes ever beheld. Then my dear boys were with me for some time.

'I was thinking of you all. A lovelier evening for meditating I never remember, and this is one of the finest mornings that eye ever beheld. But I must break off. I am delaying Stephen and the boys from a stroll in the woods.'

FOR MEDITATION: Wilberforce wrote these words in the late summer or early autumn of 1812. With Isaiah the prophet, Wilberforce knew what it was to praise him who makes evenings so lovely that it seems the very skies will 'pour down righteousness' (Isaiah 45:8).

REFERENCE: *The Life of William Wilberforce* (1838)

'Doing good to those around him'

'The steps of a good man are ordered by the Lord: and he delighteth in his way.' Psalm 37:23
SUGGESTED FURTHER READING: Psalm 119:65–72

Mr. Wilberforce was again at Sandgate, living in the midst of his children, studying the Scriptures daily with some of them, 'walking and reading with them all, and bringing them into the habits he desired by kind, not violent means.'

He was as busy too doing good to those around him, as if his sympathies had never wandered from his own immediate circle; entering eagerly into any individual tale of suffering—as when he heard this year of a case, ('the shocking account of Mrs R.'s cruelty to her child'), which he took up and carried through, at a great expense of time and trouble, and in spite of repeated threatenings of personal violence from the brutal parent—and labouring too by schools and other institutions to relieve the want and ignorance around him.

'The adult school,' wrote a friend staying at this time in his family to Mr. Arthur Young, 'is established here; a room and teachers provided, and all will be left in good train. Mr. Wilberforce went himself, read them extracts from Thomas Pole's *History of Adult Schools*,[20] and made them a little speech, saying how much he respected their good sense for coming. You would have been delighted with seeing him seated by the old ladies, with the utmost patience, kindness, and humility, fairly teaching them their letters. This was beautiful in him, and highly useful and encouraging in its effects upon the institution.'

FOR MEDITATION: The events related above took place in the late summer or early autumn of 1814. Christians are those who have known God's 'lovingkindness, and the multitude of his tender mercies' (Psalm 51:1). In Christ, we have been called to be agents of mercy, and people who exhibit something of the lovingkindness we have received to others.

REFERENCE: *The Life of William Wilberforce* (1838)

'To adjust a disagreement between two absent friends'

'And all things are of God, who hath reconciled us to himself by Jesus Christ, and hath given to us the ministry of reconciliation.'
2 Corinthians 5:18
SUGGESTED FURTHER READING: 2 Corinthians 5:10–21

Another day he was endeavouring by letter to adjust a disagreement between two absent friends, telling him who had taken the offence: 'It grieves and justly grieves me, loving and respecting you both as I do, to think that your friendship should be in any measure injured by that which is in reason an utterly inadequate cause for producing such an effect. As I hinted to you, my dear ——, you men of meditation (though I sincerely acknowledge and covet your ruminating habit) are liable to the fault of weaving a web out of your own cogitations, which has no substance but that ideal one which renders it the basis of your castles in the air, and leads you often, or at least sometimes, to false solutions of enigmas, and mistaken views of character; though I grant that it enables you to fix and retain conceptions of the passing events of life with their causes and consequences, which flit away and are forgotten by us bird-witted gentry, as Locke or Lord Bacon calls us. But I must break off.'

FOR MEDITATION: Early in 1805 another reconciliation took place between cherished friends of Wilberforce's, Prime Minister William Pitt and his immediate predecessor as premier, Henry Addington. In this case, the circumstances were much more dire: the two national leaders had fallen out over different views as to the prosecution of the war against Napoleon's France. Wilberforce received the news from Pitt himself: 'You will, I know, be glad, independent of politics, that Addington and I have met as friends.' Of this, Wilberforce's sons wrote: '[Our father] was extremely pleased with this reconciliation. He was gratified too by Mr Pitt's anxiety to acquaint him with it. "It showed me that he understood my real feelings." Upon the 1st of February Mr Wilberforce called on Mr Pitt and walked with him. "I am sure," Pitt said, "that you are glad to hear that Addington and I are at one again."'

Wilberforce had taken to heart verses found in 1 Peter 3:10–11. May we be able to go on in the same spirit.

REFERENCE: *The Life of William Wilberforce* (1838)

'Our brave fellows may be fighting hard'

'Bow down thine ear to me; deliver me speedily: be thou my strong rock, for an house of defence to save me.' Psalm 31:2
SUGGESTED FURTHER READING: Psalm 59:1–9

Sunday [18 June 1815], was spent at the parsonage of Taplow, where Mr. Wilberforce's family had been staying for a week. It is described in his Diary as 'a quiet day.'

Above measure did he enjoy its quietness. He seemed to shake off with delight the dust and bustle of the crowded city; and as he walked up the rising street of the village on his way to the old church of Taplow, he called on all around to rejoice with him in the visible goodness of his God.

'Perhaps,' he said to his children, 'at this very moment when we are walking thus in peace together to the house of God, our brave fellows may be fighting hard in Belgium. Oh how grateful should we be for all God's goodness to us.'

FOR MEDITATION: Wilberforce could not have known, but he was exactly right. The Battle of Waterloo was being fought as he uttered the words above—on the 18th of June 1815.

Prayer for those who guide the counsels of our nation, and for those who defend it, is deeply important. We receive guidance as to this from the apostle Paul, who wrote to Timothy: 'I exhort therefore, that, first of all, supplications, prayers, intercessions, and giving of thanks, be made for all men; for kings, and for all that are in authority; that we may lead a quiet and peaceable life in all godliness and honesty. For this is good and acceptable in the sight of God our Saviour' (1 Timothy 2:1–3).

REFERENCE: *The Life of William Wilberforce* (1838)

'As beautiful as they are complete'

'For all the promises of God in him are yea, and in him Amen.'
2 *Corinthians* 1:20
SUGGESTED FURTHER READING: Psalm 46:1–11

Mr Wilberforce was still ever praying to be more fully 'quickened, warmed, and purified;' and at times he complained 'from what cause soever it is, my heart is invincibly dull. I have again and again gone to prayer, read, meditated, yet all in vain. Oh, how little can we do any thing without the quickening grace of God! I will go again to prayer and meditation.'... But though occasionally harassed by such 'dullness of heart,' his ordinary spirit was far different. The full spring of love, and joy, and thankfulness was bursting forth into spontaneous expression in his conversation, his letters, and his Journal. All the natural objects round him had become the symbols of the presence and love of his heavenly Father, and like the opening of the passion flower, suggested to him some new motives for thankfulness and praise.

'I was walking with him in his verandah at Kensington Gore,' said a friend, 'the year before, watching for the opening of a night blowing cereus. As we stood by in eager expectation, it suddenly burst wide open before us.'

'"It reminds me," said he, as we admired its beauty, "of the dispensations of Divine Providence first breaking on the glorified eye, when they shall fully unfold to the view, and appear as beautiful as they are complete."'

FOR MEDITATION: The beauties of nature so often turned Wilberforce's thoughts to his Creator. In May 1824, he wrote to his great friend and fellow reformer Hannah More, telling her that taking the air and exercising were at present 'the main business of life. But for this I have Francis Bacon's authority: indeed I trust a still higher than his. For each and all of these is associated with a grateful sense of the loving-kindness of that gracious Being, whose goodness and mercy continue to be so profusely poured out on me, and who thus bountifully strews with flowers the way—the narrow way, I humbly hope, that leads ... to that better world wherein all will be congenial with the unalloyed and unobstructed influences of the God of holiness and love.'

REFERENCE: *The Life of William Wilberforce* (1838)

'I shall like the place as well again'

'For the Lord shall comfort Zion: he will comfort all her waste places; and he will make her wilderness like Eden, and her desert like the garden of the Lord; joy and gladness shall be found therein, thanksgiving, and the voice of melody.' Isaiah 51:3
SUGGESTED FURTHER READING: Isaiah 58:8–14

One of the first amongst these visits was to Barham Court, 'which is now in full beauty,' Mr. Wilberforce wrote to James Stephen on 24 July 1818, 'I never saw it in greater.

'We arrived late on Wednesday, and you would be pleased to know how much I have walked about to-day. You know the Noels: could you not come here from Saturday next to the Monday following? How you would revel in the walks of this fruitful scene of multiform production, farm, woodland, cornfields of all kinds, meadows, garden, orchard!

'Never did I see a place of such varied forms of beauty and fertility. Come on Friday after your business, I beg of you, that you may have all Saturday for your rambles. I shall like the place as well again, when I shall have witnessed the raptures which I am sure it will kindle in you. To be sure, it does forcibly impress on me Cowper's famous line, borrowed however from some preceding poet: 'God made the country, but man made the town.'

FOR MEDITATION: The natural beauty to be found in the homes of cherished friends was a recurring theme in Wilberforce's correspondence. To this friend James Stephen he wrote of Yoxall Lodge, the home of their mutual friend Thomas Gisborne: 'Well as I thought I knew this place, and much as I had admired it, I never saw its riches displayed in such overflowing profusion. I never was here before till late in the year, or saw the first foliage of the magnificent oak contrast with the dark holly, the flowering gorse, and the horse-chestnut. A fine tree always seems to me like a community in itself, with the countless insects which it shelters and nourishes in its roots and branches. It is quite a merciful ordination of Providence, that the forests of our country to which as a maritime nation we look for protection and commerce should be so admirable for their beauty. Instead of a beautiful ornament, they might have been a disagreeable object, to which we were compelled to be indebted.'

REFERENCE: *The Life of William Wilberforce* (1838)

'Sunday turned all his feelings into a new channel'

'Cause me to hear thy lovingkindness in the morning; for in thee do I trust: cause me to know the way wherein I should walk; for I lift up my soul unto thee.' Psalm 143:8
SUGGESTED FURTHER READING: Psalm 65:1–13

Writing of their father as he was in 1812, Wilberforce's sons observed: 'His affections were naturally lively, but it was not to this only that he owed the preservation, all through his busy life, of their early morning freshness. This was the reward of self-discipline and watchfulness; of that high value for the house of God, and the hours of secret meditation, which made his Sundays cool down his mind and allay the rising fever of political excitement. Sunday turned all his feelings into a new channel. His letters were put aside, and all thoughts of business banished. To the closest observer of his private hours he seemed throughout the day as free from all the feelings of a politician, as if he had never mixed in the busy scenes of public life.'

FOR MEDITATION: Wilberforce once wrote of 'that mercy of God which has never failed me.' At another time he wrote: 'I often think no one scarcely has so much cause as myself to adopt the language of the psalmist, and to say, that goodness and mercy have followed me all the days of my life.'

It was during his times of meditation upon the things of God, that he was reminded anew and strengthened in his confidence regarding God's never-failing mercy. With the psalmist he could say: 'My meditation of him shall be sweet: I will be glad in the Lord' (Psalm 104:34). Verses found elsewhere in the Old Testament are fitting here: 'This I recall to my mind, therefore have I hope. It is of the Lord's mercies that we are not consumed, because his compassions fail not. They are new every morning: great is thy faithfulness' (Lamentations 3:21–23).

REFERENCE: *The Life of William Wilberforce* (1838)

'A constant guard over his temper'

'Create in me a clean heart, O God; and renew a right spirit within me.'
Psalm 51:10
SUGGESTED FURTHER READING: Psalm 141:1–10

'Mr Sargent preached, and pleased us all greatly—simple seriousness, and consequent pathos, the character of his preaching.' These are samples of Mr Wilberforce's Sunday thoughts; and to these was joined a constant guard over his temper. 'What a blessing,' he wrote, 'is a cheerful temper! I felt most keenly ——'s behaviour about Bowdler, and his not coming to me; but for his sake, and I hope from Christian principles, I resolved to struggle against bad temper about it, and now all is over.'

Thus was his spirit kept unruffled by all the exasperating influences of the life he led; whilst he walked safely, with a cheerful seriousness and disengaged affections, in the heated and infectious air of public life—in the world, but most truly not of the world—ever remembering the end. In this vein, he wrote on one occasion: 'How will all this busy and tumultuous world appear to have been all one great bedlam when we look back on it from a future state!'

FOR MEDITATION: All his life, Wilberforce struggled with his quick temper. And he struggled too, when vexed by people and circumstances, to keep things in right perspective. He did not always succeed and even 'sparred' with Prime Minister William Pitt, one of his closest friends, over one legislative issue. But as the Victorian prose of Wilberforce's sons affirms—he kept trying to guard and govern his temper—asking God to help him to do so. That is all any of us can really do—keep trying, and keep asking for God's help.

REFERENCE: *The Life of William Wilberforce* (1838)

'Oh may I walk softly'

'Furthermore then we beseech you, brethren, and exhort you by the Lord Jesus, that as ye have received of us how ye ought to walk and to please God, so ye would abound more and more.' 1 Thessalonians 4:1
SUGGESTED FURTHER READING: Colossians 1:9–14

'I was much affected last night after seeing poor S. in an agony of pain, with thinking what hell must be—pain without hope.'

With all my defects and unprofitableness, I humbly hope that it is my main desire to please thee. Oh may I walk softly, deeply feeling my own unworthiness, repenting in dust and ashes; guarding against self-deception, lest I lose the precious opportunities of communion with God.

FOR MEDITATION: To walk softly before the Lord was a continuing desire of Wilberforce's heart. However, his experience of what it meant to walk softly before the Lord was fostered through often trying circumstances, none more so than an illness contracted by his beloved wife Barbara during her first pregnancy: 'My dear wife,' he wrote in 1798, 'is now ill. How dependent does this make me feel upon the power and goodness of God! What a humbling impression have I of my own inability—that all my happiness and all that belongs to me is at the disposal of the Supreme Being! So it ought always to be. This is to walk softly.'

God brought mother and child (son William) safely through, and a few days later Wilberforce wrote: 'Oh what abundant cause have I for gratitude—how well all has gone on both with mother and child! I will take a musing walk of gratitude and intercession. How full of mercies is God to me.'

Ye souls, redeemed with blood,	Has Jesus made you free?
And called by grace divine,	Then you are free indeed;
Walk worthy of your God,	Ye sons of liberty,
And let your conduct shine;	Ye chosen royal seed,
Keep Christ, your living Head, in view,	Walk worthy of your Lord, and view
In all you say, in all you do.	Your glorious Head, in all you do.

William Gadsby (1773–1844)

REFERENCE: *The Life of William Wilberforce* (1838)

'The same melancholy sensation'

'Her children arise up, and call her blessed; her husband also, and he praiseth her.' Proverbs 31:28
SUGGESTED FURTHER READING: Proverbs 31:10–31

'For once,' Mr Wilberforce told his wife, who was travelling with his children to the coast in the summer of 1812, 'I rejoice in an east wind, since I recollect that it will meet you and prevent your all suffering from the heat.'

I have been sitting under the trees reading and writing. The only part of the garden which I did not enjoy, was one to which I went purposely to see how all looked—the children's gardens. Even the fullest exuberance of summer beauties could not supply the want of animal life. Barbara's[21] gum-cistus is in high beauty, and the roses in full bloom. My own room produces something of the same melancholy sensation as the children's gardens.

FOR MEDITATION: None of God's gifts is dearer than that of family. Having waited until he was thirty-eight to marry, Wilberforce's love and devotion to his beloved wife Barbara and their six children was all the more ardent. He missed them dearly when he was kept in London on business and they were away on holiday. We all know the phrase 'absence makes the heart grow fonder.' The absence of his family only deepened his love for them. It was seldom far from his mind that they were a gift he thought he might never know, since he had been for so many years a bachelor.

REFERENCE: *The Life of William Wilberforce* (1838)

'In the midst of life we are in death.'

'Precious in the sight of the LORD *is the death of his saints.' Psalm 116:15*
SUGGESTED FURTHER READING: Romans 8:31–39

'Poor Perceval! You know the boys at Harrow speak publicly once a year, and all the parents and old Harrow men attend. Perceval, a week or ten days before he was murdered, had bespoke rooms at the inn that he might give a dinner to some friends and relations who were to hear his son speak Cardinal Wolsey's affecting speech in *Henry VIII*. "In the midst of life we are in death." I commend you all to God's protecting care, and to our gracious Saviour's goodness.'

FOR MEDITATION: Prime Minister Spencer Perceval (1762–1812) was the son of the 2nd Earl of Egmont. His assassination in 1812 stunned the entire nation, and Wilberforce deeply mourned his loss. Perceval was a man of deep faith, and Wilberforce cherished high hopes of what he could have accomplished for Britain as a Christian statesman. Tragically, Perceval was taken from his family and friends in the prime of his life. We never know when God may summon us home. Therefore every day is a gift. As one current songwriter has phrased it: 'Teach us to count our days/teach us to make the days count/life means so much.'

REFERENCE: *The Life of William Wilberforce* (1838)

'As we grow nearer the great change'

'He shall abide before God for ever: O prepare mercy and truth, which may preserve him.' Psalm 61:7
SUGGESTED FURTHER READING: Isaiah 64:1–8

Age is not to be measured by years, but by bodily strength. For instance, I account myself full ten years older than most men of my own age, though by care I may, through God's blessing, and calculating according to human probabilities, attain to the ordinary duration of the life of man.

In truth, if I could have been sure that this Parliament would have died in three years, I might have consented to a renewal of my lease (i.e. continued as MP for Yorkshire, rather than have resigned my seat). But six years was a longer term than I durst venture to engage for. Indeed, as we grow nearer the great change, it is well to make still ampler preparation for it; and to live under a more abiding impression of the uncertainty of life. For this end I find nothing more effectual than private prayer, and the serious perusal of the New Testament.

FOR MEDITATION: These words, written to Wilberforce's dear friend Lord Muncaster on 27 October 1812, possess a wisdom born of knowing this world is not our ultimate home. For the Christian another home awaits us. It has been well said that this life is given us so that we may rightly prepare for the life to come. Wilberforce understood this.

It is also touching to think that Wilberforce was right in humbly stating that he might, 'through God's blessing attain to the ordinary duration of the life of man.' Indeed he did, dying just shy of his seventy-fourth birthday. God had graciously granted him, though so often beset by serious illness and physical infirmity, more than 'three score and ten.'

REFERENCE: *The Life of William Wilberforce* (1838)

'By thee have I been holden up'

'Thou makest the outgoings of the morning and evening to rejoice.'
Psalm 65:8b
SUGGESTED FURTHER READING: Psalm 71:1–24

Writing of their father as he was in the autumn of 1812, Wilberforce's sons observed: To the eye of a stranger he appeared at this time full ten years older than he was; but more intimate acquaintance removed this impression. Delicacy of health had indeed set on him already some of the external marks of age, and a stoop which he contracted early, and which lessened his apparent stature, added much to this effect. But the agility of his step, the quickness of all his senses (though he only heard with one ear), his sparkling eye, and the compass and beauty of his voice, contradicted all these first appearances.

And those who listened with delight to the freshness and exuberance of thoughts, sometimes deeply serious, sometimes playful and humorous, which enriched his conversation, could hardly believe that he had long borne the weight even of manly years. At the breakfast table, and again from the setting-in of evening until midnight were his gayest times; at the last, especially, all his faculties were in the fullest exercise; and when being read to in his family circle, which was his delight, he poured forth all his stores, gathering around him book after book to illustrate, question, or confirm the immediate subject of the evening.

FOR MEDITATION: Wilberforce's revivifying sense of the goodness of God was not unlike that which had prompted the psalmist to write of the Lord: 'Who satisfieth thy mouth with good things; so that thy youth is renewed like the eagle's' (Psalm 103:5).

REFERENCE: *The Life of William Wilberforce* (1838)

'Scripture reading and meditation'

'My meditation of him shall be sweet: I will be glad in the Lord.'
Psalm 104:34
SUGGESTED FURTHER READING: Psalm 119:1–16

When not unavoidably prevented by company or House of Commons I
will take an hour, or at least half an hour, for private devotions, including
Scripture reading and meditation, immediately before family prayers.
Besides other benefits, one will be to send me back into society with a
more spiritual mind, and to help me to preserve it through the evening,
and to make the conversation more edifying and instructive. The best
hope will arise from my bearing about with me a deep impression of my
own weakness, and of the urgent need of Divine help.

FOR MEDITATION: One of the fruits of our times of spiritual reflection can
be to make, as Wilberforce writes, 'the conversation more edifying and
instructive.' He was deeply influenced in this view of things by Philip
Doddridge, who wrote in *The Rise and Progress of Religion in the Soul*
(1745): 'It should be our desire that our discourse in company may be
edifying to ourselves and others. We should endeavor to have some
subject of useful discourse always ready. We should watch for decent
opportunities of introducing useful reflections; and if a pious friend
attempt to do it, we should endeavour to second it immediately. When the
conversation does not turn directly on religious subjects, we should
endeavour to make it improving some other way; we should reflect on the
character and capacities of our company, that we may lead them to talk
of what they understand best. And in pauses of discourse, it may not be
improper to lift up a [silent prayer] to God, that his grace may assist us
and our friends in our endeavours to do good to each other; that all we
say or do may be worthy the character of reasonable creatures and of
Christians.'

REFERENCE: *The Life of William Wilberforce* (1838)

'We should give God our best time'

'With my whole heart have I sought thee: O let me not wander from thy commandments.' Psalm 119:10
SUGGESTED FURTHER READING: Deuteronomy 18:3–5

As to my being now extremely occupied, John Owen's remark in some degree applies, [as does the] inference from Malachi, that we should give God if needful our best time. O Lord, thy blessing can render far more than a day's time as nothing even in my worldly business, and if the main-spring's force be strengthened, and its working improved, (cleansed from dust and foulness,) surely the machine will go better. Lord, what I do I trust is pleasing to thee; accept and bless my service.

FOR MEDITATION: The Bible is replete with metaphors of what it means to 'give God our best time,' as Wilberforce phrases it above. Often references are made to giving God the firstfruits (or best portion) of our labours. The Book of Exodus states: 'The first of the first fruits of thy land thou shalt bring into the house of the Lord thy God' (Exodus 23:19). In the book of Leviticus we read: 'And the Lord spake unto Moses, saying, Speak unto the children of Israel, and say unto them, When ye be come into the land which I give unto you, and shall reap the harvest thereof, then ye shall bring a sheaf of the firstfruits of your harvest unto the priest: And he shall wave the sheaf before the Lord, to be accepted for you' (Leviticus 23:9–11).

In the New Testament, we read of what it means to 'gather fruit unto life eternal: that both he that soweth and he that reapeth may rejoice together' (John 4:36). It should be our prayer that God will guide us aright in all things. Then, when we strive to give him our best, we will find that our mainspring's force will have been strengthened, its working improved, and our machinery of our collective watches will go better.

REFERENCE: *The Life of William Wilberforce* (1838)

'There are two souls within me'

'For the good that I would I do not: but the evil which I would not, that I do. Now if I do that I would not, it is no more I that do it, but sin that dwelleth in me. I find then a law, that, when I would do good, evil is present with me. For I delight in the law of God after the inward man: but I see another law in my members, warring against the law of my mind, and bringing me into captivity to the law of sin which is in my members.' Romans 7:19–23
SUGGESTED FURTHER READING: Romans 6:4–8

I put these things down, that I may fix, and ascertain, and reconsider my own corruptions and the deceitful working of my mind and passions. There are two souls within me; Lord, help me to expel the fleshly occupant, [to take up] thankfulness and prayer that I may plan my system of life wisely, and execute it properly.

FOR MEDITATION: 'O Lord enable me to press on,' Wilberforce wrote on another occasion. 'How absolutely helpless I am in myself. May [my circumstances] keep me more simply dependent on the grace and Spirit of God.'

Psalm 16 contains some lovely phrases about the comforts received by those who repose their entire trust and dependence upon God. 'Therefore my heart is glad,' we read, 'my flesh also shall rest in hope.' The psalm concludes: 'Thou wilt shew me the path of life: in thy presence is fullness of joy.'

REFERENCE: *The Life of William Wilberforce* (1838)

'An habitual love of God'

'But I have trusted in thy mercy; my heart shall rejoice in thy salvation.'
Psalm 13:5
SUGGESTED FURTHER READING: Ephesians 3:14–21, Revelation 2:1–7

How sadly apt am I to lose all recollection of keeping my heart when I am in society! Lord, strengthen me with might. Let Christ dwell, not merely occasionally visit, but dwell in my heart by faith. Let me cultivate more an habitual love of God.

FOR MEDITATION: The Scriptures admonish us not to lose our first love. This is to say the supreme object of our affections should be the Lord.

Philip Doddridge wrote of this in *The Rise and Progress of Religion in the Soul* (1745): 'Now surely there is nothing we should do with greater cheerfulness or more cordial consent, than making such a surrender of ourselves to this Lord, to the God who created us, who brought us into this pleasant and well-furnished world, who supported us in our tender infancy, who guarded us in the thoughtless days of childhood and youth, who has hitherto continually helped, sustained, and preserved us. Nothing can be more reasonable than that we should acknowledge him as our rightful owner and our Sovereign Ruler; than that we should devote ourselves to him, our most gracious Benefactor, and seek him as our supreme felicity. Nothing can be more apparently equitable than that we, the product of his power, and the price of his Son's blood, should be his, and his for ever.'

REFERENCE: *The Life of William Wilberforce* (1838)

'Lord, I must flee to thee'

'But now being made free from sin, and become servants to God, ye have your fruit unto holiness, and the end everlasting life. For the wages of sin is death; but the gift of God is eternal life through Jesus Christ our Lord.'
Romans 6:22–23
SUGGESTED FURTHER READING: Psalm 139:1–18

I have had lately too little time for private devotions. I must take at least an hour for them in the morning. I can sadly confirm Doddridge's remark, 'that when we go on ill in the closet, we commonly do so every where else.' I must mend here; I am afraid of getting into what John Owen calls a 'trade of sinning and repenting.' Yet where can I go else? Thou only, Lord, canst pardon and sanctify me. Oh what unspeakable comfort it is to cast oneself on the Saviour as a guilty, weak sinner in myself, but as trusting in the gracious promises of God through the Redeemer! Let him that is athirst come. Lord, I must flee to thee, and cleave to thee. Be thou my All in All.

FOR MEDITATION: In 1896, the hymn writer Judson Van DeVenter penned verses that speak of the believer's need to cleave to God, and to let him be our all in all:

All to Jesus, I surrender;
All to him I freely give;
I will ever love and trust him,
In his presence daily live.
All to Jesus, I surrender;
Make me, Saviour, wholly thine;
Let me feel the Holy Spirit,
Truly know that thou art mine.
I surrender all, I surrender all,
All to thee, my blessèd Saviour,
I surrender all.

REFERENCE: *The Life of William Wilberforce* (1838)

'Fill me with all the fulness of God'

'My soul waiteth for the LORD *more than they that watch for the morning: I say, more than they that watch for the morning.' Psalm 130:6*
SUGGESTED FURTHER READING: Proverbs 22:1–5

Wilberforce's sons wrote of their father as he was late in 1812: 'His secret entries testify that habitual peace, combined with the deepest humility, were in him the blessed fruit of keeping God's watch carefully. They are well expressed in an entry at this time. "I am just returned from a highly impressive sermon by Mr Dunn. I hope that my sensibility is in some degree the effect of the Holy Spirit; the knocking of Christ at the door of my heart. I must not spend any of my few minutes before dinner in writing; but let me just record my feelings of deep humiliation, yet of confiding, though humble faith—looking to the Saviour as my only ground of hope. I cast myself at the foot of the cross, bewailing my exceeding sinfulness and unprofitableness, deeply aggravated by the infinity of my mercies. I plead thy precious promises, and earnestly pray to thee to shed abroad in my heart more love, more humility, more faith, more hope, more peace, and joy; in short, to fill me with all the fulness of God, and make me more meet to be a partaker of the inheritance of the saints in light. Then shall I also be better in all the relations of life in which I am now so defective, and my light will shine before men, and I shall adorn the doctrine of God my Saviour in all things."'

FOR MEDITATION: In Chapter 26 of *The Rise and Progress of Religion in the Soul* (1745), Philip Doddridge wrote: 'as we have some exercise of a sanctified reason, we shall be solicitous that we may be growing and thriving. And you, my reader, "if so be you have tasted that the Lord is gracious," (1 Peter 2:3) will, I doubt not, feel this solicitude. I would, therefore, endeavour to assist you in making the inquiry, whether religion be on the advance in your soul. You are not to measure your growth in grace only or chiefly by your advances in knowledge, or in zeal, or any other passionate impression of the mind, no, nor by the fervour of devotion alone; but by the habitual determination of the will for God, and by your prevailing disposition to obey his commands, submit to his disposal, and promote the highest welfare of his cause in the earth.'

REFERENCE: *The Life of William Wilberforce* (1838)

'May my faith and love be more active'

'Now he which stablisheth us with you in Christ, and hath anointed us, is God; who hath also sealed us, and given the earnest of the Spirit in our hearts.' 2 Corinthians 1:21–22
SUGGESTED FURTHER READING: 2 Corinthians 5:1–10

O God, make me more earnest for thy glory; and may I act more from real love and gratitude to my redeeming Lord. Let me not take my estimate of myself from others who do not know me, but from my own self-knowledge and conscience. O Lord, may my faith and love be more active, bringing forth more the fruits of the Spirit.

FOR MEDITATION: In Chapter Eight of *The Rise and Progress of Religion in the Soul* (1745), Philip Doddridge wrote: 'Blessed, for ever blessed be thy name, O thou Father of mercies, that thou hast contrived the way! Eternal thanks to the Lamb that was slain, and to that kind Providence that sent the word of this salvation to me! O let me not, for ten thousand worlds, 'receive the grace of God in vain' (2 Corinthians 6:1). O impress this gospel upon my soul, till its saving virtue be diffused over every faculty! Let it not only be heard, and acknowledged, and professed, but felt! Make it 'thy power to my eternal salvation;' (Romans 1:16) and raise me to that humble, tender gratitude, to that active, unwearied zeal in thy service, which becomes one 'to whom so much is forgiven' (Luke 7:47).

REFERENCE: *The Life of William Wilberforce* (1838)

'Sanctify me'

'The meek will he guide in judgment: and the meek will he teach his way.' Psalm 25:9

SUGGESTED FURTHER READING: Psalm 149:1–9

Alas, how little have I been exhibiting the temper of the meek and lowly Jesus! Lord, I flee to thee for mercy, and do thou guide and direct me. Lord, to thee I look, for thou delightest in mercy. O soften, quicken, warm, and sanctify me.

FOR MEDITATION: Sanctification, according to the dictionary: 'involves more than a mere moral reformation of character, brought about by the power of the truth: it is the work of the Holy Spirit bringing the whole nature more and more under the influences of the new gracious principles implanted in the soul in regeneration.'

This is how one eighteenth-century writer much admired by Wilberforce, Philip Doddridge, described sanctification: 'Behold a blessed hope indeed! a lively, glorious hope, to which we are "begotten again by the resurrection of Christ from the dead" (1 Peter 1:3), and formed by the sanctifying influence of the Spirit of God upon our minds.'

In the timeless cadences of the King James Bible, we read in 1 Peter 3:15 the following admonition from the apostle Peter: 'sanctify the Lord God in your hearts.' In his great high priestly prayer as recorded in the gospel of John, Chapter 17, the Lord Jesus had this to say concerning sanctification: 'Sanctify them through thy truth: thy word is truth' (John 17:17).

REFERENCE: *The Life of William Wilberforce* (1838)

'The spiritual interests of my children'

'The Lord is far from the wicked: but he heareth the prayer of the righteous.' Proverbs 15:29
SUGGESTED FURTHER READING: 1 John 5:10–21

His children now were much upon his mind. In midsummer 1813, they had all gathered around him at Sandgate, and he watched over them as usual with the deepest interest. 'I can scarcely,' he wrote to a friend, with an enclosure which had been sent for his perusal, 'conceive any earthly pleasure greater than that of receiving such a letter from a beloved son, who shows by his conduct that he writes the real sentiments and feelings of his heart. I humbly trust that I can say with truth that the spiritual interests of my children are my first object, I mean that I wish to see them become real Christians, rather than great scholars, or eminent in any other way; and I earnestly pray to God for wisdom to direct me, and that his grace may be given in large measure to my children. I own I am rather sanguine in my hopes of the result, on ground of the Scripture promises. Join your prayers, my dear friend, to mine, and give me also from time to time the benefits of your friendly counsel.'

In the same tone he told Mrs Wilberforce—'My best hopes for them rest on the declaration that God hears and grants the prayers of his people through the merits and intercession of the Saviour.'

FOR MEDITATION: Before his marriage in 1797, and after seeing the welcome home a friend received from his family, Wilberforce wrote in his diary that he 'felt sadly the want of wife and children to hail my return.' After his marriage and the birth of his children, he longed for his family to know God's grace. This was especially so after he resigned his seat as MP for Yorkshire in 1812 to spend more time with them. Soon after his resignation he wrote: 'I trust God will strengthen my mind, and smooth my path, and vouchsafe to prosper my labours and endeavours with my children.' History knows of Wilberforce's two celebrated great objects: the suppression of the slave trade and the reformation of manners. But now Wilberforce considered 'religious exercises [and] my children the great objects with God.' His children were to receive the best of his time and efforts. His best hopes for them should be ours as well for our children: 'God hears and grants the prayers of his people through the merits and intercession of the Saviour.'

REFERENCE: *The Life of William Wilberforce* (1838)

'The impression of invisible and divine things'

'Stablish thy word unto thy servant, who is devoted to thy fear.'
Psalm 119:38
SUGGESTED FURTHER READING: Psalm 34:1–10

Therefore though knowing that God prefers mercy to sacrifice, yet let me in faith give up this day to religious exercises, to strengthening the impression of invisible and divine things by the worship of God, meditation, and reading.

FOR MEDITATION: Wilberforce longed to know God more deeply and to follow him more steadfastly. Another diary entry attests this: 'I mean to set aside a day this week for fasting and religious exercises; for seeking God and praying for political direction, for a blessing on my parliamentary labours, on my country, and on those who have specially desired my prayers. May God for Christ's sake enable me to seek in all things to please him, and submit to his will—to repress vanity, cultivate humility, constant self-examination—[and] think of saints in past times.'

On another occasion he observed: 'the Scripture enjoins constant prayer, and the writings and example of all good men suggest and enforce the necessity of a considerable proportion of meditation and other religious exercises, for maintaining the spiritual life vigorous and flourishing. Let me therefore make the effort in humble reliance on Divine grace.'

In humble reliance on Divine grace, may we so pursue holiness.

REFERENCE: *The Life of William Wilberforce* (1838)

'The soul will grow lean'

'My soul longeth, yea, even fainteth for the courts of the LORD*: my heart and my flesh crieth out for the living God.' Psalm 84:2*
SUGGESTED FURTHER READING: Psalm 119:81–88

Surely the experience of all good men confirms the proposition, that without a due measure of private devotions the soul will grow lean. It is remarkable that at such times my business and worldly concerns have also gone on ill. O Lord, help me. Strengthen my faith, send the Spirit of thy Son into my heart, that I may call thee Father, and set my affections upon things above.

FOR MEDITATION: Because Wilberforce faithfully maintained the practice of private devotions, he knew what it was to struggle to keep to this practice. 'What a mystery of iniquity,' he said, 'is the human heart! How forcibly do thoughts of worldly pursuits intrude into the mind during the devotional exercises; and how obstinately do they maintain their place—and when excluded how incessantly do they renew their attacks!—which yet the moment our devotional exercises are over, fly away of themselves.'

Yet he never ceased to keep trying—to maintain his private devotions and to have the right attitude about them. 'Though knowing that God prefers mercy to sacrifice,' he wrote, 'yet let me in faith give up this day to religious exercises, to strengthening the impression of invisible and divine things by the worship of God, meditation, and reading. I trust he will bless me during the week.' Let us keep on in faith. And let us trust God for his blessing upon our devotions.

REFERENCE: *The Life of William Wilberforce* (1838)

'Such constant remembrances of God's goodness'

'Blessed is the man whom thou choosest, and causest to approach unto thee, that he may dwell in thy courts: we shall be satisfied with the goodness of thy house, even of thy holy temple.' Psalm 65:4
SUGGESTED FURTHER READING: Psalm 107:1–9

Wilberforce's sons wrote of him as he was in September 1814: 'There was nothing more remarkable about him than the cheerful spring of his natural affections, even under the heaviest pressure of perplexing business. "There," he said when hurried once almost beyond bearing, calling the attention of a friend to a sudden burst of voices, "how can I be worried by such trifles, when I have such constant remembrances of God's goodness to me?" It was his children playing overhead with a noisy glee which would have jarred upon the feelings of almost any one besides himself.'

FOR MEDITATION: 'If you are a Christian,' wrote Philip Doddridge in *The Rise and Progress of Religion in the Soul* (1745), 'your thoughts, your affections, your pursuits, your choice, will be determined by a regard to things spiritual.' Wilberforce concurred with this, for he revered Doddridge's 'super-excellent book.' In his own classic devotional text, *A Practical View of Christianity* (1797), Wilberforce wrote of the affections we ought to manifest towards God. To make his point, he used the metaphor of a human benefactor. 'True love is an ardent, and active principle—a cold, a dormant, phlegmatic gratitude, are contradictions in terms. When these generous affections really exist in vigour, are we not ever fond of dwelling on the value and enumerating the merits of our benefactor? How are we moved when any thing is asserted to his disparagement! How do we delight to tell of his kindness! With what pious care do we preserve any memorial of him, which we may happen to possess! How gladly do we seize any opportunity of rendering to him, or to those who are dear to him, any little good offices, which, though in themselves of small intrinsic worth, may testify the sincerity of our thankfulness! The very mention of his name will cheer the heart, and light up the countenance!' This was the secret of Wilberforce's 'cheerful spring of natural affections'—they had their root in his religious affections.

REFERENCE: *The Life of William Wilberforce* (1838)

'Acquaint thyself with God'

'Acquaint now thyself with him, and be at peace: thereby good shall come unto thee.' Job 22:21
SUGGESTED FURTHER READING: Job 22:21–30

My judgment hesitates as to the political line I should adopt; but on this blessed day, let my motto ever be, and I bless God I am enabled pretty well to make my practice accord with it, so far at least as public affairs and private business are concerned, 'acquaint now thyself with God, and be at peace.'

FOR MEDITATION: This phrase, or variations of it, occurs repeatedly throughout Wilberforce's diary. It comes originally from Job 22, and is part of the advice given by Eliphaz. It is a book which is far better known for its depictions of suffering than as a source of consolation. And yet there it is that we read: 'Acquaint now thyself with him, and be at peace: thereby good shall come unto thee.'

Does this strike us as strange? It should not. God is never closer than when we need him most. His peace is never further than the solace freely given by him. God stands ever-ready to give this consolation. Psalm 119:165 states: 'Great peace have they which love thy law,' which is another way of saying that when we commune with God and meditate upon his word—we shall find comfort for our weary soul.

REFERENCE: *The Life of William Wilberforce* (1838)

'We must acquaint ourselves with God'

'These things I have spoken unto you, that in me ye might have peace. In the world ye shall have tribulation: but be of good cheer; I have overcome the world.' John 16:33
SUGGESTED FURTHER READING: Philippians 4:4–9

What events have we witnessed both in public and private life! Poor Whitbread, what a close, alas! He was certainly however deranged. But oh, how does all enforce on us the important truth that we must acquaint ourselves with God to be at peace!

FOR MEDITATION: These lines were written in a letter to Hannah More on 19 July 1815. In 1815, Samuel Whitbread began to suffer from depression. He had been subjected to vitriolic attacks in newspapers and prints. He received persistent, rough treatment in the House of Commons. After one debate in June he told his wife: 'They are hissing me. I am become an object of universal abhorrence.' On the morning of 6 June 1815 he committed suicide.

It was a tragic loss for Britain. Whitbread was a reformer who championed religious and civil rights, the abolition of slavery. He also supported the establishment of a national education system.

Wilberforce was deeply shocked over Whitbread's death, and mourned his loss. Part of his grief sprang from the thought that if Whitbread had known something of the consolations of faith, he might not have fallen victim to despair. An old negro spiritual tells of this unspeakable comfort:

There is a balm in Gilead
To make the wounded whole;
There is a balm in Gilead
To heal the sin sick soul.

REFERENCE: *The Life of William Wilberforce* (1838)

'The hope of glory'

'Precious in the sight of the LORD *is the death of his saints.' Psalm 116:15*
SUGGESTED FURTHER READING: Psalm 133:1–3

Wilberforce's sons give this record of their father's words and actions in the days leading up to and following the death of one of his dearest friends, Marianne Sykes Thornton: 'For several days before her death, he had read and prayed with her, and written to their friends; and from her dying bed he went on the last morning of her life to a meeting of the Brighton Auxiliary Bible Society. "When he entered the room," says an eyewitness, he seemed so pale and fatigued, that his friends feared he would scarcely be able to speak. But he no sooner entered on his subject than his countenance was lighted up, he became animated and impressive."'

'Had it not been,' he said, 'for one painful circumstance, it was not my intention to have been present at this meeting today, for I have been compelled to curb the zeal which I always feel to attend on occasions like this, by making it a rule to myself to decline being present at such meetings in places of which I am not a regular inhabitant, that I may not become too obvious and intrusive. But today I have broken this rule, for I am just come from a scene in which the value of the book which it is your object to disperse, is displayed as with a sunbeam. Therefore how could I but come, and congratulate you and this assembly on being permitted to be the honoured instruments of the Almighty, in diffusing such a cordial as this through a dying world? How could I but rejoice in being allowed to join with you in endeavouring to circulate these imperishable blessings? I dare not withhold such a testimony as it furnishes to the healing and victorious efficacy of the inspired volume. I am come from a chamber, in which a widowed mother, surrounded by her soon to become orphan family, is enabled to look the last enemy calmly in the face; herself possessing a peace which even the waves of Jordan cannot ruffle, because it is the gift of God; her children in some degree enabled to anticipate for her the hope of glory.'

FOR MEDITATION: purposely omitted

REFERENCE: *The Life of William Wilberforce* (1838)

'That last enemy'

'The last enemy that shall be destroyed is death.' 1 Corinthians 15:26
SUGGESTED FURTHER READING: Psalm 30:1–12

Wilberforce's tribute to the Christian faith and passing of Marianne Sykes Thornton (commenced in the last entry) is here continued: 'It is a scene which must be witnessed to produce its full effect upon the heart, a scene such as, if I had not myself witnessed, I could not have adequately imagined a happiness felt in the moments of the deepest outward dejection and sorrow, an elevation above the evils and trials of this mortal life. Trials did I call them? Triumphs let me rather say of the believer's faith. And let me ask, is this consolation in affliction, this hope in death, any thing peculiar to their particular circumstances or temper of mind, any family secret which they alone possess, and from which men in general are excluded? No, Sir, it is that which the blessed word of God offers to all who will embrace it.

'It is true indeed, some tears of mortality will fall, when we see a friend descending into the dark valley of the shadow of death, and the mortal frame suffering its last agonies. Jesus wept, and he will allow his people to weep also; he will pardon and pity the tears we shed from human infirmity. But notwithstanding this natural sorrow, its end is glory to God in the highest, the way by which it conducts us is pleasantness and peace; and it gives us substantial victory over that last enemy, whom, sooner or later, we must all of us individually encounter. For it is not only in the din and confusion of battle that the spirit may be so raised as to brave danger, and not turn away the eye from death when it stares you in the face. This may arise from the mere excitement of the occasion, or from driving away all thought about the consequences of death. But in the cool and silent hours of reflection, a nobler and more genuine courage may be evinced; and in the chamber of sickness, and from the bed of death the soul, leaning on the word of her God, may meet that enemy without alarm, and calmly say, O *death, where is thy sting? O grave, where is thy victory?'*

FOR MEDITATION: purposely omitted

REFERENCE: *The Life of William Wilberforce* (1838)

'The pledges of our security'

'Whereby are given unto us exceeding great and precious promises: that by these ye might be partakers of the divine nature.' 2 Peter 1:4
SUGGESTED FURTHER READING: Psalm 31:1–8

Oh! how blessed will be that day, when after all our conflicts and anxieties we shall be made partakers of that rest which remaineth for the people of God! Oh let us all strive lest a promise being left us of entering into his rest, any of us should seem to come short of it. But if we give diligence to make our calling and election sure, we never shall, we never can fail, for the promises of the God of truth are the pledges of our security.

FOR MEDITATION: The promises of the God of truth are the pledges of our security. In the selection above, Wilberforce is paraphrasing the second epistle of the apostle Peter: 'Wherefore the rather, brethren, give diligence to make your calling and election sure: for if ye do these things, ye shall never fall' (2 Peter 1:10).

The promises of God, we also read in 2 Peter, are great and precious. Through these, and through the work of the Holy Spirit in our lives, we are enabled to become partakers of the divine nature. When we begin to understand this, even if only in part, it is tempting to paraphrase the psalmist by saying: 'such knowledge is too wonderful for me' (Psalm 139:6).

And yet it is not. Therein lies the wonder. If we desire holiness—that is to say, making our calling and election sure—God stands ready to help us do this. What is more, if this is continuing desire and our earnest pursuit, we shall fall. All praise and glory be to our Lord and Saviour.

REFERENCE: *The Life of William Wilberforce* (1838)

'Something better than that too, I trust, Sir'

'For the law made nothing perfect, but the bringing in of a better hope did; by the which we draw nigh unto God.' Hebrews 7:19
SUGGESTED FURTHER READING: Hebrews 10:32–39

This excuse however would not long serve, and three days afterwards he was again 'at the Pavilion—the Prince came up to me and reminded me of my singing at the Duchess of Devonshire's ball in 1782, of the particular song, and of our then first knowing each other.'

'We are both I trust much altered since, Sir,' was his answer.

'Yes, the time which has gone by must have made a great alteration in us,' replied the Prince.

'Something better than that too, I trust, Sir.'

FOR MEDITATION: Many of us have heard the phrase 'speaking truth to kings.' Scripture contains telling examples of those who speak truth to power. In Proverbs 22:21 we read: 'that thou mightest answer the words of truth to them that send unto thee.' Zechariah 8:16 declares: 'these are the things that ye shall do; Speak ye every man the truth to his neighbour.' In 2 Chronicles 18:15, we have something of a reversal: the King of Israel admonishes the prophet Micaiah not to withhold the truth: 'And the king said to him, "How many times shall I adjure thee that thou say nothing but the truth to me in the name of the LORD?"'

There had been a time in Wilberforce's life when he was nearly as much of a fixture of polite and fashionable society in London as the Prince of Wales (the future George IV). Wilberforce had gambled, danced the nights away and fought aggressively in the rough and tumble world of politics. One could be forgiven for thinking that this period of his life, on which he looked in later years with regret, would ever prove to be a basis for urging a future king to look for 'something better.' But one never knows how opportunities of this sort might arise when we seek to share our faith with others. God can raise up opportunities when we least expect it. May we be found ready—ready to speak truth to kings—ready to speak truth to our neighbours.

REFERENCE: *The Life of William Wilberforce* (1838)

'Still better reasons'

'A good name is rather to be chosen than great riches, and loving favour rather than silver and gold.' Proverbs 22:1
SUGGESTED FURTHER READING: 1 Corinthians 15:1–10

'No, my dear Stephen,' Mr Wilberforce wrote in reply to the playful taunt from his brother-in-law—'you will live to be a peer at last', I am not afraid of declaring that I shall go out of the world plain William Wilberforce. In one view indeed I seldom have had less reason to be dissatisfied with that less dignified style: I mean in the degree of civility or even respect to which even plain W.W. may be deemed entitled. For really had I been covered with titles and ribands, I could not have been treated with more real, unaffected, unapparently condescending, and therefore more unostentatious civility. But, alas still better reasons suggest the same dispositions. I become more and more impressed with the truth of good old Richard Baxter's declaration, that the great and the rich of this world are much to be pitied.'

FOR MEDITATION: 'A good name is better than precious ointment,' we read in Ecclesiastes 7:1. The Britain of Wilberforce's day had need of plain and honest men. In *King Lear*, Shakespeare praised the man who possessed 'an honest mind and plain—he must speak truth!'

The story related above unfolded after Wilberforce had been invited several times to visit the Prince Regent in the Royal Pavilion at Brighton. 'The Pavilion,' he wrote, had been designed 'in Chinese style—beautiful and tasty. Though it looks,' he added, 'very much as if St Paul's had come down to the sea and left behind a litter of cupolas.'

Wilberforce's fine and descriptive architectural eye notwithstanding, there was something compelling and winsome about him—a member, as he put it, of the gentry, whose company the Prince sought out. Several times over several weeks Wilberforce was a guest at the Pavilion. The Bible speaks of those whose lives are as salt and light. In Matthew 5, we read verses which should inform our conduct wherever we are in God's world: 'Ye are the salt of the earth' (v. 13). 'Ye are the light of the world' (v. 14). 'Let your light so shine before men, that they may see your good works, and glorify your Father which is in heaven' (v. 16).

REFERENCE: *The Life of William Wilberforce* (1838)

'God is gently leading me'

'Teach me to do thy will; for thou art my God: thy spirit is good; lead me into the land of uprightness.' Psalm 143:10
SUGGESTED FURTHER READING: Isaiah 57:15–18b—*'I will lead him also, and restore comforts unto him and to his mourners.'*

'Mrs Henry Thornton dying at this place [Brighton], it was my privilege to be much with her in her latter days, and a more peaceful, humble, grateful, hopeful death I cannot conceive. I trust, she said a few days before her decease, God is gently leading me to that blessed world which he has prepared for those that love him. I thank God we are well. We overflow with blessings.'

FOR MEDITATION: God is gently leading me. What a lovely sentiment. How very like the matchless words we find in our Psalm 23:

The Lord is my shepherd; I shall not want.
He maketh me to lie down in green pastures:
he leadeth me beside the still waters.
He restoreth my soul:
he leadeth me in the paths of righteousness for his name's sake.
Yea, though I walk through the valley of the shadow of death, I will fear no evil:
for thou art with me; thy rod and thy staff they comfort me.
Surely goodness and mercy shall follow me all the days of my life:
and I will dwell in the house of the Lord for ever (Psalm 23:1–4,6).

REFERENCE: *The Life of William Wilberforce* (1838)

'How little likely'

'How excellent is thy lovingkindness, O God! therefore the children of men put their trust under the shadow of thy wings.' Psalm 36:7
SUGGESTED FURTHER READING: Psalm 103:8–18

Sunday, Dec. 31st 1815. Church morning. After church, we and our six children together—I addressed them all collected, and afterwards solemn prayer. How little likely on the 30th May, 1797, when I married, that we and all our six children (we never had another) should all be living and well! Praise the Lord, O my soul.

FOR MEDITATION: At times, a profound sense of the Lord's blessing on our lives overwhelms us. Wilberforce had nearly died in 1788, and he thought for many years after that he would never marry. To look upon his beloved wife Barbara and their children as he did on this New Year's Eve so long ago, was to know that God had blessed him beyond what he could have asked or imagined. He had longed all his life for a family such as this—a desire all the more poignant when one recalls that he had lost his own father at age eight and two beloved sisters, Elizabeth and Anne, before he reached adulthood. New Year's Eve should prompt within us a deep sense of reflection and gratitude. It always did with Wilberforce. And given all that has been said above, he had so many reasons to praise God.

Once, upon a visit in his later years to Battersea Rise (the home he had once shared as a bachelor with his cherished friend and cousin Henry Thornton), he was struck forcibly once more by God's goodness to him in the blessings of a wife and six children: 'How naturally I was led to adopt the old patriarch's declaration: "With my staff I passed over, etc. and now I am become two bands!"'

REFERENCE: *The Life of William Wilberforce* (1838)

'The same superabundant goodness'

'I am come that they might have life, and that they might have it more abundantly.' John 10:10b

SUGGESTED FURTHER READING: Psalm 145:1–12

He who said 'Thou didst well that it was in thine heart,' will graciously forgive my sins; and that my all-merciful Saviour will take me to himself out of the same superabundant goodness, which I have ever experienced. For how true it is, I am often driven to this, 'Thy thoughts are not as our thoughts, nor thy ways as our ways; for as the heavens are higher than the earth, so are thy ways higher than our ways, and thy thoughts than our thoughts!'

FOR MEDITATION: Grace and mercy—two words that are bound to the heart of Christians. God's forgiveness was a source of never-failing wonder to Wilberforce. In his book *A Practical View of Christianity*, he wrote of how it had 'pleased God to check the future apostle of the Gentiles[22] in his wild career, and to make him a monument of transforming grace.'

Paul had been complicit in the murder of the martyr Stephen. As he recalled: 'And when the blood of thy martyr Stephen was shed, I also was standing by, and consenting unto his death, and kept the raiment of them that slew him' (Acts 22:20). More than this, Paul had ruthlessly persecuted the early church. Surely such a one was beyond the reach of grace, mercy or forgiveness.

But Paul wasn't. No one is. That is the glory of the gospel.

REFERENCE: *The Life of William Wilberforce* (1838)

'This great change'

'And he shall be like a tree planted by the rivers of water, that bringeth forth his fruit in his season.' Psalm 1:3
SUGGESTED FURTHER READING: John 4:31–38

'Above all, my dearest Samuel,' he wrote to his son on his tenth birthday, 'I am anxious to see in you decisive marks of this great change. I come again and again to look and see if it be indeed begun, just as a gardener walks up again and again to examine his fruit trees, and see if his peaches are set, and if they are swelling and becoming larger; finally, if they are becoming ripe and rosy. I would willingly walk barefoot from this place "near London" to Sandgate, to see a clear proof of it in my dear Samuel at the end of my journey.'

FOR MEDITATION: A father's love and the hopes he cherishes for his son. These were realized in Samuel Wilberforce's life. He became one of the most revered prelates the Church of England has ever known. His eloquence, his philanthropies and his faith touched countless lives.

And it all began with a father's love—a love that found expression in over 600 letters. Each of them was carefully numbered and kept by Samuel as long as he lived. Canon A.R. Ashwell, Samuel's biographer, said that these letters 'exercised the most powerful influence on the formation of [Samuel's] character. All these [were] strung upon the one thread of [the] ever-repeated inculcation of the duty of private prayer as the one holdfast of life,—these remarkable letters exhibit the influences which formed the solid character which underlay the brilliant gifts and striking career of Samuel Wilberforce.'

These letters were no less significant, Ashwell continued, considering that Wilberforce was forty-six when Samuel was born, fifty-seven when he began writing the letters. He had little leisure time, and Samuel was neither an only nor an eldest son that he could lay claim to a large share of his father's time. Add to this Wilberforce's health and eyesight were often poor, so poor that there are many letters in which he told Samuel he was writing with closed eyes.

REFERENCE: *The Life of William Wilberforce* (1838)

'Our great heavenly Shepherd'

'I am the good shepherd, and know my sheep, and am known of mine.'
John 10:14
SUGGESTED FURTHER READING: 1 Peter 5:1–11

Upon his busiest days he found time to write to them. 'Were it not,' he told one of his daughters, 'that my eyes were so weak, and that, in such a state, writing by candlelight does not suit me, especially after a full day's work following a bad night, you would have received a good long letter instead of this sheetling. My last night's wakefulness arose in fact from my thinking on some subjects of deep interest, from which, though I made several efforts, I could not altogether withdraw my thoughts. My mind obeyed me indeed while I continued wide awake, but when I was dropping half asleep it started aside from the serious and composing train of ideas to which I had forced it up; and like a swerving horse chose to go its own way rather than mine. I like to direct my language as well as my thoughts and feeling towards you on a Saturday night, because it serves as a preparation for that more continued mental intercourse with you in which I allow myself on the Sunday. When I was a bachelor, and lived alone, I used to enliven the dulness of a solitary Sunday dinner by mustering my friends around me in idea, and considering how I could benefit any of them; and now how can there be a more suitable employment of a part of the Lord's day, than thus to call my absent children round me? And you will present yourselves to-morrow; and I shall pray that our great heavenly Shepherd will number you amongst the sheep of his pasture, and guide you at last into his fold above.'

FOR MEDITATION: 'I shall pray that our great heavenly Shepherd will number you amongst the sheep of his pasture, and guide you at last into his fold above.' Wilberforce loved his daughters no less than his sons. That love found expression in letters and in his life. May it be so with all of us who have been entrusted with the privilege of parenthood.

REFERENCE: *The Life of William Wilberforce* (1838)

'Let me try'

Bear ye one another's burdens, and so fulfil the law of Christ.' Galatians 6:2
SUGGESTED FURTHER READING: Galatians 6:1–6

My dear Stephen,
You appeared to me to look unhappy last night, as if something was giving you pain either in body or mind. It will be a pleasure to me to hear that this was not so; or if it was, and I can help to remove it, let me try.
Ever affectionately yours,

W. Wilberforce

FOR MEDITATION: Few of Wilberforce's letters are as touching as this. He knew how to be a friend, and how to bear another's burdens.

Friends, wrote Philip Doddridge, show tender love. Their hearts yearn over those whom they have befriended. They shed tears when those close to them are troubled (*Rise and Progress*, Chapter 7).

Bearing the burdens of others is to 'fulfil' the law of Christ. What a powerful truth. And what a high privilege. Such a privilege lies at the heart of fellowship. It builds and strengthens not only lasting friendships, but God's church. For it is in the church that we are to find such love and fidelity. It is as John 13:35 tells us: 'By this shall all men know that ye are my disciples, if ye have love one to another.' May we resolve to be his disciples. May we remain steadfast in seeking to fulfil the law of Christ. May we bear one another's burdens.

REFERENCE: *The Life of William Wilberforce* (1838)

'At all events I shall be supported'

'Honour and majesty are before him: strength and beauty are in his sanctuary.' Psalm 96:6
SUGGESTED FURTHER READING: Psalm 18:25–36

How little have I of late been under the influence of real Christian tempers! How sadly defective am I in humility! When I look into myself I find myself poor indeed compared with my highly favoured state; but how little do I feel this habitually! How fond am I of distinction (my constitutional vice)! This would not be, if I was truly humble within, at the core. Here meditation daily, or as frequent as might be, would do much. Let me try for it. Oh may this day be of lasting service to me! and at this time, when probably war and tumult are at hand, may I serve God and fear nothing. May I boldly walk in the might of the Lord, and sigh and cry for the abominations done in the land. May I grow in humility, peace, and love, in meekness, holy courage, self-denial, active exertion, and discreet zeal.

I feel a firm confidence, that if through God's grace I am enabled to keep close to him in love, fear, trust, and obedience, I shall go on well; most likely even in this life, being perhaps remarkably preserved from evil; but at all events I shall be supported under whatever may be laid upon me. These are days in which I should especially strive to grow in preparedness for changing worlds, and for whatever sharp trials I may be called to. Oh what humiliation becomes me when I think of my innumerable mercies! I resolve to be up in time to have an hour before breakfast for serious meditation, prayer, and Scripture preparation for these dangerous times; also more time for unbroken thought.

FOR MEDITATION: Drastic times call for drastic measures, it has been said. For the Christian drastic times call for determined trust and utter reliance upon God. Wilberforce wrote the words above when the threat of invasion from Napoleon's France was very great. It was an uncertain and unsettling time. He understood, profoundly, that these are times when we must seek to draw near to God. For when we do, he will draw near to us (James 4:8).

REFERENCE: *The Life of William Wilberforce* (1838)

'Set the mainspring right'

'That thou mayest love the LORD thy God, and that thou mayest obey his voice, and that thou mayest cleave unto him: for he is thy life, and the length of thy days.' Deuteronomy 30:20
SUGGESTED FURTHER READING: Deuteronomy 30

Let me strive to set the mainspring right, and then to mend the works also. God help and direct me; and though I deserve no such honour, enable me yet to do some good. May God purify my motives, while he prompts, quickens, and strengthens me for action.

FOR MEDITATION: Wilberforce was fond of using watches as metaphors. Sometimes, he used the metaphor in a tongue-in-cheek fashion, as when he said this of a pastor following a sermon: 'Good old Mr C. preached uniformly rapid, like a watch hand when the spring chain broke.'

These words, wrote Wilberforce's sons, 'bespoke the playfulness of good-tempered humour.' But more often than not Wilberforce invoked the metaphor of a watch as a way of illustrating his desire to keep his faith in good running order—to exercise care and watchfulness over his heart.

We are not perhaps used to such a metaphor. But it is a very fine one. Watches of the kind Wilberforce would have known required care, cleaning, protection and maintenance at regular intervals. Is this not true of ourselves? The owners of watches must be good stewards, or else their watches will lose much of their usefulness. These are lessons worth remembering.

REFERENCE: *The Life of William Wilberforce* (1838)

'Let me now resolve'

'Thou wilt keep him in perfect peace, whose mind is stayed on thee: because he trusteth in thee.' Isaiah 26:3
SUGGESTED FURTHER READING: Psalm 119:89–104

This week I have got more morning time for serious reading and reflection. I have now been taking a musing walk, and alas, what cause do I find for humiliation! During the ensuing week I shall be subject to several temptations as heretofore. Let me now resolve to keep earlier hours; not curtail evening prayer; turn the conversation to profitable and rational topics; be meek, and gentle, and humble and kind.

FOR MEDITATION: Resolutions are the hallmarks of a disciplined heart. They indicate a fixed desire to serve and seek God. They are the declarations of a heart that consistently cries: 'O God, thou art my God; early will I seek thee: my soul thirsteth for thee, my flesh longeth for thee in a dry and thirsty land' (Psalm 63:1).

As Wilberforce was in the throes of the spiritual crisis which led ultimately to his self-described 'great change' or embrace of Christianity, he wrote words that spoke of his resolve to seek Christ and him only: 'Christ should be a Christian's delight and glory. I will endeavour by God's help to excite in myself an anxiety and longing for the joys of heaven ... O God! do thou enable me to live more to thee, to look to Jesus with a single eye, and by degrees to have the renewed nature implanted in me, and the heart of stone removed.'

REFERENCE: *The Life of William Wilberforce* (1838)

'What a blessing is friendship'

'Behold, how good and how pleasant it is for brethren to dwell together in unity! It is ... as the dew of Hermon, and as the dew that descended upon the mountains of Zion: for there the LORD *commanded the blessing, even life for evermore.' Psalm 133:1–3*
SUGGESTED FURTHER READING: Psalms 133–134

Kensington Gore, July 29, 1817

My dear Macaulay,

I quite envy—no, that is not true—I enjoy with you in [thought] your visit at the Temple. It would—and I trust I may justly use the indicative for the optative,[23] and say that some day or other it will gladden my heart again to revisit those haunts of my younger years. May God bless you and yours, my dear friend. What a blessing is friendship! How true is the psalmist's exclamation, 'How good it is to dwell together in unity!' It is in short a heaven upon earth. May we realize it there, from its being the reflection from the better and less imperfect state of it beyond the mountains.

Your affectionate and sincere Friend,

W. Wilberforce

FOR MEDITATION: 'I have long thought,' Wilberforce once wrote to his brother-in-law James Stephen, 'that of all the manifold blessings which Providence has heaped on me—the greatest of this world consists of kind and intelligent friends whom he has raised up for my comfort and benefit. Surely no man ever had so many; and you and my sister are amongst the very first.'

There have been many celebrated friendships in the Scriptures. David and Jonathan, Paul and Timothy, Naomi and Ruth. When we read of them, we see modelled for us devotion and fidelity, mentoring and common cause. C. S. Lewis wrote famously of 'the four loves'—storge, philia, eros and agape. When we read of and reflect upon the friendships described in the Bible, we learn anew of the richness of the love known as philia.

REFERENCE: *The Life of William Wilberforce* (1838)

'Living as it were in an atmosphere of love'

'Ointment and perfume rejoice the heart: so doth the sweetness of a man's friend by hearty counsel.' Proverbs 27:9
SUGGESTED FURTHER READING: Proverbs 16:19–24

In *The Life of William Wilberforce*, Wilberforce's sons recorded a touching instance of their father's devotion to family: 'For myself,' he said when he unveiled his heart in a letter to his family on 28 August 1817, 'I can truly say, that scarcely any thing has at times given me more pleasure than the consciousness of living as it were in an atmosphere of love; and heaven itself has appeared delightful in that very character of being a place, in which not only every one would love his brethren, but in which every one would be assured that his brother loved *him*, and thus that all was mutual kindness and harmony, without one discordant jarring; all sweetness without the slightest acescency [sourness].'

FOR MEDITATION: In Ephesians 4, the apostle Paul describes the metaphor of the human body in ways that have equal application to what it means to be a part of the family of God—that is to say, the church. His words show how we can foster that atmosphere of love of which Wilberforce writes.

Paul begins by saying 'I urge you to live a life worthy of the calling you have received' (v. 1). How are we to do this? We are to 'be completely humble and gentle; be patient, bearing with one another in love,' we are to 'make every effort to keep the unity of the Spirit through the bond of peace' (v. 2–3).

Recognizing that we all have been endowed with different gifts, we are not to give place to jealously or envy, but rather to act in concert and complement each other 'so that the body of Christ may be built up until we all reach unity in the faith and in the knowledge of the Son of God and become mature, attaining to the whole measure of the fullness of Christ' (v. 12–13).

As we do this, we must always remember that the head of our family is the Lord Jesus Christ. 'From him,' Paul concludes, 'the whole body, joined and held together by every supporting ligament, grows and builds itself up in love, as each part does its work' (v. 16—all verses from the NASB translation).

REFERENCE: *The Life of William Wilberforce* (1838)

'True Christian joy'

'Thou wilt shew me the path of life: in thy presence is fulness of joy; at thy right hand there are pleasures for evermore.' Psalm 16:11
SUGGESTED FURTHER READING: Psalm 42:1–11

'True Christian joy,' Wilberforce's sons wrote with reference to their father, 'is for the most part a secret as well as a severe thing.'[24] The full depth of his feelings was hidden even from his own family. 'I am never affected to tears,' he said more than once, 'except when I am alone.'

A stranger might have noticed little else than that he was more uniformly cheerful than most men of his time of life. Closer observation showed a vein of Christian feeling mingling with and purifying the natural flow of a most happy temper; whilst those who lived most continually with him, could trace distinctly in his tempered sorrows, and sustained and almost child-like gladness of heart, the continual presence of that 'peace which the world can neither give nor take away.' The pages of his later *Journal* are full of bursts of joy and thankfulness; and with his children, and his chosen friends, his full heart welled out ever in the same blessed strains; he seemed too happy not to express his happiness; his 'song was ever of the loving-kindness of the Lord.'

FOR MEDITATION: All of us have known what it is to cry tears of joy. There are moments when our sense of happiness moves us profoundly. Tears of this kind flow when we watch our children being born, or when we wed. Sometimes these tears flow when we are seated beside a lake at sunset and a palpable sense of God's goodness overtakes us even as it is mirrored in the sky. Wilberforce shed tears of joy when he was alone with God, and he was overwhelmed with a sense of all that God had done in his life. He knew what it was to have felt the touch of amazing grace.

REFERENCE: *The Life of William Wilberforce* (1838)

'Spirits jaded and tempers worn'

'Behold, thou hast made my days as an handbreadth; and mine age is as nothing before thee: verily every man at his best state is altogether vanity.'
Psalm 39:5
SUGGESTED FURTHER READING: Psalm 4

Wilberforce's sons wrote of him as he was in 1817: 'He occasionally met at this time with some who had entered life with him, and were now drawing wearily to its close with spirits jaded and tempers worn in the service of pleasure or ambition.' Such meetings 'brought out strongly the proof of his better choice.'

'This session,' he said, 'I met again Lord ——, whom I had known when we were both young, but of whom I had lost sight for many years. He was just again returned to parliament, and we were locked up together in a committee room during a division. I saw that he felt awkward about speaking to me, and went therefore up to him.

'"You and I, my Lord, were pretty well acquainted formerly."

'"Ah, Mr Wilberforce," he said cordially; and then added with a deep sigh, "you and I are a great many years older now."

'"Yes, we are, and for my part I can truly say that I do not regret it."

'"Don't you," he said, with an eager and almost incredulous voice, and a look of wondering dejection, which I never can forget."'

FOR MEDITATION: Pleasure and ambition are poor company in the evening of life. Age brings with it a sense of nearness to eternity. Many a man or woman has reached this point in life only to say, 'I've done all I wished to do, and what is left for me now?' Slowed by the advance of years, and left with time to reflect, they come late to the realization that pleasure and ambition are not all there is to life.

Where is life, true life to be found? In Christ. The first chapter of the gospel of John tells us: 'In him was life; and the life was the light of men' (v. 4). The apostle Paul writes of 'Christ, who is our life' (Colossians 3:4). If we surrender ourselves to him, we shall find life and that more abundantly (John 10:10).

REFERENCE: *The Life of William Wilberforce* (1838)

'The old charge of dullness'

'Happy is that people, that is in such a case: yea, happy is that people, whose God is the LORD.*' Psalm 144:15*
SUGGESTED FURTHER READING: Proverbs 16:6–20

'You must allow that Mr Wilberforce is cheerful,' said some of his friends to one who had just spent a week in the same house with him, and who was fixing on religion the old charge of dullness.

'Yes,' she said in a tone intended to convey reproach, 'and no wonder: I should be always cheerful too, if I could make myself as sure as he does that I was going to heaven.'

FOR MEDITATION: After Wilberforce's 'great change' friends noted that he was 'very cheerful.' This flowed from the abiding sense of peace that was Wilberforce's portion after he surrendered his heart to God.

That sense of peace has perhaps been written of most famously by St Augustine in his celebrated *Confessions*. In this book, Augustine wrote in the fourth century:

Nos fecisti ad te et inquietum est cor nostrum donec requiescat in te.
Thou hast made us for thyself, O Lord, and our hearts are restless until they rest in thee.

Wilberforce also penned eloquent phrases of this kind. On one occasion he wrote: 'I must awake to my dangerous state, and never be at rest till I have made my peace with God.' One of his most moving prayers reads: 'Create then in me this sacred thirst, and satisfy it with that peace of God which thou only canst supply.'

REFERENCE: *The Life of William Wilberforce* (1838)

'Teach, guide, quicken me'

'Let thy hand be upon the man of thy right hand, upon the son of man whom thou madest strong for thyself. So will not we go back from thee: quicken us, and we will call upon thy name.' Psalm 80:17–18

SUGGESTED FURTHER READING: Psalm 119:33–48

I have been a sadly unprofitable servant. Pardon me, O Lord; quicken, soften, warm, invigorate me, and enable me to rise from my torpor, and to imitate the example of holy Paul, doing this one thing, forgetting the things behind, and pressing forward towards the mark of our high calling of God in Christ Jesus. Alas, I fear I sadly neglect my duties to my children, and also to the poor, for though I serve the latter more abundantly than by individual visitation, when with the motive of Christ's speech (Matthew 25:40),[25] I attend to whole classes and masses of them, yet individual visitation has its good also. O Lord, teach, guide, quicken me. Without thee I can do nothing; with thee all things. Lord, help, bless, and keep me. Amen.

FOR MEDITATION: Wilberforce's sons wrote: 'It is well worth the inquiry by what system of self-treatment these happy fruits had been matured. They were not merely the results of a naturally easy temper leavened with religious feeling; they resulted from close and systematic discipline. He kept a most strict watch over his heart. He still recorded by a set of secret marks the results of frequent and close self-examination under a number of specific heads. He used every help he could devise for keeping always on his soul a sense of the nearness and the goodness of his God.'

REFERENCE: *The Life of William Wilberforce* (1838)

'He kept a most strict watch over his heart'

'Thou art my portion, O LORD: *I have said that I would keep thy words. I intreated thy favour with my whole heart: be merciful unto me according to thy word.' Psalm 119:57–58*
SUGGESTED FURTHER READING: Psalm 73:16–28

Wilberforce's sons wrote of their father's growth in the Christian life thus: 'It is well worth the inquiry by what system of self-treatment these happy fruits had been matured. They were not merely the results of a naturally [easy] temper leavened with religious feeling; they resulted from close and systematic discipline. He kept a most strict watch over his heart. He still recorded by a set of secret marks the results of frequent and close self-examination under a number of specific heads. He used every help he could devise for keeping always on his soul a sense of the nearness and the goodness of his God.

'"I used to have an expedient similar to the Jewish phylacteries (Numbers 15:38–39), in order to keep up the sense of God's presence. Let me try it again. I must have him for my portion and the strength of my heart, or I should be miserable here as well as hereafter."' Another custom from which he found great benefit was putting down motives for humiliation, motives for thankfulness, and so on, which he 'carried about and could look at during any moment of leisure.'

FOR MEDITATION: Wilberforce understood, along with the psalmist, that 'the LORD is my light and my salvation.' So too did he know that 'the LORD is the strength of my life' (Psalm 27:1). Those who know this and trust in these blessed truths cry 'I must have him for my portion and the strength of my heart.' May we be of that number. May this be the desire of our hearts.

REFERENCE: *The Life of William Wilberforce* (1838)

'Living almost without God in the world'

'That at that time ye were without Christ, being aliens from the commonwealth of Israel, and strangers from the covenants of promise, having no hope, and without God in the world.' Ephesians 2:12
SUGGESTED FURTHER READING: Psalm 86:1–17

In the summer of 1817, Wilberforce penned a lengthy review of his life with a view towards remembering all that God had done in his life. Though it reads in a somewhat fragmentary fashion—almost like a catalogue—what comes through is a profound sense of gratitude.

'Early advantages abused, and benefits often lost.—What an (almost) hell of bad passions (despair absent) in my soul when a youth, from emulation, envy, hatred, jealousy, selfishness! (Yet, alas! justice to myself requires my adding how ill-treated here.) Time, talents, substance, etc. wasted, and shocking goings-on (Christianity considered): and after the revellings over, as egregious waste of faculties and means among the fellows; card-playing, etc. Consequent course of living almost without God in the world, till God's good providence checked and turned me, oh miracle of mercy in 1785, through the Dean's instrumentality.'[26]

FOR MEDITATION: Upon another occasion Wilberforce wrote in a similar vein. It is a moving testimony. 'Surely when I think of the way in which I went on for many years, from about sixteen to 1785–6, I can only fall down with astonishment as well as humiliation before the throne of grace, and adore with wonder (no less than remorse and gratitude) that infinite mercy of God which did not cast me off; but on the contrary, guiding me by a way which I knew not, led me to those from whom I was to receive the knowledge of salvation.'

REFERENCE: *The Life of William Wilberforce* (1838)

'Pray for me, my dear friend'

'See then that ye walk circumspectly, not as fools, but as wise, redeeming the time, because the days are evil.' Ephesians 5:15–16
SUGGESTED FURTHER READING: Psalm 101:1–8

Wilberforce wrote these words to his brother-in-law James Stephen on 22 September 1817: 'May it please God to enable me to employ the small stock, whatever it may be, of talent and time that is left to me, more diligently and effectually than I have done hitherto. Pray for me, my dear friend, as I do and will for you.'

FOR MEDITATION: Stewardship is a recurring theme in Wilberforce's writings. It should be a consistent feature of our prayer lives to ask for the grace and determination to act as faithful stewards of all that God has entrusted to us.

We most often think of stewardship in terms of money, but biblical stewardship is far more comprehensive in its scope. It encompasses our employment of time, the cultivation of talents and abilities, and much else. Most of all, it is incumbent upon us to be good stewards of our prayer and devotional life. For if we do not know him whom we would serve, how can we serve him aright? If we give short shrift to our devotions, how can we give liberally and wisely of all that God has given us? In Matthew we read 'Seek ye first the kingdom of God, and all these things shall be added unto you' (Matthew 6:33). We must seek first the kingdom of God that we might learn how to be faithful stewards.

REFERENCE: *The Life of William Wilberforce* (1838)

'Whether in the bustle or the solitude'

'Then are they glad because they be quiet; so he bringeth them unto their desired haven.' Psalm 107:30
SUGGESTED FURTHER READING: Isaiah 35:1–10

Well, if God be with us, whether in the bustle or the solitude—if we are engaged in the work he has assigned to us, and are performing it in the proper spirit, all is well.

FOR MEDITATION: Wilberforce once wrote of the different callings given to us. 'It is evident we are to consider our peculiar situations, and in these to do all the good we can. Some men are thrown into public, some have their lot in private life. These different states have their corresponding duties; and he whose destination is of the former sort, will do as ill to immure himself in solitude, as he who is only a village Hampden would, were he to head an army or address a senate.'

Wilberforce had learned of these things from his spiritual mentor, John Newton, who had written thus to Wilberforce in 1796: 'Indeed the great point for our comfort in life is to have a well-grounded persuasion that we are, where, all things considered, we ought to be. Then it is no great matter whether we are in public or in private life, in a city or a village, in a palace or a cottage. The promise, "My grace is sufficient for thee," is necessary to support us in the smoothest scenes, and is equally able to support us in the most difficult. Happy the man who has a deep impression of our Lord's words, "Without me you can do nothing"—who feels with the Apostle likewise a heartfelt dependence upon the Saviour, through whom we can both do and bear all things that are [part of] the post allotted us.'

REFERENCE: *The Life of William Wilberforce* (1838)

'You will, please God, do great good'

'Trust in the LORD, *and do good; so shalt thou dwell in the land, and verily thou shalt be fed.' Psalm 37:3*
SUGGESTED FURTHER READING: Psalm 125:1–5

My dearest boy, remember my counsel. If you come into Parliament, let me earnestly entreat you not to expend yourself in speechifying on questions of grand political or rather I mean party contention; but while you take part in the public and general discussions that are of real moment, for this is what I have commonly done, choose out for yourself some specific object, some line of usefulness. Make yourself thoroughly acquainted with your subject, and you will not only be listened to with attention, but you will, please God, do great good. This is the mode in which I have often advised young men to proceed, but they seldom would be wise enough to follow my counsel, and hence you hear of many of them making one or two good speeches, and then all is over. This is really a sad waste of the means of prodigious usefulness which Providence has put into their power.

FOR MEDITATION: Wilberforce's advice to his son Samuel recalls the story of how Christians ought to build on a good foundation related in Matthew 7. Here the Lord Jesus declares: 'Therefore whosoever heareth these sayings of mine, and doeth them, I will liken him unto a wise man, which built his house upon a rock: And the rain descended, and the floods came, and the winds blew, and beat upon that house; and it fell not: for it was founded upon a rock. And every one that heareth these sayings of mine, and doeth them not, shall be likened unto a foolish man, which built his house upon the sand: and the rain descended, and the floods came, and the winds blew, and beat upon that house; and it fell: and great was the fall of it' (Matthew 7:24–27).

REFERENCE: *The Life of William Wilberforce* (1838)

'May God prosper it'

'They shall prosper that love thee.' Psalm 122:6
SUGGESTED FURTHER READING: Psalm 122

'Sent off a suitable letter with my *Practical View* to the Prince of Coburgh.[27] May God prosper it'—and after the notice of a 'kind answer in which he promises to read it,' follows the prayer, 'May God bless to him the perusal of it.'

FOR MEDITATION: Wilberforce wrote these words in the autumn of 1817. But this was not the first time that his book, *A Practical View of Christianity*, had influenced the lives of the prominent or of royalty. *A Practical View* had a profound effect on the Scottish philosopher Thomas Chalmers. 'About the year 1811,' he wrote, 'I had Wilberforce's *View* put into my hands, and, as I got on in reading it, I felt myself on the eve of a great revolution in all my opinions about Christianity.' Many years later, Chalmers expressed his profound indebtedness to Wilberforce: 'May that book which spoke so powerfully to myself, and has spoken powerfully to thousands, represent you to future generations, and be the instrument of converting many who are yet unborn.'

Chalmers' words proved prescient. In 1798, *A Practical View* made its way to a young curate just assuming his ministerial duties on the Isle of Wight: Legh Richmond. After reading it, he 'sought mercy at the cross of the Saviour.'

Richmond later wrote *The Dairyman's Daughter*, one of the highest-selling works of the 19th century. It told the story of Elizabeth Wallbridge, a young woman of deep faith who faced the prospect of death with great fortitude. By 1849, over 4 million copies, in 19 languages, had been sold. One copy had a profound effect on the young Queen Victoria, who made a pilgrimage to Elizabeth Wallbridge's grave.

REFERENCE: *The Life of William Wilberforce* (1838)

'Never, surely, was family religion seen in more attractive colours'

'But it is good for me to draw near to God: I have put my trust in the LORD *God, that I may declare all thy works.' Psalm 73:28*
SUGGESTED FURTHER READING: James 4:6–10

'I cannot resist,' wrote Wilberforce's young friend and biographer John Harford, 'adding the following interesting picture of Mr Wilberforce's life at Marden Park, which is partly in his own words and partly in those of his sons':—'I am profiting, I trust, from the quiet life I lead at this sweet place.' Never, surely, was family religion seen in more attractive colours. 'I only wish,' said a college friend, who had been visiting two of his sons, 'that those who abuse your father's principles could come down here and see how he lives.' It was a goodly sight. The cheerful play of a most happy temper, which more than sixty years had only mellowed, gladdened all his domestic intercourse. The family meetings were enlivened by his conversation—gay, easy, and natural, yet abounding in manifold instruction—drawn from books, from life, and from reflection. Though his step was less elastic than of old, he took his part in out-of-door occupations—climbing the neighbouring Downs with the walking parties, pacing in the shade of the tall trees, or gilding with the old man's smile the innocent cheerfulness of younger pastimes. 'The sun was very hot to-day, and the wind south; but under the beech trees on the side of the hill it was quite cool. Dined by ourselves, and walked with the boys in the evening.'

FOR MEDITATION: The apostle Paul has written of the beauty associated with those who bring the good news of the gospel of peace (Romans 10:15). But there is also a beauty, and sweetness, associated with those whose lives have been transformed and shaped by the good news.

REFERENCE: *Recollections of William Wilberforce* (1864)

'From such small beginnings'

'Another parable put he forth unto them, saying, The kingdom of heaven is like to a grain of mustard seed, which a man took, and sowed in his field: which indeed is the least of all seeds: but when it is grown, it is the greatest among herbs, and becometh a tree, so that the birds of the air come and lodge in the branches thereof.' Matthew 13:31–32
SUGGESTED FURTHER READING: Matthew 13:24–35

He spoke with high commendation of Dr Carey, the Baptist missionary, and traced him from his lowly origin as a shoemaker to his then dignified position in the learned world. He was so unskillful at his trade that he could never make two shoes alike. He felt an ardent thirst for learning, and the piety of his mind directed his studies to biblical literature. He was almost self-taught. After making a considerable progress in Greek and Latin he studied Hebrew; and being filled with missionary zeal turned his thoughts to India. The little Baptist society to which he belonged could at first raise only £13 in support of the mission of which he was to be the head. From such small beginnings emerged a society which has since produced very striking and beneficial results to the cause of Christianity. The profits of his situation and of his literary labours, to the amount of £1,500 per annum, he gave wholly to the mission. Upon this disinterested and noble appropriation of so large a sum Mr Wilberforce poured forth an eloquent eulogium.

FOR MEDITATION: 'Go ye therefore, and teach all nations, baptizing them in the name of the Father, and of the Son, and of the Holy Ghost: teaching them to observe all things whatsoever I have commanded you: and, lo, I am with you alway, even unto the end of the world'(Matthew 28:19–20).

REFERENCE: *Recollections of William Wilberforce* (1864)

'How little likely'

'How excellent is thy lovingkindness, O God! therefore the children of men put their trust under the shadow of thy wings.' Psalm 36:7
SUGGESTED FURTHER READING: Psalm 103:15–22

Sunday, Dec. 31st 1815. Church morning. After church, we and our six children together—I addressed them all collected, and afterwards solemn prayer. How little likely on the 30th May, 1797, when I married, that we and all our six children (we never had another) should all be living and well! Praise the Lord, O my soul.

FOR MEDITATION: At times, a profound sense of the Lord's blessing on our lives overwhelms us. Wilberforce had nearly died in 1788, and he thought for many years after that he would never marry. To look upon his beloved wife Barbara and their children as he did on this New Year's Eve so long ago, was to know that God had blessed him beyond what he could have asked or imagined. He had longed all his life for a family such as this—a desire all the more poignant when one recalls that he had lost his own father at age eight and two beloved sisters, Elizabeth and Anne, before he reached adulthood. New Year's Eve should prompt within us a deep sense of reflection and gratitude. It always did with Wilberforce. And given all that has been said above, he had so many reasons to praise the Lord within his soul.

REFERENCE: *The Life of William Wilberforce* (1838)

'It is by faith in Christ only'

'And if children, then heirs; heirs of God, and joint-heirs with Christ; if so be that we suffer with him, that we may be also glorified together.'
Romans 8:17
SUGGESTED FURTHER READING: 1 Peter 1:1–11

'But the nature of that happiness which the true Christian seeks to possess, is no other than the restoration of the image of God in his soul: and as to the manner of acquiring it, disclaiming with indignation every idea of attaining it by his own strength, he rests altogether on the operation of God's Holy Spirit, which is promised to all who cordially embrace the gospel. In short, it is by faith in Christ only that he is to be justified in the sight of God: to be delivered from the condition of a child of wrath and a slave of Satan; to be adopted into the family of God; to become an heir of God, and a joint heir with Christ, entitled to all the privileges which belong to this high relation; here, to the spirit of grace, and a partial renewal after the image of his Creator; hereafter, to the more perfect possession of the Divine likeness, and an inheritance of eternal glory.'

FOR MEDITATION: 'Christ in you,' the apostle Paul writes, is 'the hope of glory' (Colossians 1:27). This is among the chief privileges which belong to our 'high relation', as it were, in the Lord.

Joint heirs with Christ. How can we begin to grasp this? We cannot fully. But it is enough for us to know that God loved us so much that he has granted us this distinction in Christ—and Christ died for us on the cross that we might receive it. May we, by his Spirit of grace, strive after holiness. May it be our continual desire to be more like him.

REFERENCE: *Recollections of William Wilberforce* (1864)

'Teach, guide, quicken me'

'Let thy hand be upon the man of thy right hand, upon the son of man whom thou madest strong for thyself. So will not we go back from thee: quicken us, and we will call upon thy name.' Psalm 80:17–18
SUGGESTED FURTHER READING: Psalm 119:33–48

I have been a sadly unprofitable servant. Pardon me, O Lord; quicken, soften, warm, invigorate me, and enable me to rise from my torpor, and to imitate the example of holy Paul, doing this one thing, forgetting the things behind, and pressing forward towards the mark of our high calling of God in Christ Jesus. Alas, I fear I sadly neglect my duties to my children, and also to the poor, for though I serve the latter more abundantly than by individual visitation, when with the motive of Christ's speech (Matthew 25:40),[28] I attend to whole classes and masses of them, yet individual visitation has its good also. O Lord, teach, guide, quicken me. Without thee I can do nothing; with thee all things. Lord, help, bless, and keep me. Amen.

FOR MEDITATION: Wilberforce's sons wrote: 'It is well worth the inquiry by what system of self-treatment these happy fruits had been matured. They were not merely the results of a naturally [easy] temper leavened with religious feeling; they resulted from close and systematic discipline. He kept a most strict watch over his heart. He still recorded by a set of secret marks the results of frequent and close self-examination under a number of specific heads. He used every help he could devise for keeping always on his soul a sense of the nearness and the goodness of his God.'

REFERENCE: *The Life of William Wilberforce* (1838)

'Your temple of friendship'

'We took sweet counsel together, and walked unto the house of God in company.' Psalm 55:14
SUGGESTED FURTHER READING: Romans 12:9–21

John Harford writes that the following letter from Wilberforce reached him early in 1826:

Beckenham: Feb. 28, 1826

My dear Friend,—The three months for which we came to this place have nearly passed away and we are again meditating a visit to Bath. Shall you and Mrs H. be at home in April or May? But let me not forget to ask another question. Should the tablet which I am to send you exhibit my own arms only, or Mrs W.'s. also? After receiving your answer there shall be no delay. Indeed, I consider your request as a mark of your regard, and as a means of recording our mutual esteem in your temple of friendship. One of my compeers, Acland, has just left me, after a summer's walk, so far as atmosphere can make it such—the birds also bear their part—the foliage only is wanting. How delightful must your place be today with all your evergreens.

I am ever your sincere friend,

W.W.

FOR MEDITATION: Wilberforce had a great capacity for friendship, and his friends greatly enriched his life. So it is with many of us. Friends are the living representatives of fellowship—which is itself one of God's great gifts to humanity. The poet and divine John Donne has written some of the most famous phrases in the English language in connection with friendship and fellowship—and the ties that bind us together:

All mankind is of one author, and is one volume … therefore the bell that rings to a sermon, calls not upon the preacher only, but upon the congregation to come: so this bell calls us all … No man is an island, entire of itself … any man's death diminishes me, because I am involved in mankind; and therefore never send to know for whom the bell tolls; it tolls for thee.

REFERENCE: *Recollections of William Wilberforce* (1864)

'Oppression and cruelty'

'Behold, this was the iniquity of thy sister Sodom, pride, fullness of bread, and abundance of idleness was in her and in her daughters, neither did she strengthen the hand of the poor and needy.' Ezekiel 16:49
SUGGESTED FURTHER READING: Zephaniah 3:1–5

March 8th 1818. Sunday. Lay awake several hours in the night, and very languid this morning. My mind is very uneasy, and greatly distracted about the course to be pursued in the West Indian [slave] matters. It is hard to decide, especially where [there are] so many counsellors. This is clear, that in the Scriptures no national crime is condemned so frequently, and few so strongly, as oppression and cruelty, and the not using our best endeavours to deliver our fellow-creatures from them. Jeremiah 6:6. This is a city to be visited; she is wholly oppression in the midst of her. Ezekiel 16:49, of Sodom's crimes: Neither did she strengthen the hands of the poor and needy. Zephaniah 3:1; Amos 4:1, 8, etc.

I must therefore set to work, and, O Lord, direct, and support, and bless me. If it please thee not to let me be the instrument of good to these poor degraded people, may I still be found working, like dear [James] Stephen, with vigour and simple obedience, remembering, 'It is well with thee that it was in thy heart.'

FOR MEDITATION: Matthew 25:40 tells us: 'And the King shall answer and say unto them, "Verily I say unto you, inasmuch as ye have done it unto one of the least of these my brethren, ye have done it unto me."' The 'least of these' in our world are a source of abiding concern to our Lord. In finding ways to serve them, we find ways to honour and serve our common Lord. May we be about our Master's business.

REFERENCE: *The Life of William Wilberforce* (1838)

'My times, O Lord, are in thy hand'

'But I trusted in thee, O LORD: I said, Thou art my God. My times are in thy hand.' Psalm 31:14–15a
SUGGESTED FURTHER READING: Psalm 40:11–17

May 10th [1818]. Determined to come in again for Bramber, at least for two years. Thus Providence seems to fashion my ways, and if I should go entirely out of public life in two years, I hope to have previously sown the seeds and laid the foundation of the West Indian [slavery] reform. I shall then, if I live, be sixty as much as most men's seventy. But my times, O Lord, are in thy hand. Oh how truly may I say, that goodness and mercy have followed me all my days! What cause have I to be thankful for kind friends: Lord Gambier most affectionate. Stephen most disinterested, and kind, and generous. Babington and Inglis, Charles Grant and Macaulay too.[29] Surely no man ever had such undeserved mercies. Praise the Lord, O my soul.

FOR MEDITATION: When important decisions lie before us and we feel the weight of them, what a comfort it is to know we can rest in the truth that our times are in God's hand—and that we are always in his keeping. Then too, God also gives us the gift of friends who come alongside us in our journey of faith. God's promises and the gift of friends—they show that God knows our every need. He will supply all that we require. This the apostle Paul knew and he wrote of it, saying: 'But my God shall supply all your need according to his riches in glory by Christ Jesus' (Philippians 4:19). May we learn to trust in this truth, and in the Lord about whom these things were written.

REFERENCE: *The Life of William Wilberforce* (1838)

'A kind Providence favoured us'

'I will both lay me down in peace, and sleep: for thou, Lord, only makest me dwell in safety.' Psalm 4:8
SUGGESTED FURTHER READING: Psalm 119:113–120

Leaving Elmdon on the 10th, he reached Seaforth House,[30] near Liverpool, upon the 11th of August [1818]. 'When we got upon the paved roads, our [carriage] linch-pin twice came out, and our spring-straps broke. A kind Providence favoured us, that no accident. Praise the Lord, O my soul ... 13th. To Liverpool in Mr Gladstone's carriage, and saw the Botanical Garden—very fine.'

FOR MEDITATION: In later years, Sir William Gladstone remembered this precise occasion. He wrote: 'in 1833 I had the honour of breakfasting with Mr Wilberforce a few days before his death, and when I entered the house, immediately after the salutation, he said to me in his silvery tones, "How is your sweet mother?" He had been a guest in my father's house some twelve years before.'

Of Sir William's 1833 meeting with Wilberforce (his first) he wrote in his diary: '25 July 1833. Went to Breakfast with old Mr Wilberforce, introduced by his son. He is cheerful and serene, a beautiful picture of old age in sight of immortality. Heard him pray with his family. Blessing and honour are upon his head.'

REFERENCE: *The Life of William Wilberforce* (1838)

'The Lord shall preserve thy going out and thy coming in'

'The Lord shall preserve thy going out and thy coming in from this time forth, and even for evermore.' Psalm 121:8
SUGGESTED FURTHER READING: Psalm 121

When his family party had broken up at Rydale, he had been compelled to travel in a different direction from the rest; and on 24th of October he wrote to Mrs Wilberforce from Cambridge—'I thank God I am arrived at this place in safety, making up near 350 miles which I have travelled, full 100 of them at night, without a single accident. How grateful ought I to be for this protecting providence of a gracious God! And I just now recollect in a most natural connection, that tomorrow, the 25th of October, is the anniversary of the day on which I experienced that notable escape from being drowned in the Avon, when we lodged at Bath Easton. Praise the Lord, O my soul.'

FOR MEDITATION: Verses written by John Keble, whose book *The Christian Year* (published in 1827) Wilberforce loved to carry about with him in the last years of his life, are fitting here:

God keep thee safe from harm and sin,
Thy Spirit keep; the Lord watch o'er
Thy going out, thy coming in,
From this time, evermore.

There are times when we know, of a certainty, that God has been watching over and protecting us. It is then that we understand, in ways that are new to us and twice-blessed, what the Scripture means when it declares: 'for he hath said, I will never leave thee, nor forsake thee.' (Hebrews 13:5).

REFERENCE: *The Life of William Wilberforce* (1838)

'The aura of immorality'

'But thou, O man of God, flee these things; and follow after righteousness, godliness, faith, love, patience, meekness. Fight the good fight of faith, lay hold on eternal life, whereunto thou art also called, and hast professed a good profession before many witnesses.'
1 *Timothy 6:11–12*
SUGGESTED FURTHER READING: 1 Timothy 6:1–14

In the early spring of 1814, Madame de Stael was in London, with her son and daughter, where she mingled much in the highest society. Having expressed a particular wish to become acquainted with Mr Wilberforce, the Duke of Gloucester, in order to gratify her, made up a select dinner party, to which he was specially invited. She afterwards made a great point of his dining with her, which he did, and in addition to her son and daughter, the company included Lord and Lady Lansdowne, Lord Harrowby, Sir James Mackintosh, etc.

One of the guests afterwards assured me that, without any effort on Mr Wilberforce's part, the conversation was quickly in his hand, and that such was the brilliancy of his thoughts and remarks, that Madame de Stael herself, after thus meeting him, said, 'I have always heard of Mr Wilberforce as among the most benevolent of men: I shall now ever think of him as one of the wittiest and most agreeable.'

He told me that he had afterwards sent her his book on practical Christianity for which she had almost asked, and her remark on it to a mutual friend was, 'C'est l'aurore de l'immortalité.'

FOR MEDITATION: 'A good profession before many witnesses'—so our lives should be a winsome testimony or compelling example for those who are not of the Christian family.

REFERENCE: *Recollections of William Wilberforce* (1864)

'Turn every moment to account'

'That I may publish with the voice of thanksgiving, and tell of all thy wondrous works.' Psalm 26:7
SUGGESTED FURTHER READING: Psalm 145:1–21

In July 1822, Mrs Harford and I spent some delightful days with Mr and Mrs Wilberforce at Marden Park, on which occasion Baron de Stael passed the Sunday there—to which his sister, the late Duchess de Broglie, has particularly referred in the interesting sketch which she has published of her brother's life.

We were all very pleasingly impressed by his simple and amiable manners, and hc made himself very agreeable to Mr Wilberforce by his intelligence, and by his description of the impression produced on him by this his first visit to England. Nothing amongst us, he said, had struck him so much as the high degree of liberty we enjoyed, in union with so much respect for aristocratic institutions. Such a union, he felt, imparted great coherence to our Constitution, and was to be found in no other country in Europe.

After church, he and Mr Wilberforce took a long and retired walk together, when he opened his heart to him on religious topics, and left him with a pleasing impression that the Baron was truly seeking, and he hoped would find, the 'pearl of great price.'

Events have since proved that this hope was well founded, for though prematurely cut off in the flower of his days and usefulness, he has left behind him a character esteemed for his intellectual qualities and truly Christian virtues. He assured Mr Wilberforce that he daily read the Bible with prayer to God.

FOR MEDITATION: Early in the 20th century, the American President Theodore Roosevelt once said famously: 'Do what you can, with what you have, where you are.' Long years before, in 1786, Wilberforce said something very similar: 'In such a situation as mine every moment may be made useful to the happiness of my fellow-creatures.'—from UK Parliament talk.

REFERENCE: *Recollections of William Wilberforce* (1864)

'You are in the right road'

'As for God, his way is perfect: the word of the LORD *is tried: he is a buckler to all those that trust in him.' Psalm 18:30*
SUGGESTED FURTHER READING: Proverbs 12:17–28

I can with truth speak to you the language of encouragement. I should be sorry for your (mental) sufferings, were it not for the indication they afford me that you are in the right road. I myself have travelled it. When I was first awakened to a sense of the importance of Divine things, the distress I felt was deep and poignant indeed. I wondered, also, to find that my feelings too little corresponded with the convictions of my understanding.

But looking into the writings of many great and good men I found that their feelings and complaints had been exactly similar to my own. I felt a strange torpor and coldness which ill accorded with the mercies I had received, and the sense of obligation of which I was conscious. This led me to prayer and self-abasement—to penitential sorrow—to humble but earnest supplication for the promised aids of the Holy Spirit, for the sake of that Saviour who died upon the Cross to atone for our transgressions, in order to soften, to animate, to warm my dull heart.

FOR MEDITATION: Looking into the writings of many great and good men. How many a Christian embarking on their pilgrimage of faith has done the same. Writings that are part of the canon of Christian literature provide us with inspiration and wisdom. But perhaps the most important thing they serve to teach us is to impart the knowledge that we are a part of a story—the enduring story—of the Christian church. We are fellow-travellers with men and women of ages past who have loved and served the Lord. When this thought comes to us, we then see that reading of these men and women affords us the opportunity to walk a part of our journey of faith with them, as it were. Ours is a precious heritage, ours is the privilege of being a part of the enduring story.

REFERENCE: *Recollections of William Wilberforce* (1864)

'Christianity as practised in the world'

'be ready always to give an answer to every man that asketh you a reason of the hope that is in you.' 1 Peter 3:15
SUGGESTED FURTHER READING: 2 Timothy 2:15–26

Writing of Wilberforce's classic work of apologetics *A Practical View of Christianity* (1797), John Harford said: In this work Mr Wilberforce places in a very striking point of view the essential differences which exist between Christianity as taught in the New Testament, and Christianity as practised in the world.

He shows that the grand radical defect in the system of mere nominal Christians is, that they either overlook or disregard the peculiar doctrines of the religion which they profess: such as the corruption of human nature—the atonement of the Saviour—and the converting, sanctifying influences of the Holy Spirit. He shows, on the other hand, upon the clearest Scriptural evidence, that a consecration of the heart to God through faith in Christ, and a life daily guided, governed, and directed by the spirit and the precepts of the Gospel, is the duty and the happiness of all sincere believers. To live unto him who died for them, and daily to implore the light and grace of the Holy Spirit to enable them to do so, forms, in fact, the vital principle of true Christianity.

FOR MEDITATION: Wilberforce's words have much to teach us about what it means to commend our faith to others. First, we are to study the Scriptures diligently. Second, we are to strive, asking God to help us, to manifest in our lives the character and practices taught in the New Testament. But, as Wilberforce tells us, it is not solely the outward profession of Christian principles that we are to pursue; we are to cultivate the dispositions and affections of Christians described in the Scriptures. We are to 'set our affections on things above,' and to 'put on the new man, which is renewed in knowledge after the image of him that created him.' There ought to be, in the best sense of the word, something different about those who profess the name of Christ.

REFERENCE: *Recollections of William Wilberforce* (1864)

'What cause have we for thankfulness'

'For we have not an high priest which cannot be touched with the feeling of our infirmities; but was in all points tempted like as we are, yet without sin.' Hebrews 4:15
SUGGESTED FURTHER READING: Psalm 32:1–11

For this and all my other manifold sins, and my sad unprofitableness (God knows I say it from the heart and with a deep consciousness of its truth), I can only fly for mercy and pity to him, who is not only the propitiation for our sins, but the kind and gracious sympathiser with our infirmities. What cause have we for thankfulness who know thus where to go for pardon and for peace, as well as for grace and strength.

FOR MEDITATION: To know what it is to be forgiven of God is to possess a gift beyond price—for sometimes the sense of our sinfulness can overwhelm us. But as Wilberforce's words above remind us, when the sense of our sin runs deep, the depth of God's grace, forgiveness and love runs deeper still. As the apostle Paul wrote in Romans 8:38–39, 'I am persuaded, that neither death, nor life, nor angels, nor principalities, nor powers, nor things present, nor things to come, nor height, nor depth, nor any other creature, shall be able to separate us from the love of God, which is in Christ Jesus our Lord.' Nearly one hundred years ago, Thomas Chisholm captured the profound sense of comfort faith holds for the Christian:

Pardon for sin and a peace that endureth
Thine own dear presence to cheer and to guide;
Strength for today and bright hope for tomorrow,
Blessings all mine, with ten thousand beside!

REFERENCE: *Recollections of William Wilberforce* (1864)

'These boundless dominions'

'The heavens declare the glory of God; and the firmament sheweth his handywork.' Psalm 19:1
SUGGESTED FURTHER READING: Psalm 8:1–9; 102:25–27

John Harford wrote of his friend Wilberforce: 'It was settled between us that he should spend his seventieth birthday (24 August 1829) at Blaise Castle. He made an effort to reach us, as had been settled, on his seventieth birthday, but did not arrive till the day after.

'I never saw him in more delightful spirits. His mental powers continued vigorous as ever, and the flow of his conversation was unceasingly attractive. He had lately been reading Herschel's work on Astronomy,[31] which had greatly fired his imagination; and he said some beautiful things suggested by it on the vibrations of light necessary for the production of each of the prismatic colours. Then his wit, his ready application of fine passages of poetry to the scenery of nature, the devout elevation of his religious reflections, and the touches of feeling and tenderness which broke forth from him spontaneously all combined to shed an enchantment on the hours spent with him.'

FOR MEDITATION: Wilberforce knew what it was to love God with his mind (Luke 10:27), and he had an abiding interest in the ways in which scientific research revealed new things about the world God has made. About the same time that he visited John Harford in 1829 he recorded in his diary that he found himself 'meditating more on God as the Creator and Governor of the universe.' He marvelled at what the science of his day told him about the known universe: 'Eighty millions of fixed stars, each as large at least as our sun.' Such meditations often led him to speak of these wonders to his family. 'The discoveries of astronomy,' he said, 'warm my heart. I think of eighty millions of stars in our nebula, and of two thousand nebulae, and I feel elevated and thankful to be a part in this magnificent creation, to be the child of him who is the Governor of these boundless dominions.'

REFERENCE: *Recollections of William Wilberforce* (1864)

'A peculiar people'

'But ye are a chosen generation, a royal priesthood, an holy nation, a peculiar people; that ye should shew forth the praises of him who hath called you out of darkness into his marvellous light.' 1 Peter 2:9
SUGGESTED FURTHER READING: Matthew 5:13–16

In his memoir, *Recollections of William Wilberforce* (1864), John Harford recalled: 'Touching on the purity and elevation of heart which should mark the Christian character, Mr Wilberforce said: "The thing we are all of us—you and I and all—too much disposed to forget is, that Christians are to be a peculiar people. We are too much inclined to appear to be what other persons are. One thing I often accuse myself of is the not seeking more diligently occasions of attempting to promote the spiritual improvement of others. It is a difficult point, but we should make it the subject of prayer."'

FOR MEDITATION: When the apostle Peter writes of the need for us as Christians to be a peculiar people, he is not suggesting that we act strangely. Rather in concert with the words of Jesus in the Gospel of Matthew, he is saying that we ought to let our light—that is character of our lives and Christian testimony—'so shine before men, that they may see your good works, and glorify your Father which is in heaven.'

Jesus used a wonderful metaphor to convey the picture of how we ought to let our light shine. When men light a candle, he said, they do not put it under a bushel, but rather on a candlestick. When this is done, he concluded, the candle 'giveth light unto all that are in the house.' All of us, wherever we are in the world, are part of a community. Our relationships with our neighbours, as well as with our fellow Christians, ought to be marked by the elements of Christian character—good works born of faith and also the fruits of the spirit (see Galatians 5:22–23) 'love, joy, peace, longsuffering, gentleness, goodness, faith, meekness, and temperance.' When this is done we are, as has been often said, salt and light in our communities and our culture.

REFERENCE: *Recollections of William Wilberforce* (1864)

'The moral gravitation of the universe'

'For thy mercy is great unto the heavens, and thy truth unto the clouds.'
Psalm 57:10
SUGGESTED FURTHER READING: John 14:1–14

'When Mr Wilberforce aimed at giving peculiar force to a sentiment or a maxim,' wrote his friend John Harford, 'the point and terseness of his language could not be surpassed. As an instance of this, the topic of conversation one day being the misery to which Cowper, the poet, was exposed by his extreme sensibility at a public school, "Yes," he exclaimed, "it was a sensitive plant grasped by a hand of iron."'

Perhaps the most powerful and compelling instance of Wilberforce's gift for framing a succinct and memorable phrase took place when the subject of truth arose in conversation. 'Speaking of the value of truth,' Harford recalled, 'Mr Wilberforce remarked: "It is the moral gravitation of the universe."'

Mr Wilberforce's thoughts often passed into meditations upon the moral attributes of God. 'Retire into thy closet,' is one of the last entries [he ever wrote] in his pocketbook, 'and there let contemplation indulge her flights and expatiate.'

'I find unspeakable pleasure,' he told a friend, 'in the declarations so often reiterated in the Word of God of the unvarying truth of the Supreme Being. To me there is something inexpressibly sublime in the assurance, that throughout the whole immeasurable extent of the all but infinite empire of God, truth always extends, and like a master-key unlocks and opens all the mysterious wisdom, and goodness, and mercy of the Divine dispensations.'

FOR MEDITATION: The 'sun, moon and stars in their courses above,' wrote Thomas Chisholm, 'join with all nature in manifold witness to thy great faithfulness, mercy and love.' So too does the created world bear matchless witness to the reality—the truth—of who God is. Psalm 102:25 states: 'Of old hast thou laid the foundation of the earth: and the heavens are the work of thy hands.' Even as God is the Author of the book of nature he is also, supremely, the Author of our salvation. As Chisholm also wrote: 'As thou hast been, thou forever wilt be.'

REFERENCE: *Recollections of William Wilberforce* (1864)

'Grateful and admiring praise'

'Let the field be joyful, and all that is therein: then shall all the trees of the wood rejoice.' Psalm 96:12
SUGGESTED FURTHER READING: Isaiah 33:13–22

Highwood Hill: April 28, 1830
My dear Friend,—Let me transport myself, in this season of spring, to your rare exhibition of the sublime and beautiful. From a little spot of a dingle we have here, in which the violets (beautiful but not fragrant) and primroses are thickly sprinkled, I can form some idea of the delights of your paradise. It retains its Eve, too. When last there Mrs W. and I walked on a Sunday by the stream, reading and musing over Montgomery's *Hymns* and the interesting essay prefixed to them, and I now endeavour to take that same stroll in [thought] at this season of the year, and to people your rocks and thickets (through my mind's eye), with all the wild-flowers that they produce in such rich profusion. These objects should surely call forth in the coldest bosom warm aspirations of grateful and admiring praise.

FOR MEDITATION: James Montgomery (1771–1854) was the author of some 400 hymns, and he published two notable collections of hymns in Wilberforce's lifetime—*Songs of Zion: Being Imitations of Psalms* (1822) and *The Christian Psalmist* (1825). Among Montgomery's many hymns is one whose verses greatly resemble Wilberforce's reflections above: 'The God of Nature and of Grace.'

The God of nature and of grace
In all his works appears;
His goodness through the earth we trace,
His grandeur in the spheres.

In every stream his bounty flows,
Diffusing joy and wealth;
In every breeze his Spirit blows,
The breath of life and health.

The forests in his strength rejoice;
Hark! on the evening breeze,
As once of old, the Lord God's voice
Is heard among the trees.

His blessings fall in plenteous showers
Upon the lap of earth,
That teems with foliage, fruits and flowers,
And rings with infant mirth.

REFERENCE: *Recollections of William Wilberforce* (1864)

'The infinitely varied delights of universal nature'

'For by him were all things created, that are in heaven, and that are in earth, visible and invisible, whether they be thrones, or dominions, or principalities, or powers: all things were created by him, and for him.'
Colossians 1:16
SUGGESTED FURTHER READING: Psalm 148

I cannot but feel most deeply William Paley's exquisitely touching description of the infinitely varied delights of universal nature in all its varieties of animated being, where following the bee from flower to flower, and seeing animals so happy that they know not how to give it expression, he breaks out into the apostrophe, *'After all it is a happy world.'*

FOR MEDITATION: The hymn writer has written of the joy that comes when we 'join with all nature in manifold witness to thy great faithfulness, mercy and love.' Nature too bespeaks her Creator. Sunsets and sunrises, and all the creatures God has made—we can discern in them the hand of a master artist—the Author of all the beauty to be seen in the world around us.

REFERENCE: *Recollections of William Wilberforce* (1864)

'It is one comfort'

'Blessed be God, even the Father of our Lord Jesus Christ, the Father of mercies, and the God of all comfort.' 2 Corinthians 1:3
SUGGESTED FURTHER READING: 2 Corinthians 2–7

When I felt so comfortable in the Isle of Wight you will wonder at my not concluding my letter where I began it. Here we, however, are, conceiving myself likely to be benefited by a renewal of my annual potation of Bath water. I must say it is no very agreeable exchange to plunge into the smoke of Bath, from the pure air of the sea-shore and the Downs of the Isle of Wight, and the many coloured tints, and venerable oaks, and picturesque hollies of the New Forest, in which we halted for a day or two with an old friend. It is one comfort that we are so much nearer to you. The little you threw out as to your movements was rather unpromising as to our meeting; but I trust 'gravitation will not cease as you go by.'³² I am sure attraction will not; and a double magnet, it has long been known, is most powerful. I hope your dear lady is well. Give us a few lines, my dear friend, without delay.

Ever affectionately yours,

W.W.

FOR MEDITATION: Friends. Fellowship. There are few more precious gifts from God. A true friend comes alongside us when needed most. Friends season our lives in so many ways—imparting joy, laughter, and solace amidst tears. We walk with friends, sharing the view of a beautiful valley while hiking, or we can stand with them at the birth of a child. It is with friends that we share memorable meals and evenings—so many parts of our lives. And it is thought-provoking indeed to reflect that friendship received its most telling affirmation when Abraham was described as 'the friend of God' (James 2:23).

REFERENCE: *Recollections of William Wilberforce* (1864)

'We ought all to pray for our country'

'Continue in prayer, and watch in the same with thanksgiving.'
Colossians 4:2
SUGGESTED FURTHER READING: Proverbs 15:1–8

In October 1831 I received the following letter from Mr Wilberforce:

Bath: Oct. 7, 1831

My dear Friend,—This is an important week[33] for this country. May that Almighty Being who has so long favoured us still continue to bear with our provocations, and to hear the prayers of many among us who, I trust, do look up to him with affiance and gratitude. We ought all to pray for our country, under existing circumstances, with double earnestness. The passage in Genesis, where ten righteous would have saved Sodom, and still more that in Jeremiah 5:1: 'Run ye to and fro through the streets of Jerusalem, and see now, and know, and seek in the broad places thereof, if ye can find a man, if there be any that executeth judgment, that seeketh the truth: and I will pardon it'—are most cheering. Sursum corda.[34]

Believe me ever affectionately yours,

W.W.

FOR MEDITATION: James 5:16 tells us: 'The effectual fervent prayer of a righteous man availeth much.' 1 Timothy 2:1–3 states: 'I exhort therefore, that, first of all, supplications, prayers, intercessions, and giving of thanks, be made for all men; for kings, and for all that are in authority; that we may lead a quiet and peaceable life in all godliness and honesty. For this is good and acceptable in the sight of God our Saviour.' In whatever country we may live, we can best show that our true citizenship is in heaven by faithfulness in the office of prayer.

REFERENCE: *Recollections of William Wilberforce* (1864)

'Our Heavenly Father is constantly watching over us'

'My soul shall be satisfied as with marrow and fatness; and my mouth shall praise thee with joyful lips: when I remember thee upon my bed, and meditate on thee in the night watches. Because thou hast been my help, therefore in the shadow of thy wings will I rejoice.' Psalm 63:5–7
SUGGESTED FURTHER READING: Jeremiah 31:23–34

I heard from him as follows under date August 10, 1832:

My dear Friend,—I have been staying, for the last six weeks, with my dear friend and brother-in-law, Mr Stephen, who a few years ago built upon the summit of one of the Buckinghamshire hills a comfortable though small house, which, for a pedestrian (and his health required constant walking) is one of the most delightful spots I ever knew. There are many adjoining Downs, the herbage of which is so short and fine as to be, where not cut up, a perfect bowling-green. These extend on the chalk from fifteen and twenty miles, and there are many beechwoods for shade on the sunny days, whenever one wishes a fit time and place for meditation. My friend has given to his place the name of 'Healthy Hill;' and hitherto, even in this trying season, it has maintained its high character. We have had no appearance of cholera. Mrs W. and I, having heard of its prevalence at Bristol, have written to inquire whether it has yet visited Bath. We pause before we decide on our movements. The good Providence of our Heavenly Father is constantly watching over us wherever we are. Let us commit our ways to him, and be at peace.

Ever, my dear H. your sincere friend,

W.W.

FOR MEDITATION: Psalm 121:3 states: 'he that keepeth thee will not slumber.' The hymn writer Horatio Spafford writes of the 'peace, like a river, [that] attendeth my way.' Whether in a song of David or the refrain of a treasured hymn—we have the assurance of God's holy Word that he 'will never leave us, nor forsake us.'

REFERENCE: *Recollections of William Wilberforce* (1864)

'Christian fellowship and affection'

'A man that hath friends must shew himself friendly: and there is a friend that sticketh closer than a brother.' Proverbs 18:24
SUGGESTED FURTHER READING: Matthew 18:2–5: Luke 11:5–10

In October 1832 I received a letter from Mr Wilberforce at Bath proposing to pay us a visit in company with Mrs Wilberforce. We joyfully hailed his approach and by a happy coincidence the Bishop of Lichfield and Mrs and Miss Ryder were in the neighbourhood and gave us the pleasure of their company during part of the time. This was the last occasion on which we ever had the delight and the honour of receiving our revered and loved friend under our roof and it was one of the happiest of the many happy visits which he had successively paid us.

He was in great vigour of mind and in most animated spirits fall of affection and full of enjoyment. Sure I am that neither we nor our guests can ever forget the delightful conversations and intercourse which we enjoyed together heightened and enlivened by Christian fellowship and affection. During his stay the anniversary of our girls' school occurred when he together with several excellent clergymen who had breakfasted with us, accompanied Mrs Harford and me to the schoolroom and heard the children examined after which at our request he addressed them in a most kind affectionate and impressive manner. It was interesting to observe how adroitly the veteran statesman and orator accommodated both his language and ideas to the capacities of young children; and in concluding he made them all laugh by saying, with reference to a set of reward bonnets and plum cakes just about to be distributed, 'now, my dear children, don't eat the bonnets and put the cakes on your heads.'

FOR MEDITATION: 'I delight in little children,' Wilberforce once told a friend, 'I could spend hours in watching them.' His love for children demonstrated the extent to which he had come to, less than a year before his death, model the spirit of Christ. Our Lord loved children deeply, and invested himself in them. We ought to do the same.

REFERENCE: *Recollections of William Wilberforce* (1864)

'Love mercy, do justice'

'He hath shewed thee, O man, what is good; and what doth the Lord require of thee, but to do justly, and to love mercy, and to walk humbly with thy God.' Micah 6:8
SUGGESTED FURTHER READING: Psalm 37:1–11

On 12 April 1833, in spite of his resolution never more to speak in public, Mr Wilberforce was induced to propose, at a meeting in the town of Maidstone, a petition against slavery, to which he affixed his own signature. 'It was an affecting sight,' said his sons, 'to see the old man, who had so long been the champion of this cause, come forth once more from his retirement, and with an unquenched spirit, though with a weakened voice and failing body, maintain for the last time the cause of truth and justice. There was now no question about immediate emancipation; but the principle of compensation was disputed, and on this his judgment and his voice were clear. He hailed therefore with joy the proposal to atone for these offences by the grant of twenty millions; and in this his last speech at once declared, "I say, and say honestly and fearlessly, that the same Being who commands us to love mercy, says also, do justice ... I trust," he concluded, "that we now approach the very end of our career;" and as a gleam of sunshine broke into the hall, "the object," he exclaimed with all his early fire, "is bright before us, the light of heaven beams on it, and is an earnest of success."'

FOR MEDITATION: The noted author Os Guinness has observed that Wilberforce knew what it was to finish well. 1 Corinthians 9:24 states: *'So run, that ye may obtain.'* Three days before he died, Wilberforce was told of the safe passage of his long-cherished bill that would emancipate 800,000 slaves throughout the British Empire. His was a life of faithfulness graced by one final victory. So we ought to run, that we may obtain—in whatever it is that the Lord has given us to do.

REFERENCE: *Recollections of William Wilberforce* (1864)

'To have animated and assured our hopes'

'Therefore my heart is glad, and my glory rejoiceth: my flesh also shall rest in hope.' Psalm 16:9
SUGGESTED FURTHER READING: Psalm 33:12–22

A short time after, I heard from Mr Wilberforce in his own vigorous style as follows:

East Farleigh, near Maidstone,
Feb. 6, 1833

My dear Friend,—I ought ere this to have stated that one reason, I believe the chief, which prevented my writing to you was my wishing previously to hear the sermon of Robert Hall's[35] which you had so highly eulogized.

The particulars which Hall specifies as indicating the glory with which concealment clothes the Divine character appear to me just; yet it happened that my mind had recently been led into a different train of thought. I have been led to feel deeply how much we are called upon to admire and praise the kind condescension of the Almighty in acquainting us with his character and attributes in the degree which he has done. How embarrassing and anxiously distressing might it have been to our feelings if we had been left to judge of the qualities of the Supreme Being by the mere light of our unassisted reason. How gracious then is it in the Creator and Sustainer of the Universe to have quieted our apprehensions with such considerate kindness—to have soothed our misgivings and animated and assured our hopes by such varied means?

FOR MEDITATION: Ephesians 2:14 states: 'For he is our peace.' What a source of unspeakable comfort. What is more, the Scripture tells us the Lord is the giver of a peace that 'passeth all understanding'. We live in a world that is troubled in many ways. When we feel the weight of this, we can come to a Saviour who is, in himself, peace. He can impart peace to us. He will give us the gift of himself.

REFERENCE: *Recollections of William Wilberforce* (1864)

'Communion with my God and Saviour'

'That which we have seen and heard declare we unto you, that ye also may have fellowship with us: and truly our fellowship is with the Father, and with his Son Jesus Christ.' 1 John 1:3
SUGGESTED FURTHER READING: 1 Corinthians 1:1–9

'My soul's prosperity,' Wilberforce wrote at the close of 1799, 'it seems right to make my chief object; and at the same time to study a good deal, and cultivate faculties, my neglect of which I number among my very criminal omissions. My objects therefore in this day of solemn supplication and (in my measure) fasting, are to beg God's guidance and blessing on my endeavours to spend the ensuing interval between this time and the meeting of Parliament, piously, usefully, wisely, holily; first, however, humbly imploring pardon for all my past manifold offences, which to be particularly noted, and earnestly supplicating for grace to deliver me from the bondage of my corruptions. Then should come praise and thanksgiving, for the multiplied and prodigious mercies and blessings of God. Then resignation and self-dedication to God, desiring to submit myself to him to do and suffer his will. Lastly intercession.

'To prepare me for all the rest, let me open by earnestly praying to him to bless me in my present attempts, to chase away from me all evil spirits, and all wandering thoughts and worldly interruptions, and to enlighten, warm, enlarge, and sustain my heart, and my spirits also, that I may not weary in the work, but delight in it, and rejoice in the privilege of spending a day in communion with my God and Saviour.'

FOR MEDITATION: In 1866, Samuel Stone wrote lines that impart the sense of all that has been bestowed upon the church in communion with God:

Yet she on earth hath union
With God the Three in One,
And mystic sweet communion
With those whose rest is won ...

O happy ones and holy!
Lord, give us grace that we
Like them, the meek and lowly,
On high may dwell with thee

REFERENCE: *The Life of William Wilberforce* (1838)

'Some humble place in the better world'

'*Who shall not receive manifold more in this present time, and in the world to come life everlasting.*' *Luke 18:30*
SUGGESTED FURTHER READING: 1 Timothy 4:4–11

Wilberforce's diary entry for 12 August 1818 reads thus: 'In the evening ... Mr J. showed me Dr Johnson's affecting farewell to William Windham. "May you and I find some humble place in the better world, where we may be admitted as penitent sinners. Farewell. God bless you for Christ's sake, my dear Windham."'

FOR MEDITATION: In 1856, the poet and divine John Keble wrote the following words. They are a lovely complement to Samuel Johnson's words above.

Our hope, when autumn winds blew wild,
We trusted, Lord, with thee:
And still, now spring has on us smiled,
We wait on thy decree.

Thine too by right and ours by grace,
The wondrous growth unseen,
The hopes that soothe, the fears that brace,
The love that shines serene.

So grant the precious things brought forth
By sun and moon below,
That thee in thy new heav'n and earth
We never may forgo.

On the last day of the year, the last verse of the Watts hymn *Keep silence, all created things* seems appropriate:

In thy fair book of life and grace,
O may I find my name
Recorded in some humble place,
Beneath my Lord the Lamb.

REFERENCE: *The Life of William Wilberforce* (1838)

Endnotes

1   An English translation of the Latin proverb 'optima corrupta pessima'.

2   'dark with excessive bright'—from John Milton's *Paradise Lost,* Book iii, Line 380.

3   **William Shakespeare,** *The Two Gentlemen of Verona* 1.1.9.

4   William Shakespeare, *The Merchant of Venice*, Act 4, scene 1, line 262.

5   John Witherspoon (1722–1794), the Scottish-American divine, President of Princeton University and signer of the American Declaration of Independence.

6   A citation from **Francis Bacon** (1561–1626) *The Advancement of Learning.*

7   Lines 948–49 of Book Six of William Cowper's epic poem, *The Task.*

8   i.e. supposed.

9   Latin for 'in my opinion', literally 'I being judge'.

10 Latin for 'scattered fragments'.

11 Wilberforce is citing Book 1, lines 91–92 of John Milton's epic poem *Paradise Lost.*

12 *Hamlet,* Act iv. sc. 4. 118. 'Sure he that made us with such large discourse, looking before and after, gave us not that capability and godlike reason to fust in us unused.'

13 See **John Milton,** *Paradise Lost*, Book 2, line 432.

14 **Robert Lowth,** the author of *Lectures on the Sacred Poetry of the Hebrews* (1753).

15 The Dean of Carlisle, Isaac Milner (1750–1820).

16 Latin for 'acknowledged leader'.

17 Lines 729–46 of 'The Winter Walk at Noon'—Book 6 of Cowper's epic poem *The Task.*

18 His wife Barbara, and children William, Barbara, Elizabeth and Robert. His sons Samuel and Henry William had not yet been born.

19 Wilberforce is quoting from Book One, Letter 10 of Horace's *Epistles*: 'excepto quod non simul esses, cetera laetus.' Translated, this reads: 'happy on all counts save that you are not with me.'

20 First published in 1814.

21 Wilberforce's eldest daughter.

22 Paul of Tarsus, who was known as 'the apostle to the Gentiles'.

23 A mood of verbs in some languages, such as Greek, used to express a wish.

24 Wilberforce's sons wrote: 'Res severa est verum gaudium', Latin for 'true joy is a serious thing'.

25 'And the King shall answer and say unto them, Verily I say unto you, Inasmuch as ye

have done it unto one of the least of these my brethren, ye have done it unto me.'

26 That is the Dean of Carlisle, Isaac Milner (1750–1820).

27 This may well have been Prince Albert's father—Ernst I, Duke of Saxe-Coburg-Gotha (1784–1844).

28 'And the King shall answer and say unto them, Verily I say unto you, Inasmuch as ye have done it unto one of the least of these my brethren, ye have done it unto me.'

29 Wilberforce is referring to the British Admiral, James, Baron Gambier (1756–1833); laywer and Master in Chancery, James Stephen (1758–1832); philanthropist and politician Thomas Babington (1758–1837), politician Sir Robert Inglis, 2nd Baronet (1786–1855); statesman and philanthropist Charles Grant (1746–1823) and abolitionist Zachary Macaulay (1768–1838).

30 Seaforth House, the home built by Sir John Gladstone (1764–1851) who was MP for Liverpool and the father of Sir William Gladstone, the great Victorian Prime Minister.

31 Sir John F.W. Herschel (1792–1871) was a noted astronomer whose studies of the phenomena of light won international acclaim.

32 Line 128 from Epistle IV of Alexander Pope's poem *Essay on Man*.

33 Harford writes, 'The Reform Bill was being debated in the House of Lords'.

34 This Latin phrase means 'Lift up your hearts'.

35 The English Baptist Robert Hall (1764–1831) is remembered as a great pulpit orator whose sermons, states the *Encyclopedia Britannica*, were marked by 'undeniable vigour'. The title of this sermon is 'On the Glory of God in Concealing'. See *The Works of Robert Hall,* vol. 6, p. 32.2